Seeing Krishna in America

ALSO BY E. ALLEN RICHARDSON

Strangers in This Land: Religion, Pluralism and the American Dream, Revised Edition (McFarland, 2010)

Seeing Krishna in America
The Hindu Bhakti Tradition of Vallabhacharya in India and Its Movement to the West

E. ALLEN RICHARDSON

McFarland & Company, Inc., Publishers
Jefferson, North Carolina

All photographs courtesy of the author unless otherwise noted.

LIBRARY OF CONGRESS CATALOGUING-IN-PUBLICATION DATA

Richardson, E. Allen, 1947– author.
    Seeing Krishna in America : the Hindu bhakti tradition of Vallabhacharya in India and its movement to the West / E. Allen Richardson.
        p.   cm.
    Includes bibliographical references and index.

    ISBN 978-0-7864-5973-5 (softcover : acid free paper) ∞
    ISBN 978-1-4766-1596-7 (ebook)

    1. Vallabhachars—India—History. 2. Vallabhachars—United States—History. 3. Bhakti. I. Title.
BL1289.53.R53 2014
294.5′5—dc23   2014020925

BRITISH LIBRARY CATALOGUING DATA ARE AVAILABLE

© 2014 E. Allen Richardson. All rights reserved

No part of this book may be reproduced or transmitted in any form or by any means, electronic or mechanical, including photocopying or recording, or by any information storage and retrieval system, without permission in writing from the publisher.

On the cover: *Swarup* of Shri Nathji, Shreenathji Temple, Phoenix, Arizona (photograph by Sanjay Shah)

Printed in the United States of America

McFarland & Company, Inc., Publishers
  Box 611, Jefferson, North Carolina 28640
    www.mcfarlandpub.com

For Betty and Jimmy,
whose encouragement never wavered,
and for my many friends
in the *Vaishnava* community
who, with vision and compassion,
have brought *Pushtimarg* to America.

Table of Contents

Acknowledgments — ix
Preface — 1
Introduction — 5

Part One: Bhakti, Vallabha and the Search for the Sacred — 11

1. The Vallabha Sampradaya — 12
2. Seeing Krishna: Darshan as the Inward Journey — 52

Part Two: Early History — 69

3. Krishna's Many Mansions: Mughal Patronage and Expansion — 73
4. Of Maharajas and Maharanas: Patronage and the Development of Regional Autonomy — 86

Part Three: Pushtimarg in America — 101

5. Vaishnavism Without Borders: Shri Nathji and the Journey Abroad — 102
6. Fitting Pushtimarg into American Hinduism — 134
7. The Challenges of the Diaspora — 166

Glossary — 187
Appendix — 197
Chapter Notes — 199
Bibliography — 215
Index — 225

Acknowledgments

I am indebted to a number of people who have provided invaluable assistance in the development of this book. Dr. Alfreda E. Meyers, who supervised my dissertation on the *Vallabha Sampradaya* at the University of Arizona, offered numerous suggestions for the project and critiqued a draft of the manuscript. Colleagues at Cedar Crest College reviewed the text, including Dr. Catherine Cameron, Dr. Micah Sadigh, and Mohamed Rajmohamed. Dr. Anoop Chandola, who taught Hindi for many years at the University of Arizona, graciously assisted with issues of language and transliteration.

The text could not have been developed without the assistance of many friends and associates in *Pushtimarg*. Pramod Amin, *Paramarshak* and founder of Vraj, graciously opened the doors of the temple to me as a researcher, welcoming my students on numerous visits over the last fifteen years. Dr. Mahendra Shah offered kind assistance and warm hospitality. Navnit Shah, Hasmukh Shah, and Bharat Patel offered counsel over many years. The Vraj youth group has welcomed me for many summer and winter retreats where I have been privileged to help lead their discussions. Bhagwat Shah in London read parts of the text, offered numerous suggestions, and prepared a table of festivals and a map of India showing the location of *baithaks*. Wanda Renee Millican generously prepared a map for inclusion in the text.

Havelis throughout the United States and Canada warmly received me. Special thanks to Avni and Sandip Marfatia at the Shreenathji Haveli in Toronto, the Vaishnav Samaj of Midwest, Suresh Patel at the Texas Nathdwara, Dr. Hari Dave and Jatin Shah at the Shreenathji Temple of Phoenix, Rajeev DeSai at Vallabhdham in Newington, Connecticut, and Hasmukh Shah at the Vaishnav Samaj of New York.

I am indebted to Cedar Crest College for numerous faculty development grants that supported research trips to havelis. President Carman Ambar granted a sabbatical that allowed me to work full time on the text.

Others provided valuable assistance, including Gabrielle Augustine, Trish Field, Johanna Eddy, Jane Scott (who meticulously prepared the index), Shree Patel, and Amit Ambalal in India. Finally my love and appreciation to my wife, Betty, and son, Jimmy, who supported me every step of the way.

Preface

I first encountered *Pushtimarg* (Vallabhacharya's "the way of grace") while living in New Delhi in the summer of 1973 on a language fellowship from the American Institute of Indian Studies. I had traveled to Mathura, the gateway to the homeland of the god Krishna and the site of the beginnings of Vallabha's sectarian tradition. Located about 35 miles from Agra and the Taj Mahal, Mathura is an ancient city with an important past. The region has deep connections with both Hindu and Buddhist mythologies. However, to the casual tourist, these mythologies are nowhere to be found. Instead, the city presents a formidable countenance. Filled with narrow, winding streets, the sounds of itinerant cattle and small herds of water buffalo, it seems to belong to another time.

But for Hindu pilgrims, Mathura is much more. The city is a sacred space that is connected not only to the birth of Krishna but also to the god himself, who is understood to be inseparable from the terrain. Connected to a rich tapestry of tradition, the region has been captured by numerous schools of Hindu religious art that depict an idyllic world filled with a verdant landscape that becomes the playground of the "dark god."[1]

For pilgrims, Mathura reveals the divine in its landscape of temples. At the Dwarkadhish temple, deeply embedded in the city, I joined pressing throngs of pilgrims all awaiting the noon *darshan*, or viewing, of the central icon. Within India's ancient history the temple is "new" and was constructed in 1814 by a wealthy devotee in honor of Krishna.[2] Now, managed by the *Vallabha Sampradaya*, it is an important center of *Pushtimargiya* devotion and pilgrimage where the image of Krishna receives a public audience several times each day.

The moment when the curtain is drawn to reveal the icon is a time of enormous excitement and anticipation. In 1973, the crowd was so large that uniformed police kept the pressing throng of devotees back with long batons as the assembled mass reached a frenzy, shouting praises to Krishna. A group of women sang *bhajans,* devotional songs to Krishna that evoke a vibrant mythology, becoming a bridge between the senses and the transcendent. I saw a tear in the eye of one man who was overwhelmed by the spontaneous outpouring of emotion. Another devotee who sat next to me was dressed in ochre, the color worn by *sadhus*, or holy men. As we talked he commented that he lived in New Delhi but came to this temple every month, a trip of more than ninety miles that was complicated by his poor health. As the moment for unveiling the deities drew near, he paused and spontaneously erupted into song, calling out in a melodic voice that seemed to fill the temple. The intensity of the emotions and the pressing rush of humanity made the experience both overwhelming and exhausting. When the curtain was finally drawn the crowd erupted into a frenzy that overflowed into the streets.

I never forgot the intensity of this experience but confined it to a host of memories of South Asia that seemed far afield from American religion. Little was I to know that 18 years later in the heartland of rural Pennsylvania, this same experience that I had realized in Mathura would be brought to America. In 2002, amidst twenty-two thousand devotees, a new temple at Vraj (which devotees term a *haveli* or home), the spiritual headquarters of the Vallabha Sampradaya in the West, was formally dedicated. In the intervening period since the dedication, other American and Canadian havelis have been erected as Pushstimarg has rapidly expanded into the North American religious landscape. Each is a door to a labyrinth, defining a path that connects the senses of the external world to the dimensions of the inner mind. Linkages between god, stone, priest, and pilgrim become a single, flowing river of consciousness that transports the pilgrim into the realm of the deep, abiding mystery of the child god.

Visiting American havelis conveys the same sense of fervent adoration of the child Krishna that was so evident in India. In most havelis in the United States and Canada, the deity receives his public six times a day. He is adorned with fresh clothing and jewelry, given toys to play with, and fed lavishly. The complex patterns of rituals that define his day continue no matter who is there to greet him. The priest who attends him ensures that his every need is met in a level of self-sacrifice so intense that the bond between them becomes a continuous expression of devotion.

In North America, Krishna is no longer a visitor. In just forty years from that day in Mathura, Pushtimarg has become an American religion. Like the vast majority of religions in America, it is an immigrant tradition, seeking to protect and preserve its rich cultural heritage and at the same time adapt to life in the West. Like its predecessors in the Christian and Jewish traditions, it navigates its way through American ideas such as the separation of church and state and the role of non-profit, tax-exempt organizations. At the same time, in its growing configurations of havelis, in its recurrent festivals, and in the devotional life centered in the home, Pushtimarg has brought another rich level of diversity to the American religious landscape.

Transliteration of Hindi, Braj, and Sanskrit Words

In order to facilitate the use of this text by persons who are unfamiliar with the *Devanagari* alphabet, transliterated spellings of Hindi, Braj, and Sanskrit words that are the most common in academic literature and are easily understood are used.

In the glossary, terms that appear frequently in the text are defined. Diacritical marks are provided and alternate transliterations are indicated. When diacritical marks were provided in transliterated quotations in the text and in titles in the bibliography, they have been retained. If a transliterated Hindi source did not use diacritical marks, they have not been added.

Names of Goswamis

In order to assist with the flow of the text, titles of *goswamis* are abbreviated. Titles of current goswamis are included in the appendix. Names are combined as they appear in common use. However, some sectarian sources may separate them (e.g., Vrajeshkumar may be written as Vrajesh Kumar).

Introduction

There are many Krishnas. As the central divinity in the epic *Bhagavad Gita* and as an important figure in the wider *Mahabharata*, Krishna is a counselor to Arjuna, a warrior, and an ardent purveyor of bhakti, or devotion. In the *Bhagavata Purana* his entire life is represented, including birth, adoption by foster parents Nanda and Yasoda, childhood, and numerous exploits as an adult. In these traditions and in still other sectarian accounts, Krishna is viewed as an *avatar*, or incarnation, of Vishnu. As a form of this powerful and pervasive god, he helps the *Vaishnavas*, who worship him, understand the true nature of reality, which is centered in his *lila*, or play.[1] Yet, much like the almost endless corpus of stories that surround him, Krishna cannot be contained. When his consort Radha attempts to find him she discovers that his appearance is fleeting. Those who try to fully comprehend him discover that as a trickster he changes his form and moves beyond the human focal plane. As an infant he yawns and in that moment reveals the entire universe. As an adult he lovingly tends his cattle but becomes an entire herd of cows.

Just as there are many Krishnas, so Vallabha's tradition of Pushtimarg emphasizes a variety of manifestations of the dark god in a complex pantheon. Shri Nathji, a seven-year-old child, is the central deity of the faith and contains the male form of Krishna as well as the female presence of Radha, his consort. Another form of the child Krishna, Shri Navanitpriyaji, is mischievous and carries a butter ball in his right hand, as does Shri Balakrishnaji. Shri Gokulchandramaji is associated with the moon of Gokul and is often depicted playing a flute (as is Shri Madanamohanji). Still other manifestations are connected with place. Shri Mathureshji is Krishna, the Lord of Mathura, while Shri Gokulanathji is the central deity of Gokul. Other aspects of Krishna are related to the feminine side of religion. As Shri Vitthalnathji, Krishna is endeared to the female deity Shri Swaminiji, while the river goddess, Shri Yamunaji, is given a special place, first introducing Vallabha to Shri Nathji. Similarly, an adult

Krishna, Shri Dwarkadhishji, sports with Radha. Finally, other deities recognized by Vallabha's son, Vitthalnath, are also venerated and include Shri Mukundrayji and Shri Kalyanaraiji.

This range of forms of Krishna and other deities emphasizes an experience of the sacred that is a sharp contrast to religion in the West. Participants enter a mystical realm of sight and sound in which each visual and auditory image is focused on an iconographic form of the god Krishna, who is most often depicted as a child. Enthroned on a raised dais only accessible to a priest, a stone image is dressed, fed, offered toys, and presented with a mirror so that he can admire himself. The icon is considered alive and the form is understood to be actual presence. Nothing in this mystical realm of experience and transformation of the senses is commonplace in American religion, nor can the encounter be understood entirely through logic. For example, when Pushtimargiyas worship Krishna as a child, the worshipper is confronted with a consuming contradiction. The youthful Krishna is assumed to be dependent—everything in the temple is there because he needs regular attention and is fed, dressed, and entertained daily. Yet behind this form of the child god lies a singular level of reality that is transcendent and cannot be dependent. Beyond thought, freed from the conventions of subject and object, Krishna collapses the distance between deity and devotee, wresting the mind away from logic and into a unitary realm of mysterious presence.

While Pushtimarg maintains a distinct form of worship and religious identity, it is also part of a diverse fabric of sects, or *sampradayas*, that have been part of the historical bhakti movement in North India. Most Americans in the 1960s became aware of one of them—the Hare Krishna movement, which, through the International Society for Krishna Consciousness (ISKCON), became the first organized expression of bhakti to reach the United States. With origins in a fifteenth century founder figure, Chaitanya, ISKCON initially borrowed from evangelical Christianity to create an American interpretation of bhakti based on proselytism. Carried here by Abhay Charanaravinda Bhaktivedanta Swami Prabhupada, a devotee of the Chaitanya bhakti tradition, the faith became popular among the American counterculture of the 1960s. Other forms of bhakti followed that were less controversial. The *Swaminarayan* tradition, a later North Indian bhakti movement, brought the teachings of Sahajanand Swami, an early nineteenth century Gujarati reformer, to the United States. Now in a variety of forms, including the original tradition, a later sectarian movement called BAPS (*Bochasanwasi Shri Akshar Purushottam Swaminarayan Sanstha*) and a recent derivative body, the Anoopam Mission, *Swaminarayan bhakti* has become a visible part of the American religious landscape. Large temples exist in more than 18 states and have been erected near major cities including Chicago, Atlanta, and Toronto. BAPS is planning to build Akshardham in Robbinsville, New Jersey, replicating the grandeur of a temple of the same name in New Delhi.

The presence of these bhakti traditions in America is part of a larger migration pattern that has brought 2.7 million South Asians to the United States following the 1965 immigration reforms.[2] This occasioned what researchers now describe as the Hindu diaspora, the flow of Hindus abroad in which patterns of cultural and religious identification are maintained outside of the country of origin.[3] In the diaspora, bhakti traditions have encountered a religious landscape that was itself in the midst of a dramatic change. This transition was documented by *The Pew Report on Religion* (2008), which concluded that

> the United States is on the verge of becoming a minority Protestant country; the number of Americans who report that they are members of Protestant denominations now stands at barely 51 percent. Moreover, the Protestant population is characterized by significant internal diversity and fragmentation, encompassing hundreds of different denominations loosely grouped around three fairly distinct religious traditions—evangelical Protestant churches (26.3 percent of the overall adult population), mainline Protestant churches (18.1 percent) and historically black Protestant churches (6.9 percent).[4]

This reality, coupled with the increasing xenophobia following the 9/11 tragedy, has produced an American context for non–Christian religions that offers increasing latitude for growth and simultaneously is often distrustful of any unfamiliar religion. However, as religion in America also moves increasingly out of the public square and into a more privatized environment, bhakti sects have achieved an insular quality, protected by the formidable boundaries of religion and culture within the South Asian community. For the majority of Americans, Hindu temples are viewed as an occasional part of the religious landscape still identified by its steeples and other symbols of the nation's Christian heritage. What they don't see are the complex socio-religious networks within American Hindu temple traditions or the differences between classical expressions of the tradition and newer sectarian movements. For those bhakti sects such as Pushtimarg, which focuses its devotional life in the home, American Hinduism retains a further level of invisibility.

Seeing Krishna in America argues that the presence of Pushtimarg in North America cannot be understood without a working knowledge of its social history in India. That history is important for a number of reasons. The text shows how the sect used regal imagery for its principal deities, creating temples with the aura of palaces, and how this expense was sustained through patronage. The discussion also demonstrates how the sect used this royal support to expand, developing autonomous regional centers in Rajasthan and the Gujarat. Finally, the book explores how in the late twentieth and early twenty-first centuries, lay entrepreneurs assumed an increasing role in developing the sect in India. Becoming part of the American Hindu diaspora in the 1980s, Pushtimarg temples were created in the United States by laity who sought affiliation with traditional seats of authority in India.

All of this was supported by a metaphor. Krishna has always been defined by movement, changing locations at will and leaving one center for another. In Pushtimarg, while such sacred journeys may have been occasioned by oppression or economic opportunity, it was always the deity who was understood to sanction each transition. The journey took multiple forms beginning in Krishna's heartland, Braj, and continuing to the holy city that was named in his honor, Nathdwara. From there the journey broadened further into Rajasthan and the Gujarat as seven of Vallabha's grandchildren were entrusted with other naturally formed images of the deity. Their descendants provided initiation to the ritual life of the sect and used their wealth and prestige to guide expansion.

In America, the metaphor has been extended to the West. Using their business acumen and ability to maximize social capital, in just twenty-four years Pushtimargiya leaders developed a spiritual headquarters in Pennsylvania and temples in a number other states. In New York City, a haveli was founded in June 1988. A year earlier founders of the Vraj temple in Pennsylvania had acquired land where they would erect the spiritual headquarters of the faith in North America. By 2012, havelis in North America had been constructed in New York, Pennsylvania, Illinois, Texas, Arizona, New Jersey, Connecticut, Georgia, and Ontario, Canada. Groups of devotees also organized associations in Atlanta, Savannah, San Jose, San Francisco, and parts of Florida. While the total number of devotees remains small in comparison with more established forms of religion in America, the growth rate is rapid.

Using skills developed in professions and industries, Pushtimargiya leaders established havelis in metropolitan areas near large Gujarati populations. In America, these temples are removed from traditional sources of revenue. Patronage is not a possibility and there are no communities with historical ties to the temple. American temples do not own large tracts of land and cannot rely on income from crops. Instead, American havelis must depend on contributions from principal donors and on a continuing flow of support from devotees.

As Pushtimarg was carefully transplanted abroad, the decedents of the founder also became increasingly globalized. Bringing the theological traditions of their seats of spiritual authority to America, Vallabha's patrilineal descendants (goswamis) entered the jet age, spending weeks at a time in the United States meeting the needs of their devotees. They have helped start new havelis and have nurtured them as they developed. They have also learned to utilize the social media, developing pages on Facebook in order to carry out continuing conversations with their followers.

Although not seeking assimilation, havelis began to adapt. When priests and musicians could not be obtained from India, laity were trained to take on their duties. Temples created administrative structures compatible with American denominations. Fundraising programs suited to non-profit, tax exempt religious institutions were devised. Educational programs for the second generation were developed to assist them in their struggle with conflicting Indian and American identities.

In order to help the reader understand this total process, *Seeing Krishna in America* is written in three parts, each containing two chapters from a similar perspective. The first part, "Bhakti, Vallabha and the Search for the Sacred," takes the reader through the Indian origins of the faith. Chapter 1 helps to put Vallabha in context, describing the role of North Indian bhakti traditions and the milieu that shaped the sect's beliefs and praxis. Chapter 2 helps the reader understand the role of image worship in the sect through the lens of material culture and textual studies.

Part Two, "Early History," focuses on the early history of the sect and helps the reader understand how the Vallabha Sampradaya used patronage to expand its geographical base while maintaining ritual symbols of enthronement for Krishna. Chapter 3 explores the role of the Mughal Empire in first granting patronage. Chapter 4 demonstrates how patronage was continued by *Rajput* princes who sustained the geographical spread of the sect in a series of independent states.

Part Three, "Pushtimarg in America," looks at the evolution of the Vallabha Sampradaya in the West and the role of laity as developers. Chapter 5 discusses the history of American Hinduism and the way in which Pushtimarg fits into this globalized tradition. Chapter 6 describes the evolution of havelis in the United States and the success of immigrant entrepreneurs in constructing them. Chapter 7 looks at the challenges to Pushtimarg as an American religion.

Part One

Bhakti, Vallabha and the Search for the Sacred

Part One focuses on the convergence of myth, ritual, and literature in the *Vallabha Sampradaya*, exploring the ways that Krishna is perceived and worshiped. In scripture, including the *Bhagavad Gita* and the *Bhagavata Purana*, Krishna emerges as a divine folk hero whose manifestations are so unpredictable that he cannot be contained. *Pushtimarg* approached this theological challenge by bringing Krishna into the home where, in iconographic form, he developed lasting relationships with the families who attended him. Chapter 1 describes the beginnings of this tradition and the theophany that led Vallabhacharya to initiate a *bhakti sampradaya*. Chapter 2 explores *darshan* (the central act of viewing Krishna), and the role of *seva* (service) that undergirds it.

1

The Vallabha Sampradaya

When the milkmaids heard the flute in the woods.
They were disquieted and forgot their household work.
They did not at all fear family honor or the sanction of the scriptures.
Like rivers they rushed toward the ocean–Krishna.
They began to anoint their bodies with oil and ointment
And those standing in the forest that night set out as they were.
They neither cared for the love of their sons and husbands,
Nor feared their family, nor felt any shame.
Sūrdās says that the beautiful and clever Hari drew their hearts.[1]

—Surdas (fifteenth century)

Understanding North Indian Bhakti Traditions

In India's more than 638,000 villages the signs of bhakti or devotion are not hard to find. During festivals groups of women may join impromptu celebrations of dance and song called *bhajans,* praising Krishna and singing the poems of bhakti saints. To the casual observer, the bhajan appears to be just a circle dance. However, to those who participate in it, the circle is defined not as much by the dancers but by the deity who may appear in the center. For those who see him, the sight of Krishna is ephemeral and spontaneous. As the dancers long for a glimpse of the god, so the circle is also a metaphor for ultimate reality with the center its focal point. Convinced that he is there just for her, each dancer may experience *lila,* the sport of the dark god in which the true nature of reality is revealed.

As the bhajan sets the stage for Krishna's appearance, so another bhakti tradition, the *Ras Lila* or miracle play, does the same thing. These open air dramas attempt to recreate the pastoral, wooded landscape of Krishna's heartland—*Braj.* Dancers take on the roles of Krishna, his consort Radha and the members of Krishna's family, including his elder brother Balarama and his foster mother, Yasoda. Like the bhajan, the Ras Lila is more than an art form. It sets the stage for the intervention of Krishna in human affairs and for the fleeting, miraculous appearance of the god among those who desire him the most.

Bhajans and the Ras Lila are visible expressions of bhakti and typify the complex outpouring of love that many Hindus regularly express to a variety of deities including Rama, Shiva, and Krishna. Bhakti is surrender and may be marked by expressions of emotion so intense that the boundary between self and god begins to disintegrate. This critical idea of submission is central to all forms of bhakti and frequently contrasts with American expressions of religion, which are focused on the development of the individual. These ideas will be further explored in chapter 7.

The frequently voiced interpretation of bhakti as devotion "does not accurately convey the issues at stake"[2]—a more accurate interpretation is necessary. *Participating* is more appropriate, drawing from the Sanskrit root of bhakti, *bhaj*—to partake or participate:

> Participation signifies the bhaktas' relationship with God; it is a premise of their poetry that they can participate in God by singing of God, by saying God's name, and in other ways. As a representation in English of the bhakta's relationship with God, the term *participation* has the advantage of not resonating with something we think we already know but encourages us to understand the relationships of bhakti as represented by its promoters and interpreters in history.[3]

This interpretation is helpful not only in understanding bhakti as a state of mind but also in looking at the ways that it conditions the devotee to participate in the direct experience of ultimate reality.

However, bhakti is also more than an attitude. It also reflects a historical movement that has deep roots in South India. There, in the sixth through the ninth centuries, the writings of the Tamil *Alvars* and the *Shaiva Nayanmar* poets directed the attention of their followers toward intimate, personal understandings of god. Later, in the fourteenth through seventeenth centuries in North India, a number of poet-saints continued the same emphasis. At times, the movement became so intense and popular that it crossed sectarian and religions divisions. In Varanasi, the mystic poet Kabir folded intimate expressions of love for Allah in the Sufi tradition into the wider fabric of bhakti. In Rajasthan, Mirabhai devoted her writings to Krishna, further spreading the mystique of the mischievous god whose passion for Radha became a cultural expression of the fleeting nature of religious ecstasy. Other sects followed, including the *Radhavallabha Sampradaya*, a revival of the *Nimbarka Sampradaya*, the *Haridasa Sampradaya*, and the *Gaudiya Sampradaya* of Bengal.[4] Of these, the *Gaudiya* tradition became the most readily identifiable in the West in a form known as the Hare Krishna tradition.

As the number of bhakti sects increased in northern India, so the images of Krishna also changed. Gone was the penultimate warrior of the *Mahabharata* and *Bhagavad Gita*. The warrior was replaced by equally dominant images of Krishna as a child and a young man whose mysterious presence occupied the wooded terrain of Braj.

Of the array of deities who have become focal points of bhakti devotion, Krishna alone seems to exist both in history and beyond it. Most scholars have maintained that his origins may have been as a folk hero:

> The empirical evidence of inscriptions, dated monuments, and original manuscripts is not perhaps as strong for Krishna as some of the other examples of religious figures. However, most scholars of Hinduism and Indian history accept the historicity of Krishna—that he was a real male person, whether human or divine, who lived on Indian soil by at least 1000 BCE and interacted with many other historical persons within the cycles of the epic and puranic literatures.[5]

Yet, despite these assumptions, inscriptions and numismatic evidence provide traces but offer no firm historical footing for Krishna's identity.[6] In short, as Wendy Doniger concludes in a quote from Garrison Keillor, "There are stories, and that is all we have."[7]

Interpreting Bhakti

As images of Krishna in art and poetry circulated in India's religious landscape for more than two millennia, bhakti also seemed to challenge the status quo, creating a popular expression of devotion that went well beyond the traditional boundaries of authority. To Western Orientalists in the nineteenth and early twentieth centuries, this seemed to be analogous to the challenges to Roman Catholicism that led to the sixteenth century Reformation.

Scholars soon abandoned these attempts to find such seemingly simple European parallels, realizing that in its literature and social implications, bhakti was more complex. As studies in bhakti literature became more prevalent in the West, the devotional movement was further understood as an egalitarian tradition that rejected caste and challenged reliance on Sanskrit. The bhakti movement seemed to shift the lens of the faith, granting unrestricted access to the divine for anyone who entered its path of self-surrender, offering unlimited access through vernacular languages and the absence of caste restrictions.

There are a number of inconsistencies in these interpretations, particularly around the questions of caste and scripture.[8] While the bhakti movement was often presented as a challenge to caste, the dynamic of purity and pollution that undergirds it could frequently still be found in bhakti sects. Moreover, the assumption that the rise of the tradition in vernacular languages meant that bhakti traditions eschewed Sanskrit could not be easily supported. Although the bhakti movement did present a broadening of the Hinduism, it was not a movement away from Hindu Sanskrit tradition as much as it was an augmentation of it. Perhaps most important, what the earlier perspectives failed to understand fully was the nature of reform in Hinduism.

Reform has had a very different connotation in the history of Hinduism than in the West. As the world's oldest living religious tradition, Hinduism includes no founder figure, no single point of origin and an often confusing array of practices that incorporate elements that extend to the dawn of the Indus Valley Civilization. As the religion of the Aryans was recorded in the closed canon of the Vedas, so Hinduism also developed an entirely different, non-canonical set of scripture dubbed *smriti*, which were expansive and open ended.

Within this context, Western presumptions about the nature of reform would hardly apply to Hinduism. Reformist traditions that often emphasized a purification of the faith, returning to a more pristine form of doctrine and praxis, are inapplicable. In the Hindu religion and culture are expressions so diverse that beliefs and practices vary from household to household and village to village.

Assumptions of linear reform have had some interesting implications for understanding the nature of bhakti. What scholars initially perceived as reform was not reform but a continuation of past practices. The egalitarian philosophical roots of bhakti may have opened up a caste bounded tradition to the masses. But it could hardly be argued that the emerging bhakti sects were separated from the hierarchical nature of Hindu culture. At the same time, some bhakti sects worked hard to demonstrate their close connections to the larger corpus of Hindu tradition. Generations of bhakti saints became charismatic, populist leaders, frequently aligning themselves with the wider fabric of the great teachers (*acharyas*) of Hinduism. Further, as the history of the Vallabha Sampradaya demonstrates, the sectarian bhakti movement was often aligned with traditional avenues of support that were common throughout Hindu history. Just as the large temples in South India were often supported by the patronage of princes and kings, so North Indian bhakti sects often used the same technique as a mechanism to spread their own traditions. In the case of the Vallabha Sampradaya, these practices were developed during a period of transition in North India.

Bhakti Sampradayas in Context: North India in the Early Sixteenth Century

As bhakti sects competed for patronage in the sixteenth century, North India experienced enormous cultural flux. Vallabha's life spanned both the demise of the Delhi Sultanate and the rise of the Mughal Empire. By the time of Vallabha's birth in 1470 CE the Delhi Sultanate was in its final stages of disintegration.[9] It was founded in 1206 CE by an Afghan, Muhamad Guhri, who, following the exploits of Muhamad Gazni over a century earlier, entered India from the northwest for plunder and profit. By the time of its demise over three hundred years later the Sultanate had left a succession of warring states, the "slave dynasties."[10] Each dynasty was governed by a ruler or sultan and an array of lesser nobles and officials. By 1470 CE, the Sultanate had also established a number of independent Muslim kingdoms in the Gujarat, Bengal and other locations in the north. These areas, along with Hindu principalities in Gwalior, Rajasthan and Orissa, produced a climate of competing religious and cultural interests and little overall unity.[11]

Among the results of political instability were intricate levels of Hindu and Muslim culture. Urdu was synthesized as a mixture of Hindustani and Persian, including many Persian loan words and cultural symbols, and used its own Persian script that replaced the conventional *Devanagari*, which had evolved from Sanskrit. Persian miniature painting swept into the north. Indian music took new forms, evolving into mixtures of expression that drew from Hindu tradition and from the utterances of Sufi saints.

Within this complex and diversified world varying degrees of cooperation among Hindus and Muslims emerged. While the era is replete with examples of intolerance by Muslim rulers, it is not difficult to also find levels of cooperation. During the Lodi dynasty, which had accrued power at the time of Vallabha's birth, "in the cities the Hindu population had come to terms with their Muslim overlords: some enterprises, like the royal mints, remained exclusively in Hindu hands; and some converts had achieved high office."[12]

In a diverse and religiously competitive atmosphere, the kingdom of Vijayanagar was established in South India as a bastion of orthodox resistance to Mughal incursions. As an independent state, Vijayanagar became a center of classical Hinduism and South Indian *Vaishnava* tradition. In its capital city of the same name, a labyrinth of Hindu temples included elaborate patterns of South Indian architecture and iconography, attracting Vaishnava philosophers such as Vallabha who challenged the traditional tenets of non-dualistic Hindu thought.[13]

1. The Vallabha Sampradaya

By the time Vallabha died in 1532 CE, the fragmentation of the north had been replaced by a more unified empire. The Mughal Empire arose with the invasion of Babur, who achieved a military victory in 1526 CE at Panipat. A descendent of Genghis Kahn, Babur continued the pattern of movement into India from the northwest. His dynasty was designated as Mughal, a corruption of the term "Mongol," and used the militaristic image of Mongol warriors to

Fig. 1. Map of India showing Rajasthan and Gujarat (courtesy Wanda Millican).

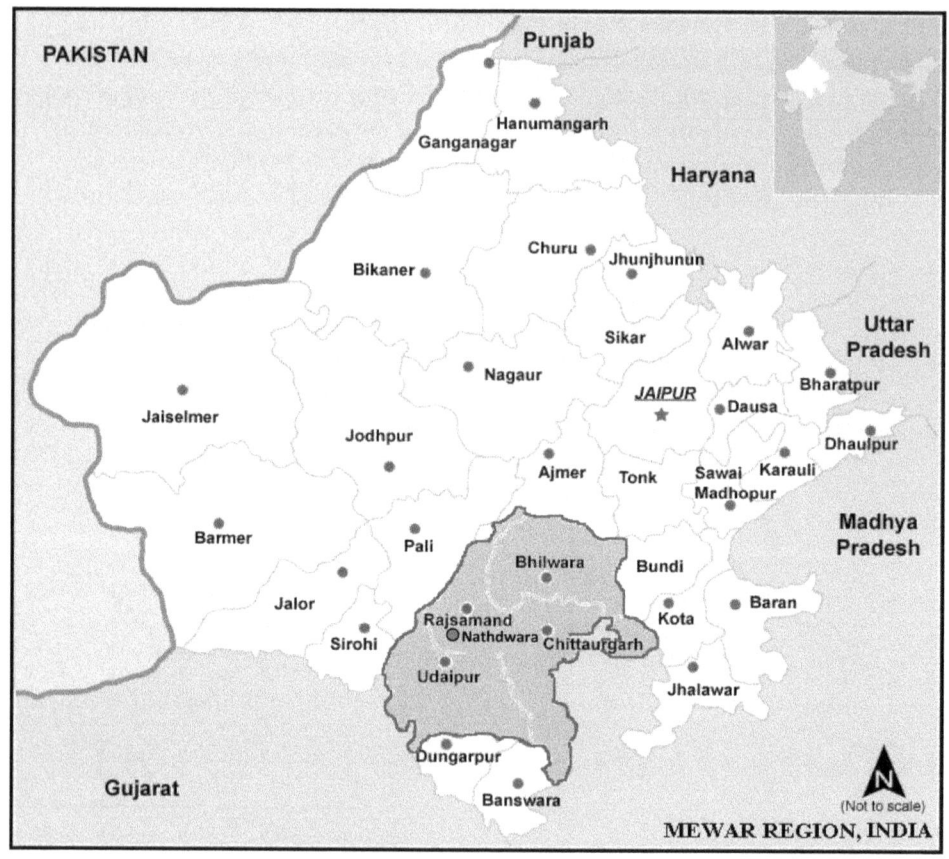

Fig. 2. Detail of Rajasthan showing Nathdwara (Wikipedia).

its advantage. For Babur and his descendants, the emperors Humayun (1530–1556 CE), Akbar (1556–1605 CE), Jahangir (1605–1627 CE), Shah Jahan (1628–1658 CE) and Aurangzeb (1659–1707 CE), Islam became the official religion of the land while court life was modeled after high Persian culture.

In Rajasthan and the Gujarat (figs. 1 and 2), champions of Hindu independence struggled to retain their land and traditions, creating an atmosphere that was rife with patronage. In the seventeenth and eighteenth centuries as the British East India Company assumed political power, both the British and the Mughals forged alliances with *Rajput* leaders. Writing as late as 1829 CE, British official James Tod was acutely aware of the fierce Rajput independence and the feudal system of land tenure that easily created the possibility of patronage.[14]

As bhakti sects proliferated in the north in the medieval period, the villages of Brindaban and Gokul, long associated with the myths surrounding Krishna, became increasingly important centers of Vaishnava culture and tradition. The surrounding landscape, punctuated by the flow of the Yamuna River, became a mythologized terrain where the dark god intermittently appeared before his devotees, nurturing a rich array of art and culture.

Vallabha

Vallabha Bhatt was a Tailangana Brahmin whose parents were from a region currently in the Telugu-speaking state of Andra Pradesh. His father, Laxman Bhatt, was a religious man who the tradition says had completed many pilgrimages. His mother, Yallamagaru, is described as the daughter of a priest from the independent Hindu state of Vijayanagar.[15]

Vallabha's birth is shrouded with images of mystery and divinity. The narrative, written with symbols of purity and authority, reflects a cultural understanding of holy men in South Asia. The birth of the Tamil Alvars and Krishna himself are described using many of these symbols. (The birth stories of the Buddha, conceived in a forest and protected by a deity, were presented in a similar fashion.) According to several early sectarian biographies (the most well-known being *Sri Vallabhacharitra*, written in the sixteenth century), Vallabha was born while his parents were en route from Varanasi to South India, fleeing the threat of attack by Muslim armies. In the lunar month of Vaishakh, 1478 CE, Vallabha's parents are said to have stopped in the Champaranya forest for rest. During their sojourn Yallamagaru gave premature birth. The infant was stillborn and was placed beneath a large Champa tree before the group departed the next day. However, unwilling to believe the infant dead, Yallamagaru persuaded the others to return to the place where the baby had been placed. There, beneath the Champa tree, the party found much to their surprise the child alive and miraculously surrounded by a protective fire.

As Vallabha's birth was described in the context of divinity, so his life was interpreted as the biography of a great teacher (acharya) in the Vaishnava tradition. When Vallabha was 20 (following the death of his father in 1490 CE), he began a series of pilgrimages that would take him around India three times.[16] Such lengthy and arduous journeys were expected by teachers who sought to establish themselves within Vaishnava tradition and were a normative means of garnering authority. Pilgrims usually completed these arduous journeys barefoot and wearing only a simple *dhoti*.

According to Pushtimargiya tradition, Vallabha's first pilgrimage (1488–1495 CE) led him to the Hindu kingdom of Vijayanagar.[17] As a young boy of eleven he traveled with his mother and a number of other pilgrims. There, the ruling monarch, Krishnadevray, organized a formal debate including proponents of Shankara's non-dual philosophy of *advaita* and the dualistic tradition of Madvha.[18] In presenting his interpretation of Hindu monism Vallabha achieved victory and was proclaimed by the court as an acharya, firmly rooting his philosophy within Vaishnava orthodoxy.

As an acharya, Vallabha was attached to the lineage of Vishnuswami. As described in a late thirteenth century commentary, *Bhaktamala,* Vishnuswami was perceived to be an established Vaishnava leader whose teachings had formed the basis of a sect known as the *Rudra Sampradaya*.[19] However, Vishnuswami's historicity is uncertain, and he occupies a curious role within the development of Vaishnavism: The scholarly opinion does not accept any "real connection between the thought of Vallabhācārya and that of Viṣṇuswami."[20] What mattered about the linkage to Vishnuswami was not his historical identity as much as the conduit that his hagiographic imagery provided for Vallabha. Now, as the heir to a recognized current of Vaishnava thought, Vallabha anchored his teachings within established parameters of tradition.

Once this recognition had been achieved Vallabha continued his pilgrimage in South India where, beyond his role as an established philosopher, he began to have mystical encounters with deity. In 1493 CE he had a vision in which Krishna told him that he had appeared in a cave on Govardhan Hill as Shri Nathji and would meet him there.[21] Returning to Braj, Vallabha reached Gokul in 1494.[22] Again he experienced a theophany, informing his disciples that Krishna had talked to him and had described the initiation (*Brahmsambandh*) that would be required of all who would follow him.

Acting on this vision, Vallabha traveled to Govardhan Hill in Braj, where he encountered a farmer, Sadu Pandey, who had begun to worship an arm of Shri Nathji that protruded from the ground. Decades before Vallabha's birth, the tradition says, the arm had been fed and bathed by a cow. At the time of his birth the face had been excavated from the mountain. Reaching the place where the icon was buried, Vallabha heard Shri Nathji calling out for more milk. He recognized the voice as belonging to Krishna and immediately began to worship the image.

This etiological myth not only defined the relationship between Vallabha and Krishna, but also rooted the evolving *sampradaya* in a metaphor of a continuing physical and spiritual journey. Not only would Vallabha construct yet another temple for Shri Nathji, but his descendants would once again move the icon to Mewar. In turn, the sons of Vitthalnath would transport other forms of Krishna to the far reaches of Rajasthan and the Gujarat.

Continuing his own pattern of movement, Vallabha began a second pilgrimage in Rajasthan and the Gujarat. After stopping in a number of places he continued to Ayodhya, Prayaga and Varanasi.[23] There, he married Mahalakshmi and, in traditional Hindu fashion, became a householder and the father of two sons, Gopinath (born in 1511 CE) and Vitthalnath (born five years later in 1516 CE).[24] These events placed Vallabha in the mainstream of familial life, removed from the role of a renunciant and establishing his sampradaya as a form of bhakti that would generate mass appeal.

On his third pilgrimage, which lasted for four years, Vallabha revisited many of the sites he had seen in his earlier journeys. The tradition suggests that it was during this time that he encountered the poet Surdas, who also had gained a popular following.[25] In time, Vallabha's religious significance increased, and he was recognized not only as a philosopher but as an incarnation of the same god whose form he had unearthed on Mount Govardhan. He settled into a regimen of worship, teaching, and writing, penning over thirty books. By adopting the traditional fourfold stages of life (*brahmacharya* or student, *grihastha* or householder, *vanaprastha* or supplicant engaged in religious study, and finally *sannyasi* or renunciant), Vallabha championed the established lifestyle of a Hindu householder. Defining his understanding of surrender to Krishna as firmly embedded in a home centered tradition, he modeled a path that, while accepted within patterns of Vaishnava orthodoxy, challenged the traditional role of utter renunciation. Instead, he argued, service to Krishna, or seva, was the means to achieve salvation. Finally, in 1532 CE, entering the Ganges for the last time, he vanished into the waters after having only adopted the role of renunciation immediately before his death.[26]

Philosophical Underpinnings: Vallabha's Philosophy of Shuddhadvaita

As a philosopher, Vallabha developed a system of thought called *Shuddhadvaita*, or pure non-dualism. Within this worldview reality was divine, with Krishna fully manifested both at its center and in the periphery. Non-duality, the perception that all reality is of one nature, had been an important part of Vaishnavism prior to Vallabha. The school of non-dualism, or Advaita, was developed in the eighth century by Shankara, who was one of the most significant teachers of the Hindu tradition.

In Shankara's system, which drew on the monistic worldview evolved in the *Upanishads*, reality is of one substance that is identified as *Brahman*. Brahman is beyond the distinction of subject and object. Neither male nor female, and not a god, Brahman could be seen as possessing attributes (*saguna Brahman*) or, on a far deeper level, as being attributeless (*nirguna Brahman*). Within this understanding there can be no creation or first cause of existence since there is no separation between Brahman and the world. Similarly, good and evil contain no ontological reality since the ultimate nature of all things is one.

However, despite this oneness, the day-to-day experience of reality is often perceived as dual and separate from the self. Shankara dubbed this misperception as illusion or *maya*, understanding it as a powerful and pervasive force driven by a larger karmic reality that obscures the true nature of all things. Since the human soul (*atman*) is the product of an endless process of rebirth it becomes bemired in negative karma even if its current life is relatively pure.

Shankara posited that maya was pervasive and that it was further propelled by human desire. Maya fueled perceptions of individualism and separation, creating levels of desire so strong that many persons never awoke from the nightmare of self-indulgence that it presented. For Advaitans, meditation was singled out as the most productive form of eliminating maya and experiencing the true nature of reality. In its emphasis on meditation, Advaitan thought discounted the role of image worship. This position was challenged by a number of classical theistic schools including Ramanuja, Madvha, Nimbarka, and Vishnuswami.[27] In the eleventh century, Ramanuja posited a qualified non-dualism in which theism became linked to Brahman, opening the way for renewed emphasis on image worship. In the thirteenth century, Madvha developed a more dualistic attitude that also had no conceptual difficulty with icon worship. Similarly, the school of Nimbarka (which may have arisen in the thirteenth century) and that of the more historically elusive figure of Vishnuswami also emphasized the worship of a personal god in iconographic form.[28]

Shankara's approach ultimately led to the path of renunciation that was actualized in Hindu culture through the role of the holy man or *sadhu*. Leaving their families, sadhus renounce their identity, abandoning all forms of attachment. Their lives are spent in rigorous patterns of meditation that often involve physical austerities and deprivation. However, to Vallabha, the identification of maya as a separate level of reality was an untenable compromise of pure monism. Attempting to purify a philosophical system he judged corrupt, Vallabha posited that maya was part of Krishna and a form of his lila, or sport. Further, Vallabha suggested that because all reality was singular the inability to perceive the true nature of things was due to different levels of awakening.

Vallabha described three kinds of souls. The first, or *pravaha*, looked at the world as a physical reality and as unaware of its deeper manifestations. The second, or *maryada*, followed principles drawn from the Vedas. It saw more of the true nature of things but was still unaware of their essence. The third or *pusht* saw the divine and understood that all reality was one. For Vallabha, this meant that Brahman (which Shuddhadvaita philosophers term *Parabrahman* or the supreme form of Brahman) was Krishna.[29]

The implications of Vallabha's path of Shuddhadvaita were significant. Rejecting aestheticism, Vallabha argued that access to the divine could be actualized in the natural course of family life. The vehicle for this access was a form of devotion and service to god called seva. Seva and the mystical role of the darshan became the context for personal transformation. Although souls were inherently of different natures, Vallabha's approach was highly democratic. Through the darshan, each person could learn to access the divine.

As a post–Vedic tradition, Pushtimarg incorporates the insights of the tradition into a vast array of texts, all of which would be considered smriti (or scripture) beyond the Vedic canon. For Pushtimargiyas, the Vedas are not studied; smriti literature is. This includes the *Bhagavata Gita* and the *Bhagavata Purana*, a treatise of special significance for bhakti sects in the Vaishnava tradition.

As a philosopher, Vallabha was also a prolific writer, incorporating his thoughts into a number of philosophical discourses including the *Subbodhini* (a commentary on the *Bhagavata Purana*), the *Anubhashya* (a commentary on the *Brahma Sutras*), and a large number of other discourses. These include the *Shodash Granth*, which contains 16 volumes and is an influential body of literature that is viewed with special reverence because it was written by Vallabha for guidance of the sect.

Other tracts important within the sect include 31 treatises written by Vitthalnath, and a corpus of other commentaries written by lineage holders. These include five pieces written by Shri Balkrishnalalji (the third son of Vitthalnath) and 75 texts penned by Shri Hariraiji, a highly revered teacher. A number of other literary works were written by significant descendants of Vallabha including Dwarkeshji, Brajbhusanji (II), and by the *Tilkayat*, the spiritual head of the sect who is the senior *goswami* of Nathdwara.[30]

Still other literature that has become part of the sect's devotional life is hagiographical. These individual stories describe the role of Pushtimarg in the lives of followers during the formative history of the tradition and often incorporate significant points of doctrine and teachings. Of this genre, two texts, the *Chaurasi Vaishnavan ki Varta* or *Stories of Eighty-Four Vaishnavas*, and

Do Sau Bavan Vaishnavan ki Varta, Stories of Two Hundred Fifty-Two Vaishnavas, have assumed special importance. Scholars have observed that "both texts are ascribed to Viṭṭhalnāth's son Gokulnāth (c. 1551–1647), though their actual history is uncertain."[31]

Vitthalnath

After the death of Vallabha in 1532 CE, leadership of his emerging sampradaya passed to his two sons, Gopinath and Vitthalnath. In 1564 CE Gopinath left the leadership of the sect and disappeared—an act that the sect interprets as a theophany, positing that he merged into the image of Shri Baladevji in Jaganathpuri.[32] While some members of the sect have continued to follow Gopinath, the majority of devotees look to Vitthalnath, whom they lovingly refer to as Shri Gusaiji (an honorific form of the term *goswam*—"lord of the cows") as the heir to Vallabha's authority.

Vitthalnath became the tutelary leader of the tradition, eventually passing the mantle on to his seven sons, who created a dynasty (*Vallabhkul*). The purity of the dynasty was insured through a pattern of marriage in which sons married wives who were *bhattas*, from the same *Tailanga* caste as Vallabha.[33] Each son was given an icon (*swarup*) of Krishna[34]:

Son	Swarup
Giridharji	Mathureshji
Govindarayji	Vitthalnathji
Balakrishnaji	Dvarkadhishji
Gokulanathji	Gokulanathji
Raghunathji	Gokulchandramaji
Yadunathji	Balakrishnaji
Ghanashyamji	Madanamohanji

As this process expanded, the eldest son, Giridharju, inherited primary care of Shri Nathji, Shri Navnitpriyaji, and Shri Mathureshji.

Swarups, which will be discussed in more detail in chapter 2, are seen as the actual presence of the deity. These special swarups, worshipped by Vallabha, were called *nidhi swarups* and were thought to be self-manifested.[35] Pushtimarg makes a distinction between these images and the swarups that are consecrated and used in private homes.[36] While both forms are fully Krishna, the deity is understood to be even more visible in the nidhi swarups, which have occupied a special place within the faith.

Vitthalnath organized the teachings of his father into a bhakti sampradaya, borrowing concepts associated with royalty, which helped secure the patronage of the Mughal Empire. He established seva as a specific form of worship, organizing it into a regular pattern of eight daily viewings, or darshans, that were to be conducted in temples. Adopting the term darshan was astute since it was widely known in Hinduism and had also been employed by Mughal emperors to describe large public audiences in which the regent was viewed by his subjects. Vitthalnath also employed the term *gaddi*, used to designate the throne of the emperor, to describe the seat of authority given to his seven sons as they cared for nidhi swarups. In a similar fashion he used the term *haveli* (mansion) to refer to Pushtimargiya temples, again connecting the deity with opulence and position. While the correct term for the identification of a Pushtimarg temple is *nandalay*—the house of Krishna's father, Nanda—the term haveli connoted splendor and prestige.

A common interpretation of the sect's early history suggests that the use of the term haveli avoided the risk of publically identifying a Hindu temple during periods of Mughal persecution. However, this understanding risks oversimplifying the complex relationship between the Mughal Empire and bhakti sects. As the following chapters will show, the Vallabha Sampradaya was the recipient of a steady stream of Mughal support, enjoying a symbiotic relationship with the authority of the empire. When persecution did occur, the sect had already established royal favor in Mewar by employing the same pattern of patronage and reward that it had used during the early period of its formation.

Under Vitthalnath's leadership, havelis were created in which the deity was provided a bedroom and a private kitchen as well as a more public area in which he could greet his devotees. Darshans in which a public audience with the god was permitted took on the aura of the Mughal *darber,* an ornate court in the palace where the emperor conducted public audiences. However, the haveli was also designed as a bastion of absolute purity free from the ritual pollution of the outside world.

In these and in other innovations, Vitthalnath acquired all of the characteristics of a sectarian organizer and developer. He successfully recruited members of the mercantile castes, generating a body of believers among a large segment of Gujaratis.[37] Devotees were drawn to the sect for a number of reasons. Vallabha was increasingly seen as an incarnation of Krishna and a source of divinity. The dominant form of Krishna in the sampradaya was a child, Shri Nathji, who became increasingly popular with families. Using this to its advantage, the sect developed the image of family, even applying the term Vallabhkul (used to refer to Vallabha's descendants) to all Pushtimargiyas.[38] As family traditions are constructed around shared cuisine, food became central to the tradition. During large festivals including *Annakut* and *Chappan Bhog* large quantities of sanctified food were distributed, becoming a medium for ritual exchange. Devotees not only were fed but also acquired merit. Even to this day, "Pushtimarg pays particular attention to the feeding of *svarups* and the sect has evolved a sophisticated cuisine made up of dishes from the regional cuisines of Braj, Gujarat, Rajasthan, and South India."[39]

As the faith attracted increasing numbers, Vitthalnath reinforced the worship of other deities in order to compete with the Gaudiya sampradaya of Chaitanya. He included the female deity, Swamini, and the manifestation of Krishna as Shri Mathuradhishji, popular among Gaudiyas.[40] Like his father, he utilized pilgrimage as a means of gathering support, touring "the Gujarat six times between 1543 and 1581 with the intention of raising money to fund the luxurious programme of devotional worship he had introduced in his temple on Govardhan Hill in Braj."[41] Continuing the tradition of his father, he expanded the cadre of poets whose poems (*padas*) become integral with seva, eventually leading to the group of eight who formed the *Astachap* tradition. Perhaps most significantly, as the following chapters will show, he established relationships with the Mughal court, which resulted in the beginnings of the patronage as a continuing means of support for the sect.

Astachap

In codifying the teachings of his father into an effective sectarian corpus of doctrine and practice, Vitthalnath established the authority of a small core of poets, the Astachap ("eight seals"), whose devotional poems became integral with darshan. Each poet was understood to have had lasting relationships with Vallabha or Vitthalnath. Four poets who had known Vallabha were included in this cadre: Kumbhan Das, Surdas, Paramanand Das, and Krishna Das. Four others were recruited by Vitthalnath: Govind Swami, Chitaswami, Nand Das, and Chaturbhooj Das.

Of the eight, Surdas has drawn the most interest from literary critics. Surdas is acclaimed for his sensual, devotional verse, and the padas attributed to him are contained in a mammoth collection of 5,000 entries called the *Sursagar*. However, this collection was compiled well after his death and probably only included 400–500 padas that can actually be attributed to him.[42] John Hawley concludes,

> If one examines the oldest manuscripts of the *Sūrsāgar*, one finds collections comprising only a few hundred poems. The number grew in the course of time as other poems—some of them originally "signed" by other poets—were added to the corpus; and over the course of time there was a general shift in the tenor of

the poetry too. All this makes clear that what we have in the *Sūrsāgar* is not the monumental work of a single poet that was early dispersed and had to be reassembled over the generations, but a sprawling, gradually evolving tradition that undoubtedly includes poems composed by several authors. Yet, each of these poems bears a single poet's name.[43]

The lore that came to surround Surdas connected him with royalty. According to sectarian tradition the poet received an audience with the Mughal emperor Akbar, who recognized the inner vision of the blind poet. Yet, Surda's padas are silent about history:

> His poems tell us nothing of the emperor or his empire, although its busy center was a scant hundred miles from the poet's home. The poems are silent on the fall of the Delhi Sultanate and the ascendancy of the Mughals, yet these events occurred within the span of the poet's life. Absent too is all comment on the progress of a fragile peace between Muslim rulers and Hindu populace.[44]

Surdas' padas provide a window into a developing tradition. In a manner similar to the growth of the Islamic Sufi tradition, the sensual verses of the Astachap poets were part of a devotional movement that lifted devotees out of a mundane environment, transporting them into a sacred (*alaukika*) realm. There, all reality was Krishna.

Creating a Pushtimarg Sacred Geography

When Mircea Eliade wrote *The Sacred and the Profane* in 1956 he conceived of a pattern of transcendence that was qualitatively related to the nature of physical reality.[45] Eliade posited that the experience of the sacred could be directly connected with place and that the resulting characteristics of sacred space differed from the ordinary.[46] For Eliade, sacred space was a center, an *axis mundi*, that connected heaven and earth in a way that ordinary space could not. Whereas everyday space was defined by maps, scale, and measured distances, sacred space was not linear and carried the promise of transformation and change.

Drawing on these ideas, Diana Eck suggests that India's topography is a vast web of sacred sites or *tirthas* ("crossing places") that together form a unitary landscape.[47] In *India: A Sacred Geography,* she shows how these networks connect and what gives them meaning.[48] Within the interconnecting networks of sacred geography some places, such as Varanasi (Banaras), are more obvious centers of the holy than others: "Banāras does not stand alone as the great center of pilgrimage for Hindus, but is part of an extensive network of pilgrimage places stretching throughout the length and breadth of India."[49]

Eck calls the process of creating a landscape in which one aspect of a holy place can become another "spatial transposition":

> Spatial transposition is a fascinating fact of India's spiritual geography. Kāshī, of course, is present in a thousand places in India, each with its own temple of Kāshī Vishvanātha, some even boasting a Panchakroshī Road. Kāshī is the paradigm of the sacred place, to which other places subscribe in their claims to sanctity. At the same time, Kāshī includes all the other *tīrthas* within it.[50]

Within this perspective, sacred places are fluid realities that can be recreated and even contained within each other. They are geographical and historical but their essence is shrouded in accretions of myth.

Since the origin of the tradition in the late fifteenth century, Pushtimarg has identified sacred space with a rural area in North India called Braj, which in its Sanskritized form is called Vraja. Located in North India within an easy drive from New Delhi, Braj is not hard to find:

> Braj is located along the Yamuna River about ninety miles south of Delhi. It lies in the middle of that fertile heartland of northern India created when the South Asian subcontinent crashed into the continent of Asia some 50 million years ago, forming a huge ditch to be filled in with the rich alluvial soil from the rapidly rising Himalaya Mountains. The area of Braj is somewhat circular, with a diameter of roughly sixty miles, and is situated in the cultivated river valley of the western Mathura district in the modern state of Uttar Pradesh, extending into the desert terrain of the Bharatpur district of eastern Rajasthan.[51]

As a unique historical region in North India defined by the meandering Yamuna River, forests and small villages, Braj has been a spiritual center for a number of Vaishnava sects including the Pushtimarg tradition, the Gaudiya Sampradaya, the Nimbarka Sampradaya, the Radhavallabha Sampradaya, and the Haridasi Sampradaya.[52]

Braj has become portable, replicating its mystical imagery wherever devotees have migrated. Every haveli, whether in India or abroad, recreates this imagery. Life size images of *gopis*, cattle, and depictions of rural, agrarian life frame the darshan. Krishna is awakened, fed and tends his cattle not in Mumbai, London, or rural Pennsylvania but in a timeless environment, skillfully recreated in each haveli. Within the temple, Braj emerges as a spiritual realm that is not dependent on geography, but instead on a state of awareness that relies on a metaphor of movement in which the god moves through time and space.

The mythology of Braj emerged in the *Bhagavata Purana* and particularly in the tenth book, which describes the birth of Krishna. For Pushtimargiyas, the *Purana*'s description of Krishna lifting up Mount Govardhan in the heart of Braj forms one of the most important connections between topography and myth. Facing Indra, who became jealous when devotees sought him out, Krishna, an incarnation of Vishnu, offered protection:

> 18 Therefore, I make this pledge: I shall bring about the protection of the cowherd community by my own mystic power. They accept me as their Lord, their shelter is in me, and they are my family.
> 19 Saying this, Vishnu lifted up the mountain of Govardhan with one hand and held it effortlessly just like a child holds a mushroom.
> 20 Then the Lord spoke to the cowherds: "Mother, father, and residents of Braj, enter the cavity under the mountain along with your herds of cows at your leisure."
> 21 "Please do not entertain any fear that the mountain might fall from my hand during this time. Enough of your fear of the rain and wind! I have arranged shelter from them for you."
> 22 At this, their minds were pacified by Krishna, and they entered the cavity with their wealth, herds, and dependents in accordance with the available space.
> 23 Giving up concern for hunger and thirst, and any expectation of comfort, Krishna held up the mountain for seven days. Watched by those residents of Braj, he did not move from that spot.[53]

As a central theophany within Pushtimarg, Govardhan is a focal point for pilgrimage and is associated with an intense measure of devotion. The mountain is also seen to *be* Krishna. For example, in the *Govardhana-lila*, Surdas concludes:

> "That Mountain looks so much like 'Syām ...
> So hungrily it feasts,
> Stretching out its thousand arms;
> And this child standing here, holding Nanda's hand—
> He's the very same form as the Mountain!" ...
> Little Rādhā stood stunned by the beauty of it all,
> As little 'Syām fixed his eyes upon her;
> The Beloved succumbed to the glances of desire
> Cast sidelong by the Lord of Sūrdās.[54]

Because of its special significance, Govardhan is carefully watched over by Vaishnavas.[55] The mountain has also become an object of pilgrimage in an arduous, physically demanding form of devotion:

> Some people circulate the hill.... This involves prostrating along the whole length of the sacred circuit at every step, lying flat on the ground with arms outstretched and then moving forwards to prostrate again at the place last touched by one's fingers. This takes between ten and twelve days; but there is an even more arduous form ... undertaken by those who wish to repay a boon, acquire merit, or feel

that they have a heavy burden of karma to work off. They perform one hundred and eight prostrations on the spot before they move one body-length forward, counting their prostrations by moving a small stone from a diminishing pile at their feet to a growing one at the point reached by their outstretched hands.... [This] takes between two and four years.[56]

Difficult rituals such as the circumambulation of Mount Govardhan also call attention to the sacred journey as a way to "see" Krishna. From the earliest days of Pushtimargiya tradition this metaphor has been employed as part of a larger Braj pilgrimage called the *Ban-Yatra*. The Ban-Yatra is a transformative journey that for many dissolves the spiritual separation between pilgrims who take it and god. Devotees course through the landscape of Braj visiting holy sites associated with the life of Krishna. David Haberman recounts his personal experiences:

> The boundary of Braj functions to focus the attention of the pilgrims on higher truths. Pilgrims come here accepting that they have arrived at Krishna's dham (sacred abode), in which everything that happens is Krishna's lila (play). Several told me that the Ban-Yatra is an exercise for seeing things as they really are, namely lila. What Ban-Yatra pilgrims come to realize in Braj is that much of the lila looks like ordinary activities, or conversely, that ordinary activities are Krishna's lila. This opens the way for a perspectival awakening: that which is present in Braj in an intensified form is also available elsewhere. There is no need to search for a passageway out of this world, there is no need for a radical change, for this very world is itself divine. Once this realization takes place, the frame suddenly appears artificial.[57]

To experience the spiritual awakening that accompanies the Ban-Yatra is to perceive Braj at the intersection of geography, history, and mythology. It is also to participate in the process of spatial transposition in which each part of the whole can contain the sum of its parts.[58] This experience is part of a visit to the village of Vrindaban, deep in the heart of Braj. Vrindaban is not only a focal point in the life of Krishna, but also the province of a local god, Vrinda. River banks, or "*ghats*," such as *Chir Ghat*, mark familiar stories and are seen as the "place where Krishna is said to have stolen the Gopis' clothes and hid them in a tree."[59] Yet another part of Vrindaban is Govind Dev, dedicated to Govinda, the central deity of Vrindaban, but also associated with Krishna and specifically with the sound of his flute.[60] Within the body of Krishna lore, the flute assumes a magical quality, luring devotees who leave what they are doing to follow the sound.

The sanctity of Vrindaban is well known to every participant in the Ban-Yatra. Yet, beyond such heavily mythologized sites, even villages that are off of the beaten path carry intense levels of meaning. One example is Shyam

Dhak. Located at a distance from the pilgrimage routes and rarely frequented by travelers who come to Braj, Shyam Dhak nevertheless has numerous connections with the life of Krishna. For example, "some modern sources refer to the area here as Kaj(j)ali Ban and say that it is where Krishna used to graze cattle. He is believed to have made the leaves of one of the trees here turn into cups so that he and his companions could eat their curd."[61] References to Shyam Dhak also abound in sacred literature, including several post–Vedic texts such as the *Mathuramahatmya* in the larger *Varaha Purana*, which is part of a group of five treatises.[62] It is also described in the *Bhushundiramayana*, as a retelling of the story of Rama"[63] and in the *Vrajabhaktivilasa* of Narayan Bhatt, written in the eighteenth century.[64] Shyam Dhak is further discussed in the *varta* literature that "describe the activities of Vallabha, Vitthalnath, and their disciples"[65] and in the *Braj Manndal Kamalakar Bhavana*, a prose text written in Braj Bhasha.[66] Shyam Dhak is also mentioned in pilgrimage literature including the works of Brajnath.[67]

In sum, Braj is a network of well-established sites and more obscure places such as Shyam Dhak, whose connections to mythology are easily revealed. Within its total expanse of villages, fields, and forests, Braj is public space that is easily accessed within India's larger sacred geography.

This is also the case with the 84 *baithaks* (fig. 3), places sanctified by Vallabha, Vitthalnath, and his seven sons that publicly mark events in their lives. Some baithaks are seen as so connected to deity that they may be foreboding and restricted. Writing in a blog, a Pushtimargiya devotee described visiting one such baithak in a wooded area near Mysore that was so intensely associated with the experience of deity that visiting the region was seen as prohibitive:

> It was not even more than five minutes, when the forest officer advised us to leave. He only then revealed that this place is never visited by anyone, not even by the tribals. He said that without divine intervention it was not possible to visit the spot, and said that you people have been able to do so only because of the grace of the god. Myself and Shree Vrajeshbhai exchanged meaningful glances, knowing fully well that it was because of the divine presence of Shree Vallabhkul that we were able to make this journey, if not it would not have been possible.[68]

While not all baithaks would create this intense level of experience, they remain a formidable, public sacred geography of their own. In addition to the 84 baithaks attributed to Vallabhacharya, 28 baithaks are attributed to Vitthalnath. Another 30 baithaks are attributed to the seven sons of Vitthalnath. Together, these sites form a network of 142 sacred spaces throughout the Indian subcontinent. Because of their number, diversity, and association with

Fig. 3. Distribution of the principal 84 baithaks (courtesy Elizabeth Richardson, Bhagwat Shah and Seth Rehrig).

other parts of India's sacred geography, the baithaks form an important linkage between Pushtimarg and the larger Hindu tradition.

Expanding Sacred Space Through the Gaddis

Within Pushtimargiya sacred geography, not all holy places are public. Private sacred space developed in the seats or gaddis ("thrones") where the descendants of Vallabhcharya established centers for the care of the swarups. Peter Bennett notes that the *maharajas* or goswamis, together with those disciples who support them in the matter, claim that the temples under their jurisdiction are not public places of worship, but their own private (*nij*) houses, all rights over which, and benefits accruing from which, belong exclusively to them.... The rights which they claim amount to control over the temples as privately owned houses: devotees are allowed to enter the *haveli* only after receiving the *guru's* permission; they may offer donations in cash and kind only with the *guru's* consent; all priests and temple functionaries are appointed and removed by the *guru's* will; offerings become the property of the *guru* to be disposed of according to his own wishes, while some Maharajas have even claimed that they may close the havelis and remove the deity if they think fit to do so.[69]

While the theological expression of Pushtimarg emphasized the movement of Krishna, who appeared and disappeared at will, the geographical expansion of the sect was influenced by two symbiotic processes. The first was the dispersal by Vitthalnath of the nidhi swarups to his sons and the establishment of gaddis or seats with a spiritual center at Nathdwara in the Hindu state of Mewar. The second process was a series of movements, beginning with the transfer of the swarup of Shri Nathji to Mewar at the end of the seventeenth century and continuing with the relocation of other swarups during the course of the next two centuries. Undoubtedly, as Norbert Peabody concludes, this process was also influenced by the economy of pilgrimage:

> When economic conditions in the bazaar were weak, as a result of a disruption in pilgrimage due to political instability, for example, then donations to the temple decreased which was immediately reflected in the abridgment or illumination of costly rituals performed for the deity. This, in turn, adversely affected the reputation of the deity, leading to a further reduction of pilgrimage. A significant drop-off in pilgrimage then undermined the bazaar economy so that temple donations from the local business community also declined and so on. When downward economic spirals became prolonged, economic pressures mounted on the presiding goswami to move his statue to another kingdom as in the cases of Shri Mathureshji's and Shri Vitthalnathji's travels to Kota in 1744 and 1802 respectively.[70]

At times, rivalry within the sect expanded the sacred geography. In order to insure the preservation of the Vallabhkul, the dynasty had created sublineages and had even permitted (in the absence of a male heir) adoption of boys from one gaddi to another.[71] Gaddis became increasingly competitive. In 1670, rival claims were made that led to the formation of the sixth gaddi (see chapter 2). In other instances gaddis were consolidated. The swarup of shri Vitthalnathji was taken to Nathdwara in 1821 to remain installed in a haveli next to the central shrine of Shri Nathji. The swarup of Shri Dwarkadhishji was taken to Kankroli in Mewar in 1719 as the *maharanas* of Mewar accrued greater gain from the continued presence of the sect. After considerable travel, the swarup of Shri Mathureshji was installed in the village of Jatipura. Three other swarups, Shri Madanamohanji, Shri Gokulanathji, and Shri Gokulachandramaji, had been in Jaipur and were removed to Gokul at the end of the nineteenth century. In still further expansion, a group of supplemental nidhi swarups were venerated including Shri Kalyanraiji, Shri Mukundaraiji, and Shri Natvarlalji. Finally, an adopted son of Vitthalnath, Tulsidasa, established another swarup, Shri Gopinathji, who was taken to the Sindh and then moved to Brindaban in Braj.[72]

By the end of this complex process the gaddis included the following[73]:

Son's name	House	*Swarup*	Location
Giridharji	First	Shri Nathji	Nathdwara (Rajasthan)
		Shri Navanitpriyaji	Nathdwara (Rajasthan)
		Shri Mathureshji	Jatipura (Braj in Rajasthan)
Govindarayji	Second	Shri Vitthalnathji	Nathdwara (Rajasthan)
Balakrishnaji	Third	Shri Dwarkadhishji	Kankroli (Rajasthan)
Gokulanathji	Fourth	Shri Gokulanathji	Gokul (Braj in Rajasthan)
Raghunathji	Fifth	Shri Gokulachandramaji	Kamban (Rajasthan)
Yadunathji	Sixth	Shri Balakrishnaji	Surat (Gujarat)
Ghanashyamji	Seventh	Shri Madanmohanji	Kamban (Rajasthan)

During the process of moving and relocating swarups, goswamis also independently established havelis. While the eldest goswami in each gaddi was charged with maintaining the seat, other family members often opened havelis. The total process of expansion became a confederation loosely organized around the seven gaddis but incorporating a significant number of havelis throughout Rajasthan and the Gujarat.

Seva as Vallabha's Primary Expression of Bhakti

The North Indian bhakti movement of the fifteenth and sixteenth centuries redefined the relationship between devotee and deity by introducing an intimate, highly personal form of worship called seva (service). In Pushtimarg, seva is a diversified, home centered practice offered to any swarup, either in the form of a physical image or a visual representation. Often done in the morning, seva may collapse the ritual day into a single period. But, no matter when and for which swarup seva is offered, its detailed component parts are done with the authorization of a goswami who also functions as a *guru*.

Ritual requirements for performing seva at home are included in scripture. Descriptions can be found in a number of sectarian sources including the *Bade Shikshapatra*, an early manual for devotees.[74] The *Bade Shikshapatra* is a relatively brief document that achieves importance through its selfless descriptions of seva and the centrality of the swarup. A more detailed description of seva is contained in the *Sadhan Dipika,* an early text from the time of Gopinathji, the brother of Vitthalnath. Traditions related to the performance of seva also emanate from each of the seven gaddis, where generations of goswamis have defined the practice.

While, like most Hindu rituals, seva is governed by rules and traditions from these sources, devotees stress that its performance must also be spontaneous. Seva is done with the love that a parent provides to children and requires an attitude rooted in nurture and in the immediate concern for the well-being of an infant. Beyond the individual variations within the Vallabhkul, certain parts of the practice of daily seva are common. Most supplicants perform seva in the morning after bathing in order to preserve their ritual purity. Clean clothes are worn. A *tilak* is placed on the forehead before the rite begins. In many homes the swarup is kept in a small temple; a travel box or *japiji* (fig. 4) may also be used. Both contain a space for the deity's bedroom, which is equipped with a bed, a mirror and space for storage of blankets and substances used during the seva. Japijis also provide screened openings so that the bedroom receives an adequate supply of air.

A morning seva can be completed in a half hour or may continue for a much longer period. In the simplest and most abbreviated form, the swarup is awakened with a bell or by clapping hands. His face is cleaned and a bath may be given as determined by the guru. When a full ritual immersion is done, herbal substances such as *abhyang* powder and paste may be used. Oils and perfumes may also be applied to the swarup, who is adorned with a *Gunja Mala*—a special garland of red and white beads associated with Krishna. Sugar is presented and milk and fruit may also be offered. The devotee asks the deity to accept the food and prostrates in full *dandavat,* with arms stretched out and feet pressed against the floor. Once the deity has been fed and bathed his bedroom is cleaned and preparations are made for sleep. Additional food may be offered. Swarups are traditionally placed on the mattress so that the left hand holding the butter is elevated with the god's head against the pillow. In colder weather, blankets are provided.

In more extended versions of daily seva additional preparations are necessary.[75] A *tulsi* leaf, which is particularly associated with Krishna, may be placed in front of the deity. The *Brahmsambandh mantra* may be repeated several times.[76] Other *mantras* and prayers may also be offered. After being offered milk and sugar, and after the prostration of the devotee, the deity is left to consume his food in a period lasting 48 minutes. While the food is being consumed by the god the kitchen is cleaned; special attention is given

Fig. 4. A japiji.

to the utensils that have been used as part of the meal. Hands are washed again to be sure of absolute ritual purity. When the deity is again awakened, his face is again cleaned with water and dried. A *mala*, or garland, made from fresh flowers is presented to him. The deity is placed on the temple and given toys. His flute is placed next to him and a mirror is presented so that he can admire himself as the supplicant repeats a full prostration. Hands are washed again. The garland and flute are removed and placed on the side. Recitations are done as the swarup is placed on his bed, where he falls asleep.

In still other more extended forms of seva, the morning food offerings are more extensive and include milk, cream, butter, crushed sugar powder, curds and pickles. When a bath (*snan*) is provided the swarup is placed on an octagonal platform, bathed with four vessels of warm water and patted dry with a soft cloth. Two garlands may be offered instead of one. He is shown a mirror, after which the supplicant touches the deity's feet, bringing his hands to eyes, head, and heart. Milk may be offered before the larger meal, after which toys are presented. In the evening, food is again offered and includes seasonal fruits that have been peeled and cut. At bedtime a light snack of milk and rice is presented. Perfumes are applied on the bed, pillow, and bed cover. Sleeping clothes are provided and the swarup is carefully put to bed.

Because there is no single, unifying source of instruction for devotees, and because American Pushtimargiyas come from all seven gaddis, some Vaishnava leaders have attempted to standardize the tradition in the United States. *Tavasmi* has published a step by step manual, *Krishna Sewa Primer*,[77] which is provided to initiates to the sect. Recognizing that not all devotees have access to swarups, the *Primer* includes pictures of Shri Nathji, Vallabhacharya, and Shri Yamunaji suitable for worship. Prayers are offered and may include the *Shri Vallabh Stuti,* the *Shri Krishna Stuti,* and the *Shri Yamuna Stuti* in a form known as *Shri Yamunashtak.*

In all forms of seva, attention is focused on the swarup. Extraneous thoughts are eliminated during the ritual, which is only begun when standards of purity can be maintained. During the seva, the sight of Krishna's face is greatly anticipated, becoming the focal point of the ritual. The *Bade Shikshapatra* concludes:

> If the heart hankers
> For a spiritual reward,
> Let it be Krishna's face.
> The ever-blissful Krishna
> Is the reward,
> For he is the essence
> Of your love.[78]

Ritual Functions of Seva

Seva incorporates many of the same acts that are part of *puja*, yet the two rites do not have the same functions and are understood through different theological lenses. Puja is a generic expression of devotion and is done to receive the god as an honored guest. Embodying pan–Hindu symbols of hospitality and royalty, puja is performed in temples and in homes to a single deity or to a variety of gods and emphasizes a series of actions:

Awakening and bathing	gods are bathed in water and in a number of other substances including milk and ghee (clarified butter).
Feeding	bronze or stone icons are fed a number of times during the day. Food offerings may also be left at the base of the shrine. Once food has been ritualistically consumed by the deity it is considered prasad ("grace") and may be consumed by the deities' attendants.
Anointing	the deity may be anointed with powders including sandalwood paste, given as a mark of respect.
Entertaining	temple musicians may entertain the god as part of the puja.
Sleep	the deity rests during the day (frequently in the afternoons) and also at night. In some temples, the doors to the inner sanctuary are kept closed during this period.

While *seva* includes many of the same elements, for Pushtimargiyas it is more focused and carries specific theological meaning. The swarup defines the home: the family and all material wealth are understood to belong to the deity. As complete surrender, seva focuses the attention of the worshipper on this presence and is constructed around an ongoing ritual relationship that is repeated daily. Because many swarups have lengthy familial histories, *seva* may also evoke a host of memories within the extended family. Once initiated, devotees are obliged to perform seva for the rest of their lives. Unlike puja, which is frequently performed but rarely required, seva is obligatory and is linked to the traditions of the extended family within which it is practiced. Supplicants are required to perform it daily and even to carry their images with them during periods of travel.

Seva becomes a doorway to a higher realm (alaukika) and is defined by strict thresholds of ritual. The supplicant must have received initiation (*Brahmsambandh*) and must be free from all pollution. Successful performance of seva depends not only on physical purity but also on the absence of mental restrictions,[79] since Pushtimargiya tradition requires purity of thought and total surrender for transformation to take place. Seva becomes an experience of truly "seeing" Krishna and at the same time expressing gratitude for those souls that have been created for his pleasure.

Above all, seva is defined by a level of mystical awareness known as bhava, which moves the devotee from the egocentric domain of emotion to a higher state. This can be difficult for Western minds to fathom, since it depends on the absence of linear time and denies history any connotation of absolute reality. David Haberman suggests that bhava arises at the intersection of imagination and emotion:

Such questions as "Did this really happen here?" are really concerned with the issue of historical authenticity, but this way of thinking is somewhat alien to the religious thought of Braj. For most of the people with whom I discussed this problem, it had more to do with the issue of *bhava*, that is, with the investment of a certain kind of emotional and imaginative energy.[80]

Drawing on bhava, the devotee adopts one of several attitudes toward Krishna. Perhaps the most common of these moods is *Vatsalya bhava*, in which the worshipper assumes the role of a parent, caregiver and provider.[81] *Dasya bhava* defines the relationship between deity and supplicant as master and servant. Another bhava, *Madhurya*, is understood as an expression of love based on the romantic longing of Krishna's female followers and especially his consort, Radha. She may be painted in an amorous embrace with the dark god or seeking his company in the heart of the forests of Braj. *Madhuyra bhava* is also the domain of Krishna as a trickster. In numerous schools of art produced by bhakti sects, Radha is shown seeking her lover when, all the while, he is sporting with other women. In the context of bhakti, this situation is rarely understood to produce either anger or jealousy. Instead, Krishna is longed for even more.[82] Finally, *Shanta bhava* is the emotional state that results from seeing Krishna as transcendent.[83]

In each of these forms of bhava, finding Krishna became a metaphor for religious experience. Fleeting but totally transforming, the encounter is always sought but never permanently gained. It cannot be possessed and can only be understood through an attitude of surrender so complete that pride cannot be connected with its loss or gain. Bhava can only be cultivated over time:

> *Bhava* is not suddenly acquired; it grows in intensity within the mind of the worshipper; and as it grows the *svarup*, being the object of *bhava*, is infused with divine love, thereby gradually assuming an independent personality in the eyes of the devotee. Ultimately, when the devotee acquires perfect *bhava*, then the *svarup* appears as a perfect manifestation of Krishna and both sport together in *lila*.[84]

For devotees who have cultivated bhava over a lifetime, the relationship with the swarup can be intense. For example, a woman visiting the Vraj temple in Pennsylvania for a festival remarked that she would never consider leaving her home unless someone could be found who would do her daily regimen of seva. She talked about a month-long vacation and the care that she took to be certain the infant Krishna in her home shrine would be attended and cared for.

The transformation that accompanies seva and the acquisition of bhava is rooted in liminality—an "interstructural situation," in between two states.[85] This perception, developed through the ritual studies of Arnold van Gennep and later by Victor Turner, was initially applied to rites of passage.[86] However, since Turner's initial analysis, liminality has been understood as a component of a broader base of rituals in both secular and religious domains. A liminal experience is defined by ritual separation and produces a sense of disorientation that is also associated with vulnerability. As supplicants move through a liminal ritual environment, disorientation leads to the reconstruction of meaning, often accompanied by the support of other supplicants in an experience that Turner defined as communitas.

As a recurrent rite, seva is dependent on thresholds that separate the ritual area and create a liminal environment. To perform seva is to experience this environment, only available to initiates. As in all liminal spaces, the ritual space contains the possibility of transformation. It becomes a place where

> men and gods are held to be transparent to one another. It is a place, whereas in all forms of communication, static and noise (i.e. the accidental) are decreased so that the exchange of information can be increased. In communication, the device by which this is accomplished is redundancy ... through repetition and routinization.[87]

While on the surface this exchange seems much the same as generic forms of puja, Pushtimargiya tradition understands it quite differently. Whether in the haveli or in the home, the liturgical foundations of seva are threefold: *raag* (music), *bhog* (food that is offered to the deity), and *shringar* (clothes and ornaments that the deity wears).[88] These are the primary responsibility of the musicians (*kirtankars*) who participate in the darshan and the priest. In smaller havelis, the priest (or laity with musical training) performs the functions of a kirtankar. In the home, the person performing the seva may also sing *kirtans*.

Bhog is equally important in the temple and is focused on the transformation of food (bhog) into grace (prasad): "The central transformation in food ritual occurs when bhog ... is set before Krishna's image and Krishna himself is believed to consume it, through the image's eyes or mouth. In this act of consumption bhog is metonymically transformed into more love-laden prasad."[89]

The food that is offered to the deity must be of the utmost purity. In a haveli it is prepared by the priest and his family while in the larger havelis there may be a second priest to assist. Once ritualistically consumed this food becomes prasad and is distributed to devotees. Most havelis provide a meal after the noon *Raj Bhog darshan* that is freely presented to everyone who has attended. There are considerable expenses associated with these traditions that are often provided for through a tradition called *manorath*, in which devotees may donate funds to cover the cost of the darshan.

Toomey suggests that as a bhakti tradition, the process of food exchange in Pushtimarg looks at the transformation of bhog to prasad as a form of wealth since "food offerings are one of the primary means by which wealth is expressed in this sect."[90] Since seva also expresses the dedication of the devotees' minds, bodies, and wealth as part of the process, the "entire ritual system is shaped by a maternal metaphor, *pushti*, or nourishing grace. Like mothers, devotes are expected to nourish *svarups* with material offerings. Offerings are ritually channeled to sacred images by *gosvamis* and their priestly intermediaries and returned to devotees suffused and enriched by Krishna's pushti."[91]

The deity's dress (shringar) reflects the season of the year. Jewelry and other types of adornment are precisely altered to meet these requirements. Shringar is far more than embellishment. It exists for the comfort of the deity and is also connected with the ability of the worshiper to connect form and appearance with inner reality. For this reason, havelis always have on hand several pairs of binoculars for devotees who note what Krishna is wearing and how he appears.

The complex relationship between raag, bhog, and shringar is continued in the home where the ritual day is often collapsed in order to fit with busy life styles. Seva in the home is an important step in the larger ritual process of the sect where the family establishes a link with the larger Vallabhkul. The swarup, blessed by the goswami and ritually prepared for use in a family domain, connects the Vallabhkul with the devotee. While recorded in sectarian literature such as the Shikshapatra, regulations for conducting seva ultimately are the province of the goswami, who remains a living link with Vallabhacharya and at the same time is a guru who nurtures devotees to experience higher states of bhava.

Devotees wishing to do the full seva are required to seek permission from their goswami whose hereditary office combines the religious roles of teacher and spiritual adviser. Performing a full seva is a lengthy and time consuming process that may take four to six hours. In addition, supplicants observing the full ritual are also required to offer all food that is cooked in the house to Krishna before consuming it. This requires hours of preparation, since the food must meet exacting standards of ritual purity before the process can begin.

Seva is both an intensely private experience and a cultural norm. Outsiders rarely have the opportunity to view it. In India, and in the United States, seva also becomes a vehicle for social relationships. Women may gather to share food that is offered to the deity and to discuss other details of the ritual. In Chicago, one family discussed taking the images (referred to as *Thakorji*— "Lord") on a picnic where the appropriate kirtans (songs) and padas (poems) are sung and food from a number of families are offered.[92]

At the Vraj haveli in Pennsylvania, in the spring of 2011, Pushtimargiya devotees from all over the United States brought their swarups together.[93] The gathering of almost 100 women required significant preparation not only among the organizers of the event but also by each participant. Each image, carefully protected, was attended by a devotee.

Grandmothers frequently instruct their daughters and daughters-in-law in the procedures for doing seva. As a result of the continuous cycle of worship the deities may possess a complex retinue of clothing, oils for anointing, furniture and bedding, all designed to provide for the god's comfort and care. For most practitioners of seva, who are frequently female but sometimes male, the ritual is an important component of the day and sets the stage for all of the events that follow.

Pushtimargiyas[94] in the United States often identify a more rigid group of practitioners known as *marjadi*. These orthodox devotees were commonly found among Pushtimargiya communities a generation ago, but their numbers have waned. Dominated by detailed regulations governing purity and pollution, they practice a form of seva so austere that they are often hesitant to touch anyone outside the tradition for fear of being contaminated. In India, some marjadi worshippers are so devout that they move into the haveli, volunteering all of their time in service of the deity. Marjadi devotees will only consume food that has been prepared in Pushtimargiya homes, never eating outside. Everything that is done is for the sake of the deity, who cannot be approached except by persons in a high state of ritual purity.

Seva as an Expression of Boundaries

As the Vallabha Sampradaya evolved in the sixteenth and seventeenth centuries it created boundaries that distinguished it from other North Indian bhakti traditions. These boundaries, which were associated with ritual purity, included the role of caste in attracting followers and the authority of mukhiyas and goswamis.

The ability of religion to create and sustain a variety of boundaries is not unusual. In *The Psychology of Religion and Coping: Theory, Research, Practice,* Kenneth Pargament discusses the role of boundaries in religion as a means of conserving significance.[95] He suggests that boundaries protect and preserve tradition and lifestyle and "draw an unmistakably clear line between one's own world and the forces outside it."[96]

As a form of boundary, the Vallabha Sampradaya developed a widespread following among several caste groups.[97] *Banias*, "whose members tend to be engaged as retail shopkeepers, brokers, moneylenders, and merchants,"[98] formed the nucleus of the tradition. Pushtimarg also became popular with *Bhatia* merchants who had developed patterns of intermarriage with the goswamis.⁹⁹ While access to Pushtimarg was not restricted to these groups, these caste affiliations created a boundary that further defined the faith.

Yet another form of boundary was the designation of Vallabha's patrilineal descendants as goswamis ("lord of the cows"), who carried ultimate spiritual authority. Forming a dynasty (Vallabhkul), goswamis developed marriage patterns that could be sustained by their descendants without compromising their purity. Practicing caste (*jati*) exogamy, members of the dynasty evolved a pattern of marriage using Vallabha's daughter-in-law, Padmavati, who was *Bhatta*, as a prototype.¹⁰⁰ Since Bhattas were also *Tailangana Brahmins*, as was Vallabha, this tradition insured the continued purity of his descendants.

The Vallabhkul authorized devotees to perform seva through an initiation ritual called Brahmsambandh, modeled after Vallabha's own pattern of seva to Sri Nathji. Brahmsambandh is a form of initiation or *diksha* that has a wider context in Hindu bhakti traditions. Diksha can connote an initiation to a sampradaya or, within a sectarian tradition, initiation to a monastic order. A layperson who joins a sampradaya

> can have a Guru, and he picks himself out one from amongst the many monks and holy men available, choosing one who suits his own character, which he now hopes to perfect with the aid of his Guru. The Guru gives him a secret *mantra*, a formula which the pupil will repeat a million times in the course of the years, and at the same time he will meditate on the Godhead in the form evoked by his *mantra*, which is the key to that aspect of the Godhead which is chosen, the aim being to win emancipation from the chains of life and rebirth.¹⁰¹

In a monastery, diksha is more complicated. Agehananda Bharati describes the process in the Ramakrishna tradition:

> The authority to give *dikṣā* vests in the very senior monastic personalities, and as seniority is frequently tantamount with fame, and as fame decreases accessibility the individual novice must often wait for quite a while until he gets his *dikṣā*. In the Daśanāmi Order some have to remain without it for twelve years, some just never get it.¹⁰²

While in each of these cases the diksha serves a different purpose, in both instances it confers the spiritual authority that makes the mystical and devotional practices possible. In all cases diksha is bestowed by a guru and requires significant changes in lifestyle. The diksha that accompanies initiation into a sampradaya may require that the supplicant become vegetarian and practice daily seva. More rigorous forms of monastic diksha require much more, as novices adopt the lifestyle of a mendicant, cutting their worldly ties. For *sadhus*, this form of diksha may also require a symbolic funeral in which the supplicant participates in the death of their former self, creating a new person with no ties to their former existence.

Diksha is not the same as membership rituals in the West. In many sampradayas, diksha carries no organizational responsibilities nor does it confer the expectations of membership common in American denominations. Rather, the focus is on the individual who through diksha is authorized to participate in the spiritual requirements of the tradition necessary for accessing the central, numinous experience that is at the heart of bhakti traditions. For Pushtimargiyas, as a form of diksha, Brahmsambandh authorizes the supplicant to perform daily seva. In turn, seva is the gateway to the experience of the lila of Krishna.

In India, Brahmsambandh is often conducted at a young age. Parents prepare children. However, the initiation ceremony may also be offered to adults. No appointed year for the rite is specified, and it is understood to be a ritual that is performed when the devotee feels ready and spiritually mature. When that time comes, arrangements are made for a visiting goswami.

The goswami assesses the level of sincerity of the supplicant and his or her readiness to perform seva. The conversations are serious and involve a commitment that will endure through the candidate's lifetime. Once initiated, the supplicant must continue to perform seva regularly each day. Candidates are also expected to be vegetarian and to participate in a lifestyle consistent with complete surrender to the deity.

In preparation for Bramsambandh or for a festival, visits with the goswami are conducted in a haveli or in the home of a prominent devotee. A visit from the goswami carries the symbolism of an audience with royalty and necessitates careful preparation. Arrangements must be made for the goswami's entrance into the home; this may necessitate a special runner that he can walk on from car to the home. Runners and carpets may be sprinkled with flower petals, and the goswami's entrance into the dwelling may be marked with shouts of praise from the assembled family. Once in the home, the goswami's needs are carefully met. If he stays for a meal, no one will eat with him, since commensality is a vehicle for ritual contamination. The goswami's authority rests on a level of purity consistent with his lineage that cannot be compromised.

In the Pushtimargiya diaspora these conventions are strictly observed. Most goswamis have identified homes near the haveli that hosts them. While prominent Vaishnavas in the community may seek out the responsibility of hosting them, this effort is not taken lightly. It involves maintenance of a home in perfect ritual purity, careful monitoring of all food that is cooked in the house, and the requisite monitoring of the purity of the kitchen. When the time arrives for the audience with the prospective candidate for Brahmsambandh, the meeting must be arranged so that the goswami sits elevated from the devotees, who normally will sit cross legged on the floor. As is often the case with traditional Indian gurus, any teaching that is done begins with a question from the devotee rather than a didactic pronouncement from the goswami.

The ritual is rooted in cultural perceptions of purity that are maintained as a formidable boundary. Initiates must be vegetarian and must accept standards of purity that regulate seva. The rite is administered in the haveli, usually at a time between darshans when the deity is screened from the public. Before the ritual can be conducted the recipient bathes and dons traditional clothing. He or she is not permitted to touch anyone. If for any reason the supplicant is polluted they must wash again. The candidate also wears a necklace (mala) made from Tulsi seeds and sits in a prominent position in the haveli. At the conclusion of the darshan the goswami asks the devotee to step barefooted behind the closed doors or screen that hides the deity. Once inside, the goswami may further question the recipient to be sure of their readiness for the rite. Once this is ascertained and all is satisfied, the devotee must recite a mantra. This is often the Brahmsambandh mantra—"*Sri Krishna Sharanam Mama*" ("I surrender to Lord Krishna"). When this has been completed, the candidate is led back to the assembled crowds and often invited to publically address the gathering.

Brahmsambandh is a formidable boundary that not all Pushtimargiyas are prepared to take. It is often accompanied by a rite called Pusht. The Pusht ceremony is done in secret by the goswami and involves a variety of mantras, formulas and ritualistic washings of the image. This ritual renews the life of the image if it has become dormant or brings new life into an icon of recent manufacture. This ritual has parallels in other parts of Hinduism in a ritual called *Pranpratistha*[103] in which Brahmin priests evoke the presence of deity within an icon in a temple. In other traditions that have been influenced by Hindu culture, similar rites can be found. For example, in Thai forms of Buddhism, images of the Buddha are consecrated in ceremonies within the temple or *wat,* transforming icons into awakened forms of the Buddha.[104]

At the moment that Bramsambandh is given, the goswami also assumes the role of guru. During successive visits to the haveli he or she will meet with the initiates, providing counsel and instruction. Goswamis keep track of where their students live and may meet with them during their travels within the United States.

After Pusht has been done, seva must be offered daily in a protective boundary that insulates the devotee from complete immersion in secular life. If the householder must be away for any period of time, other Vaishnavas must be found to complete the seva. If the swarup is to be moved, transport is accomplished with a small box called a japiji (fig. 4), which can also be used as a miniature temple where the deity sleeps at night. Transport of the deity can be a time of anxiety. For example, a Pushtimargiya family talked about what it was like when their parents carried their swarup from India to Canada when they came to live with their son.[105] In Nathdwara they had a silk-lined jute japiji constructed to house the deity. Within the box, they placed some of their Thakorji's favorite objects as well as the blankets and coverings that he would need for the journey.[106] When the airport security forces questioned them about the wooden container, they proudly exclaimed that this was their god in an affirmation of Krishna's ability to move with those who worship him.

Darshan as an Expression of Seva

As a form of seva, darshans are performed by a resident mukhiya and his assistants every day. Darshans establish a regimen based on the time of day, the needs of Krishna in a pastoral setting related to this period, and the mood that is to be established. The traditional eight darshans are as follows:

Mangala   During this morning darshan the image of Krishna is awakened and given a light breakfast. In havelis, arati (the waving of a lighted wick) may be performed. The offering of food to the deity at this time is done in a very private manner. Bennett concludes, "Not even *Mukhiyaji* [the priest] may see *Thakurji* taking food, so he leaves the *nijmandir* (inner temple) for some fifteen to twenty minutes before returning to open the main doors for devotees to take *darshan*."[107]

Shringar   Krishna is given a bath. Perfumes or scented oils are applied to the deity, who is dressed so as to be absolutely comfortable in any season—warm clothes in winter and light garments during the summer. Jewels and garlands of fresh flowers are used to adorn him. A mirror is shown to him so that he may check his attire before going out for the day. Arati, or the waving of a lamp, is done to remove the evil eye while painted screens are sometimes hung behind him, providing the atmosphere of the festival being celebrated on that day. Food may also be presented.

Gval   This darshan marks the journey of Krishna from his house to the fields where he tends cattle during the day.

Raj Bhog   Raj Bhog is the most popular darshan of the day. Krishna is given a full meal followed by a public darshan after the food has been consumed. Garlands and flowers are offered. Arati is also performed by the mukhiya. After the arati, chopat (a game) is presented so that the deity can play with his friends. Just before the doors of the inner sanctuary are closed the water jugs are changed, garlands are removed, and the game is put away. Following the feast Krishna is given an afternoon nap. In most havelis in the United States, Raj Bhog is also a time when food offerings which are now understood to be prasad, are distributed free of charge to persons who have attended the darshan.

Utthapan The deity rests between 11 a.m. and 4 p.m.[108] He is awakened and may also receive light food.

Bhog Light foods are given to Krishna.

Sandhya-Arati This twilight darshan marks Krishna's return from the fields. In temples, arati is again performed.[109]

Shyan The deity is given an evening meal and put to bed.

Lacking the requisite herds of cows, the Vraj temple in Pennsylvania omits the Gval and Bhog darshans. Havelis in the United States and Canada frequently reduce the liturgical schedule to six rituals; most other havelis have followed suit. At home, the schedule of sevas may be far simpler and often focus on morning darshans in which elements of the remaining periods are collapsed into a single period of worship. Arati is not performed. In many Pushtimargiya homes in the United States, it is the women who perform the rituals.

The Role of Priests (Mukhiyas)

In havelis, the responsibilities for conducting seva rest with the mukhiya (derived from the Sanskrit word *mukhya*—"primary" or "main"). Mukhiyas are a special kind of priest who live in a state of ritual purity. The requirements for ritual purity in the conduct of the darshans are especially rigid: they must bathe twice a day and cannot touch persons who are not of the same ritual status. Their role is further defined by caste in India. Mukhiyas can only be selected from specific lineages of Brahmins.

The training for mukhiyas is done within the context of the family and is frequently passed from father to son. Mukhiyas often assist their fathers in the performance of darshans before doing them independently. In the village of Sanchor in the Gujarat, one devotee estimated that 80 percent of the male population becomes mukhiyas, revealing the dominance of the sect in that part of the state.[110]

Once installed in a haveli, the mukhiya is virtually wedded to his ritual obligations and must maintain a high level of purity. He cannot touch attendees at the darshan nor can he hand them any object directly. If he shares a book with a friend he must drop it in their hands without contact. When he fully prostrates before the deity his palms cannot touch the floor. Instead, mukhiyas rely on their knuckles to get the leverage they need to move off the floor to return to a standing position. During seva he must also refrain from touching either his wife or his children. At times of birth or death in the extended family, he may abstain from doing seva for 3 to 15 days in order to regain ritual purity. During those times an assistant may stand in for him.

The mukhiya is not like other clergy in America. He has no regular hours and no vacation unless an assistant is available. He rarely goes outside the ritual environment. He attends the central icon six times each day depending on the number of darshans the haveli celebrates. He (and his assistants) are the only ones who can touch the swarup; thus he becomes the deity's primary servant. When he is married and raises a family it is always in the context of the haveli. On those rare occasions when he does leave it is within the three- to four-hour period in the afternoon when he has no formal responsibilities or when his helper can briefly take over for him. The mukhiya is also the guardian of the deity's kitchen, the purest portion of the haveli. Just as in the Indian home where the kitchen is maintained in a state of ritual purity, so only the mukhiya and his helper are permitted near food cooked for Krishna. His every move is circumscribed by the purity laws in the haveli.

In the United States, areas for seva may be set aside in a bedroom, or in larger homes an entire room may be given to the deity. This space, much like the inner sanctuaries in the larger havelis, is extremely private and is rarely shown to outsiders. Utmost levels of purity are preserved. Devotees keep a wide variety of ritual paraphernalia for darshans including foodstuffs, sweets, toys for the infant to play with, perfumes and oils, and scented pastes for bathing. Many of these materials are homemade, while others are imported from India and include bedding, furniture and swings on which Krishna sits or plays.

Bhakti in Transit: Pushtimarg and the Gujarati Diaspora

Among Gujaratis, emigration from India has a long history that has also affected Pushtimargiyas. As a seacoast mercantile population, the migration patterns of Gujaratis are ancient and may extend back over two millennia. In British India during the nineteenth and twentieth centuries, as Gujaratis migrated to Great Britain and East Africa, Pushtimargiyas could be found in significant numbers. Later, at the end of the twentieth century, they also migrated to Australia and parts of the Middle East, including Oman and Dubai.[111] Names like Shah and Patel became common from Leicester to Kampala.

Following Indian independence in 1947 the out-migration of Gujaratis from these areas increased. Then, eighteen years later following the U.S. immigration reforms in 1965, Gujaratis looked increasingly to the West for economic opportunities. Many became small business persons, purchasing fast food franchises and entering the lodging industry. In some larger American metropolitan areas, Gujarati populations swelled. In central New Jersey, where Gujaratis and other South Asian populations became highly concentrated, a section of Edison was converted into a "Little India" containing over 400 Indian-owned businesses. In Houston, where the metropolitan area became home to a large number of South Asians, over 20,000 Gujarati immigrants established residence. In other metropolitan areas such as Chicago and Atlanta, sizable Gujarati communities formed ethnic and cultural associations.

Reflecting this growth, and seeking to meet with his devotees in the American diaspora, goswami Mathureshwarji, the head of the sixth gaddi, came to the United States in 1984 as the guest of the *Vishwa Hindu Parishad*, an emerging international organization of Hindus. The goswami's visit had enormous significance for Pushtimargiya devotees in New York City, who began conversations about the construction of a haveli. Led by an oncologist, Dr. Avril Shah, *satsangs* were held in members' homes, leading to the creation of the Vaishnava Temple of New York. Shah's effort was assisted by professional networks. Physicians from the Baroda Medical School found ready entry into the United States at a time when doctors were needed, increasing the Gujarati diaspora in North America.

The identification of diasporas is a recent trend among anthropologists and sociologists, who have recognized a number of characteristics of overseas ethnic communities. These include a "dispersal from an original homeland to two or more countries,"[112] a collective memory of the homeland, a mythology of return that offers ways of coming back to origins, and a sense of empathy with other transnational groups.[113] In addition, "there must be a collective— often idealized—memory/myth of the homeland."[114] Theorists also suggest that diasporan groups also have a strong consciousness about overseas ethnic communities and "a sense of empathy and solidarity with similar groups elsewhere in the world and/or with events and groups in the homeland."[115] Diaspora, then, is a contemporary term used to describe transnational populations whose social, economic, and political networks often make international borders irrelevant.

In American metropolitan areas with high concentrations of Gujaratis, the Pushtimargiya community frequently also retains the characteristics of merchant diasporas in which members have become highly entrepreneurial, a concept that will be developed in part 3. Merchant diasporas are "characterized by a higher degree of mobility, a greater amount of communication between communities, and a higher degree of interaction with the indigenous population."[116] They

> tend to differ from other types of diasporas in several important respects. Most notably, they are characterized by a higher degree of mobility, a greater amount of communication between communities, and a higher degree of interaction with the indigenous population. Unlike other diaspora categories, merchant diasporas may even be peopled by a rotating, gender-specific (generally male) population.[117]

These characteristics have made Gujaratis into a highly mobile and easily adaptable culture that has taken advantage of a variety of economic opportunities. Many are businesspeople who have become active in American franchise industries. In 2006 the *Times of India* estimated that 42 percent of the U.S. hotel businesses were Gujarati.[118]

As Gujarati Pushtimargiyas have entered America, they have also adapted to the denominational system, which is very different from traditional societies. This process will be described in more detail in chapter 5. In America, Pushtimargiyas have also experienced competition, especially from another Gujarati form of Hinduism, the *Swaminarayan* tradition. For some Pushtimargiya communities in the United States participation in both traditions does not pose a problem. In central New Jersey, buses frequently carry Gujarati Hindus to both the Anoopam Mission (a branch of the Swaminarayan faith) in Coplay, Pennsylvania, and to Vraj, near Pottsville, the spiritual headquarters of the Vallabha Sampradaya in the Western Hemisphere. For first generation devotees who grew up in India among both faiths, this juxtaposition does not present theological difficulty. Yet, in America, some Pushtimargiyas view this as a form of competition. Perceptions vary from community to community. In Toronto, for example, where a substantial Swaminarayan temple exists only miles from a smaller Pushtimarg haveli, Pushtimargiyas do not voice much concern about competition.[119]

While patterns of competition among religions may be more typical in the United States than in India, Pushtimarg has easily adapted in a pattern of growth well beyond the gaddis in India. At the same time Pushtimargiyas have erected havelis and celebrated festivals much as they would in Rajasthan or the Gujarat. Using the abilities of first generation immigrant entrepreneurs as their primary means of recreating religious institutions, they have transplanted their faith irrespective of national boundaries.

2

Seeing Krishna

Darshan as the Inward Journey

> *Dawn has come; wake up, O Gopāl*
> *The young girls have come and all the children of Braj*
> *are calling you.*
> *The sun has risen; the moon—the lord of stars—has grown dim and the*
> *young Tamāl trees have flowered.*
> *The women of Braj wait for your Darśan; in their hands are*
> *garlands of flowers which they have woven.*
> *O my son, full of beauty and power, wash your face and have*
> *your breakfast.*
> *Sūrdās says, the Lord is a treasure of bliss, his lotus*
> *eyes are large.*[1]
>
> —Surdas

In havelis worshippers regularly encounter the holy through complex, mystical rituals called darshan, a term that has a wider meaning in the Hindu tradition. Darshan literally means "seeing" and in most forms of Hinduism refers to a visual encounter with god in iconographic form. But, seeing is not unidirectional. It is reciprocal—to see god is also to be seen by him.[2] For Pushtimargiyas, this central experience is portable, transforming a home or haveli into a recreation of the inner experience of Braj.

In Pushtimarg, darshan also refers to a series of specific rituals that are performed six to eight times each day and are intended to meet the needs of the deity. In each ritual, Krishna is unveiled at a precise moment and is presented publically to his devotees. During the ritualized day he moves through a complex cycle of bathing, dressing, anointing, and feasting. He naps, leaves his home to tend the cattle under his charge, and returns home again. Each stage of his life is assisted by a priest and by the devotees' ability to enter the life cycle of the dark god vicariously. Each darshan recreates a unique mood associated with Krishna's activity at that time of day and at the same time centers the devotee in a realm that is sharply distinguished from everyday experience.

At first glance, the cycle of darshans may appear to have some similarities to typical patterns of liturgy that North Americans are used to encountering. Within the rich tapestry of visual imagery that accompanies each darshan, music and verse seem to be independent parts of the experience. Priests chant and musicians sing to accompaniment. Symbols of the sacred are placed on a central, elaborately decorated altar. All of these elements would be expected in common patterns of worship in the United States. However, once immersed in Pushtimarg, this impression quickly fades to reveal a pattern of activity rarely encountered in American religion. Instead of negating the world or renouncing it, the darshan lifts the participants out of it and plunges them into an intimate form of theism that undergirds perceived reality. In the language of the tradition, Krishna is Brahman, the one timeless embodiment of all phenomena.

The experience of finding Krishna is ineffable and at the same time ephemeral. As the mythology contained in poetry and painting confirms, to have him is to lose him as he slips out of sight. In many ways the experience of seeking and momentarily finding Krishna is a metaphor for the search for the transcendent in human religious experience. Always fleeting, never predictable, and ever transforming, the experience of the sacred can never be contained since to do so would be to negate it. In much the same manner Krishna remains elusive. His devotees may seek a fleeting glimpse of him in the clouds of dust surrounding the cattle returning home at the end of the day. Similarly, in the dim light of the early evening, gopis tending their cows search for him, lured by the distant sound of his flute. Others look for him in the mischievous antics of a child god. In each case he never does what is expected and is the consummate trickster, vanishing without prior warning and appearing in the flash of a moment as his devotees long for his presence.

In Pushtimarg, the desire to "see" Krishna is a pivotal experience. In darshan, image, sight, and sound are carefully balanced not to generate a different level of reality, but to strip away all vestiges of the mundane world, revealing the true nature of things. The transformation that accompanies "seeing" Krishna also changes the way that the world is understood, moving the perception of duality into a single, seamless experience. Once seen, even if for a moment, the devotee discovers that the vision of Krishna can only be realized through the complete destruction of the ego and surrender of the self. Without this one cannot truly see. As a response to this mystical experience, darshan moves the senses so that touching through seeing becomes a way of knowing.[3] The distinction between the human and the divine collapses, all there is, is Krishna.

Icons and Murtis

As a ritual, darshan is linked to the concept in Pushtimarg of swarup as a living presence. While the faith rejects the term *murti,* or image, understanding this Hindu concept is necessary before the meaning of swarup can be fully appreciated. In Sanskrit, murti means "embodiment" and in its original context meant a full presence of the deity in iconic form. Murtis are carefully crafted by *shilpis,* artisans who for generations have followed the dictates of the *Shilpashastras*—treatises that carefully describe the manner in which icons are to be created through the lost wax casting process. Each icon intended for liturgical use is carefully cast so that it will be a perfect vehicle for the god. The casting process also involves a priest who follows the artisan throughout the process, gradually bringing life to the metal form:

> As the artisan sets to work carving, the priest simultaneously performs ritual work: he repeatedly recites the mantra that most fully invokes the deity onto the image as it comes into form. When a sculptor makes a bronze image ... following the lost-wax method, the priest swaddles the initial beeswax model in cloth, places it on a bed of grain and sacrificial grass, honors it with a series of oblations, and recites the mantra evoking the deity over it. He returns the wax effigy to the artisan, who encloses it in a clay mold, and the priest once again treats the shell to the same actions of swaddling, honoring, and invoking.[4]

The final phase of the process is done by a priest who "opens the eyes" of the murti:

> After a sacrificial pavilion and a pedestal within it have been carefully constructed, the newly made image is placed atop the pedestal, and the priest uses a golden needle to draw on the outlines of Siva's three eyes.... The sculptor then opens the eyes with a diamond needle, and opens the other apertures as well with a chisel. The priest rubs the eyes of the image with unguents and displays before it a series of highly auspicious objects; ghee, a pot of honey, heaps of grains, brahmans reciting praises, virgins in full decoration, and the assembled crowd of devotees.... The priest immediately washes and purifies the image with clay, ashes, cow dung, and other substances, and then dresses it in clean clothes and adorns it with all suitable ornaments. Temple servants take the image on a palanquin and circumambulate the village. By this point the image has clearly reached an initial stage of livelihood, where it can see objects placed before it and is worthy of going in procession among its community of worshippers.[5]

Even at this stage the process is not yet complete.[6] A number of substances are poured over the god, anointing the image that now achieves its full level of power.[7]

Although Hinduism is a rich tapestry of beliefs and different traditions, the concept of embodiment is pan–Hindu and has also reached contiguous cultures, including Buddhist societies. For instance, in Thailand, an icon of the Buddha only gains life after a ceremony of invocation and instruction that lasts through the night. The *dharma* or teachings of the Buddha are chanted after a silk cord is tied to the central Buddha in a wat or temple and then to each of the figures that will experience this awakening.[8] Following the periods of invocation and instruction, the icon enters the third watch of the night—that time when the historical Buddha confronted the temptations of Mara and entered the final moments before his awakening and enlightenment. At this point the eyes of the new Buddha are opened in a manner reminiscent of the rituals performed in India to Hindu icons.

Few parallels or metaphors exist in the Western experience of religion that provide this understanding of embodiment. One of the parts of Christian ritualistic tradition that approaches this understanding is the process of transubstantiation in the Roman Catholic tradition, in which bread and wine are understood to be transformed through the mass into the body and blood of Christ. While this is a seminal point for Catholics, even here, the transformation is not perceived in the same way as the presence that is associated with the murti. The Catholic altar is sacred space, but the deity does not "live" on the altar in the same way that a murti resides in a temple. In Catholicism, bread and wine are not anthropomorphic and are not analogous to the presence that is understood in Hindu pujas.

In India, traditions surrounding the concept of embodiment are ancient and have matured to produce some interesting anomalies. For example, June McDaniel describes an aspect of folk religion in West Bengal in which "the New Year is celebrated by having a Thākur Pañcāyat, or council meeting of deities in the form of statutes."[9] In this rite, "the statues are carried in procession, feasted, and left to discuss the village budget and future celebrations."[10] Similarly, in South India, the courts have agreed that Shiva has a legal personality and has proprietary rights to temple property.[11]

For non–Hindus, the difficulty of understanding the idea of embodiment is complicated by the distinction between matter and spirit that dominates philosophy and religion. When exceptions to this distinction have been noted, they have often been profoundly negative. For example, in the English civil war as Puritan forces gained the upper hand, soldiers lashed out at Roman Catholic churches and icons. In at least one recorded incident, the Puritan soldiers treated the crucifixes they encountered as something more than symbols. In Radwinter in Essex in 1640,

> the soldiers were headed for Scotland, pressed into service, and probably angry: "The Soldiers went into the church and pulled up the rails and pulled down the images (which as I hear cost the parson to set up thirty pounds) they tied the

images to a tree and whipped them then they carried them 5 miles to Saffron Walden and burnt them and roasted the roast and heated the oven with it, and said if you be gods deliver yourselves."[12]

The soldiers publically humiliated the icons in a way that would have been unimaginable if they were strictly material objects that could not experience ridicule or shame. In their challenge to the images the soldiers did not appear to deny their presence but instead dared them to prove that they were gods.

Apart from such rare occurrences, material objects in Western societies have rarely been associated with embodiment. In a postmodern materialistic world governed by Enlightenment rationalism and scientific empiricism, the tendency to dismiss the distinction between symbolism and embodiment is strong. Reinforced by the history of Christian missions that condemned idolatry in the religions they encountered, the dialectic between material and spiritual has dominated Western thinking. The problem is further compounded by language and the lack of terms in English to convey the intimate connections between material form and embodiment that are so much a part of the Hindu tradition.

Yet another difficulty in bridging the chasm between symbol and embodiment has been the discovery of Hindu iconography by the American and European art world. In the nineteenth century Hindu icons were rarely associated with higher art and were more often dismissed as aberrant. However, as Orientalist scholars delved more into the complex dimensions of Hindu image worship, the West was gradually made aware of the aesthetic qualities of the images. Ironically, this awakening was also advanced by the wholesale looting of archaeological sites in Egypt, Persia, and Iraq. In Persia, American missionaries collaborated with archaeologists to unearth and ship large stone panels of Assyrian art depicting deities to church-related colleges.[13] In the Indian art world, institutions such as the Metropolitan Museum of Art, the Smithsonian Museum, and other major repositories of art have amassed significant collections of icons, each carefully preserved but entirely removed from context and the daily pattern of worship. In many cases objects that had been seen as idols were reframed as art. Museums began to collect them. One official "instructed his readers to 'concentrate upon the thing itself,' to attend to significant form, to view Indian sculpture with much the same visual attentiveness one would devote to any other works of sculpture from other cultural traditions."[14]

Understanding Embodiment Through Material Culture

The meaning of objects in material culture has been a subject of academic discussion in a number of fields including linguistics and anthropology. It has drawn particular interest among museum studies and in the field of semiotics. In *Museums, Objects, and Collections: A Cultural Study,* Susan Pearce argues that meanings are relative through time and choices are made in different periods.[15] Drawing on the work of Ferdinand de Saussure and Roland Barthes, she concludes that objects may act as symbols and have an arbitrary level of meaning with "no intrinsic relationship."[16] Or, objects may have meaning as metonyms and may represent entire categories. In making this point Pearce uses the example of a Scottish sword carried by Alistair Macdonald of Keppoch at the decisive battle of Culloden in 1746. The battle was the climax of the Jacobite Rebellion and the attempt of Charles Stuart to regain the throne. On one hand, she argues, the sword "stands for the message (the signified) as a result of human choice."[17] But on the other hand, it operates as a sign, standing for the whole—the entire battle of Culloden and the failure of Charles Stuart to regain the throne.

This approach can be used to help understand the significance of icons that function in a number of ways. In the manufacture and use of murtis, meaning is not arbitrary and is carefully constructed and connected to a greater whole. For example, an image of the Hindu god Vishnu does not have an arbitrary meaning and instead has a very specific connection with Vaishnava mythology. But, the same icon has an important level of meaning as a metonym. Each consecrated icon is an embodiment of the deity and at the same time is fully the deity. To take this further, Hindu deities are often equated with Brahman, the singular essence of the universe. In this sense the metonymic meaning of the icon carries the broadest possible reference to the whole.

However, the meaning attached to Hindu murtis is also connected to the question of authenticity. To be authentic, a murti not only must have the appropriate appearance but also must carry the level of detail that comes through the traditional means of production. Icon manufacture is done by *shilpis,* artisans who follow the exact standards that are described in the *Silpa Shastras,* treatises on the production of murtis. This traditional process is different from the commercial production of Hindu statuary that floods the international market and is often connected to the tourist economy. While these pieces may be recognized as art, they are not the same as the handcrafted murtis that are made as devotional objects and intended for regular puja or worship.

The question of authenticity is also related to the ability of the murti to contain the presence of the deity. This requires the action of a priest who, using Sanskrit formulae, invites the deity to reside in the casting. In order to accomplish this, the casting must be perfect and without flaws. The manufacture of murtis is carefully done. It often involves priests in the process who prepare the murti with incantations and formulae. When this has been accomplished and the image is ready for use, it is brought to life.

One way to bridge the gap in understanding between meaning and presence or symbol and embodiment is through the evolving study of material culture in anthropology. Michael Thompson's *Rubbish Theory* offers a typology of material objects that can be used to provide an entry point into the Hindu worldview.[18]

Thompson suggests that most goods in the modern world belong to three categories: durable goods, transient material, and rubbish. Within this typology, "objects in the transient category decrease in value over time and have finite life-spans. Objects in the durable category increase in value over time and have (ideally) infinite life-spans."[19] Durable goods include art, antiques, and objects of religious devotion.

Within this context Thompson suggests that the treatment of an object relates to its category.[20] Copies or reproductions of durable goods, for example, are not treated as reverently as the original. Meaning is carefully rationed in each socially constructed category to represent the accumulation or loss of value. For example, material goods frequently move from the transient category to garbage. However, under the right conditions, this process can be reversed— what is considered garbage can gather increased value and be reinterpreted as durable. The process of assigning value to material goods acquires a mystique— the proverbial story of finding hidden treasure in a garbage can.

Within material culture studies, debate about the influence of these categories upon the objects themselves persists:

> The way we act towards an object relates directly to its category membership. For instance, we treasure, display, insure, and perhaps even mortgage the antique vase, but we detest and probably destroy the secondhand mate. Obviously, when it comes to objects, there is a relationship between our view of the world and our action in that world, but what is the nature of this relationship? Does the category membership of an object determine the way we act towards it, or does the way we act towards an object determine its category membership?[21]

Clearly, language is essential and integral to category membership and relative value. This also suggests that language plays a role in our understanding of durable goods, which must have a proven level of authenticity in order to remain in the category. A copy of a major work of art, for example, could also be described as a "museum reproduction." The museum industry thrives on the reproductions it sells, which it hopes will convey some of the aura of the original and at the same time avoid the more degraded category of "fake."

Yet, despite these levels of association and the problems in discerning authenticity, a qualitative difference between durable objects in the art world

2. Seeing Krishna: Darshan as the Inward Journey

and murtis remains. A murti, unlike other types of durable objects, is defined by embodiment and presence rather than explicitly by form or period of fabrication. Richard Davis concludes:

> Most art historians and religious historians writing about Indian religious icons and temples focus primary attention upon the moment of creation. This too casts identity in a particular mold. Knowledge of the iconographic form of an object and the date and place of its fabrication come to be seen as the constitutive knowledge of the object. In its focus on material creation, this perspective has the effect of restricting our sense of the meaningful possibilities of an object and it draws our attention away from the object's participation in the ongoing social life of its communities.[22]

This unique quality of icons can be thought of as aura. Lynn Meskell uses this designation to describe the appeal of Egyptian artifacts, suggesting, "Works of ancient art are auratic because they have cult value and exhibition value, historically both salient properties of Egyptian things."[23] These connections to ritual also can create associations with magic. She continues, "In a Maussian sense, collectors operate on a part-whole notion of magic, whereby possessing a relic from antiquity imbues them with connectivity to ancient power, ritual knowledge and utopian wisdom."[24] It is this level of auratic connectivity with sacred power that is at the heart of the murti.

But despite their lasting power, the auratic quality of murtis can be fragile and easily diminished when, removed from their ritual settings, icons are redefined as durable goods. This happens when museums acquire murtis and they are perceived as art. Instead of being defined by presence and participation in a community of believers, murtis are seen as museum exhibits, emphasizing their aesthetic beauty and history. Richard Davis suggests that this transition from cult to museum began in the early twentieth century when Western observers began to interpret Hindu icons as objects of art:

> Objects that had been termed "idols" in 1900 found themselves metamorphosed into works of art. One can specify endpoints to this transformation. The taxonomic shift began with the writings of E.B. Havell and A.K. Coomaraswamy in the 1910s, and was institutionally completed with the great show of "The Art of India and Pakistan" held at the Royal Academy of Arts in London, 1947–1948. This shift grew out of a larger intellectual movement that we might call, by analogy, *indophilia*. Certain aspects of Indian culture were selected and given a positive valence as embodying "spiritual" values, and these were contrasted with the negatively valued "materialism" of late Victorian British culture.[25]

As Indian religious art became a category for museum collections, the appearance of murtis on public display was altered. Unlike their role in a temple or home where icons are regularly dressed and embellished with the ritual paraphernalia that further defines them, the icons in museum collections are devoid of clothing or any ritualistic accoutrements.[26] Stripped of the daily cycle of rituals and pujas, they are not awakened or fed. No longer treated as embodiments of the deity, they are not washed or dressed nor are they anointed with sacred substances. Instead, their value becomes aesthetic and monetary, rooted in their authenticity, age, and artistic merit.

This reductionism not only signals the movement of icons from auratic to durable objects, but establishes patterns of shifting identity within durable goods as they are transported globally. Davis describes the case of a twelfth century figure of Shiva. The *Pathur Nataraja*, an expression of dancing Shiva (*Nataraj*), had been buried outside the Vishvanathasvami temple in Pathur, Tamilnad.[27] The ceremonial interment of the large, 150-pound figure and a number of other murtis had undoubtedly been done to protect the icon during Portuguese incursions in the sixteenth century, or later in British attacks on Mysore in the eighteenth century. The cache remained hidden during the intervening years as the temple deteriorated and drifted out of use. Unearthed in 1976 by a laborer who was building a cowshed, the murti was quickly discerned to be ancient. Through a number of clandestine connections it entered the international art market. Transported from India to London, it wound up in the Asian antiquities collection of Robert Borden, and was subsequently sold to the Bumper Corporation for the incredible sum of £411,111.

Davis describes how the identity of the figure shifted within the international art and antiquities market. When found to be stolen, the icon quickly became identified as cultural property. The discovery was made when the figure was being cleaned at the British Museum in preparation for display. A trial ensued in the English court system in which the murti acquired yet another identity as a "juristic personality."[28] This perception of identity evolved from the god as "lord" and "owner" of the temple in which it was worshipped and as the recipient of "gifts of land, money, jewelry, [and] animals."[29] The deities' "juristic personality" evolved from the curious combination of Anglo-Indian law in which the deity could hold property in an "ideal sense."[30] In deciding the case Justice Kennedy ruled that as a juristic person the murti represented a legal claim that was higher than that of its current owner, the Bumper Corporation.[31]

The case was resolved with a mandate to return the icon to India. Once in Tamilnad, a Ceremony of Return was held re-establishing the ritualistic position of the murti and reinstating its original auratic identity.[32] However, wishing to further protect it, the Indian government took the icon to the Icon Centre in Tiruvarur near the *Shaivite* temple of Tragaraja. Unfortunately, the attempts of the Indian government to safeguard the deity meant that it would no longer be the recipient of daily pujas and instead joined other murtis in the Icon Centre where they could be protected from further theft.

This example confirms that while the auratic nature of murtis can be compromised, it is rarely completely lost. Hindus view murtis as divine figures whose presence enables a wider view of ultimate reality (Brahman). The process of creating them is symbiotic, involving the roles of traditionally trained artisans and priests, all of whom work together to create a suitable habitation for the deity. Once evoked, the presence is dependent on the ability of the murti to remain free from damage, although patterns of wear and minor damage are seen as acceptable.[33] While periods of disuse can move the deity into a dormant state, the full auratic quality of the god can be recovered through rituals that again make the presence more visible. In all of these ways, auratic objects present a different countenance than durable goods. As embodiments of the sacred their identities are deeply connected to the cultic community, past or present.

Swarups as Auratic Objects

Vallabha's experience of swarup took the concept of auratic embodiment and elevated it. Literally meaning the deity's "own form," the swarup was understood to be self-created and composed entirely of bliss. This idea also relied on the Hindu understanding of a tripartite form of reality including *sat* (truth), *chit* (consciousness) and *anand* (bliss). Anand was absolute energy and a source of complete tranquility. As the swarup was anand so it was also understood to be the absolute (rather than relative) essence of the one, singular level of reality. From this perspective, the aura of the swarup is by definition transformative, with enormous power.

As the sect grew under the guidance of the emerging dynasty of descendants, the primary nidhi swarups (including Shri Nathji, Shri Navnitpriyaji, and the swarups distributed among Vitthalnath's seven sons) acquired still greater auras.[34] They were understood to embody the most intense level of human experience possible. Nidhi swarups were more than just presence. Instead they were the ultimate form that reality can take—the center through which all other forms found their definition and meaning. In turn, the essential nidhi swarups that defined the faith were distinguished from the swarups that devotees maintained in their homes, which were perceived as *Thakur* ("Lord").[35] However, neither was considered murti:

> In the view of this sect *svarups* are opposed to *murti,* the common Hindi term for idol, because, unlike *murti,* they do not require a consecration ritual

(*pranapratishtha*) when they are installed in a temple. An image is transformed into a *svarup* by a *gosvami*, who bathes it in *pancamrt* (the five sacred substances) and feeds it consecrated food from an established *svarup;* devotees, it is maintained, undergo an analogous transformation in the *brahmasambandh* ceremony. So close is the relationship between *sevaks* and *svarups* that a *svarup* is likely to experience actual feelings of discomfort if his devotee neglects some aspect of *seva* (e.g. not serving him his meals on time or dressing him in warm enough clothes during cold weather). In addition, it is commonly alleged that *svarups* may become fully animate in the presence of spiritually advanced devotees and engage with them in *lila*.[36]

The idea that reality is configured in a variety of levels is foreign to many forms of American religion. Yet the experience of material culture offers some analogies that can be helpful in understanding the nature of swarups. Among durable goods, for example, authenticity is critical and often relies on a provenience as a way of establishing it. For example a violin's provenience can create an almost magical quality.

The question about what makes a truly great violin is an endless topic of debate that in recent years has also been approached by the scientific community. Some have argued that the majestic sound was the result of varnish, while others looked to the age and quality of the wood. Once a great violin has garnered a well-established provenience, its sound achieves a dimension that is almost equated with a living presence. A famous violin also may acquire a name, which further elevates it from the larger category of durable goods, establishing its unique aura and presence. John Marchese recounts his observation of a Stradivarius that had achieved this level of existence:

> "There really is something about its tone," Faber wrote later. "Warm and vibrant, it seems to inhabit the room." I remembered that Sam Zygmuntowicz had recounted a similar experience, when the soloist Daniel Heifetz visited the Violin Making School of America in Salt Lake City during Sam's first year there and played some of Bach's Chaconne on his Strad in a small room filled with prospective luthiers. It was Sam's first hearing one of the old guy's instruments close up. "I'll never forget that sound," Sam told me.[37]

As swarups are dependent on the level of awareness of a devotee, so the identification of the quality of a fine instrument is also dependent on the listener. A trained, highly skilled classical violinist uses a finely honed set of skills to identify a particular quality of sound in a violin. To a casual observer the full dimensions of the instrument may not be easily discernible. Developing the eyes to see the difference and the ears to hear it is often the product of a lifetime of attentive study. Sometimes, even highly sophisticated audiences are unable to identify the sound of a truly great violin. This was the case with the great violinist Fritz Kreisler, who once played an entire concert on a cheap manufactured fiddle. Of course, he was known for playing the great Guarneri that would later be named for him. As he basked in the warm applause this night, the story goes, Kreisler lifted the fiddle in the air, smashed it to pieces, and enjoyed the shocked gasps of the audience before summoning his del Gesu from the wings. You have to wonder if the audience really got what must have been the point of his theatrics. Many can recognize the sound of Kreisler, but almost no one can actually spot the sound of a great Cremonese fiddle.[38]

While the analogy of a great violin is helpful in understanding the category of durable objects, it pales in comparison to the perception of a swarup, which is seen not only as actual presence but also as transformative. After cultivating a lifetime of bhava, devotees establish deep and lasting relationships with swarups. For this reason, after death swarups are often given to a goswami if they cannot be passed down to family members.[39]

Seeing Krishna

Context is also an important element in understanding the role of darshan. Vallabha postulated that there were different levels of awareness among individual souls.[40] The most pure jivas are the most complete (pushti) and fully cognizant of Krishna's grace. Other souls are not as complete and have decreasing amounts of awareness. The completeness of a soul helps determine its ability to perceive the inner alaukika, non-dual nature of reality—to see things as they really are. By contrast, the mundane, ordinary laukika world is not a separate realm of illusion in the sense of Shankara's maya but a manifestation of the sport or lila of Krishna. Some souls never rise above the perception of illusion while others are rewarded as Krishna freely and independently bestows his grace.[41]

Members of the Pushtimarg tradition frequently comment that this level of grace cannot be earned and cannot be obtained through effort. Instead, it is totally within the prerogative of Krishna to bestow it on those souls he wishes to reward. Grace is bestowed as the ability to see the transcendent, which is always a fleeting, ephemeral experience. In the darshan, language is neither a symbolic device that creates a reflection of reality nor a means of consolidating a thought process that defines the nature of things. Instead, with music and ritual, it allows reality to be seen. The poetry and the devotional songs (kirtans) that are sung in each darshan are highly refined and intended for this specific purpose. The poetry is based on a form of poetry unique to India called padas. Padas are rhymed lyric compositions of about six or eight lines in length (although occasionally they can be much longer) that center on religious themes; each *pad* bears a refrain and is intended to be sung. *Pads* have been composed in most of the major literary dialects that contribute to what can broadly be called the Hindi language family.[42]

Padas are a convention of Indian literature specifically related to bhakti. Padas frequently carry the stamp of authority of the Astachap poet who wrote them in a final line that identifies the author. This is much more than simple attribution.[43] It is the testament that the poet wrote his lines in the context of the mystical alaukika realm and that the verse was composed within the experience of darshan rather than outside it. Padas are never afterthoughts and are themselves manifestations of the inner, hidden realm of Krishna. Composed within it, they are instruments of transformation.

Padas are written in a dialect of Hindi called *Braj Bhasha*. This highly Sanskritized dialect was popular in the fourteenth century along with *Avadhi*. Together these became the dominant literary expressions of Hindi.[44] These two dialects remained until the mid-nineteenth century when *Khari Boli*, which became the foundation of modern Hindi-Urdu, took form.[45]

The daily regimen of darshans was integrated with padas and kirtan*s* by Vitthalnath. As the sect spread across Rajasthan and the Gujarat, regional styles of the synthesis of kirtans and padas were created, including those from Nathdwara and Kankroli and a variety of other sites including Gokul, Mathura, Kamvan, Kashi, Ahmedabad, Vadodara, Surat, Jamnagar, Junagadh and Porbandar.[46]

Padas are always intended to be heard. Moreover, the music that undergirds them is uniquely partnered with the verse and, together, tied to a mood and time of day. For example, a brief pada attributed to the Astachap poet Paramanand Das paints a verbal image of Krishna (*Shyam*) returning home at the end of the day with his cattle:

> See Gopal is coming.
> My mind desires Shyam's beautiful lotus-eyed form.
> He is wearing a *chandan,* a crown, and the *Gunjamani mala.*
> Paramanand's lord Giridhar dances.[47]

Each image that the poet creates is rooted in his own perception of the hidden (alaulika) level of reality that only the darshan offers. The images are also conditioned by a host of cultural nuances. For example, the chandan, or sandalwood paste, anoints the deity, continuing a common Hindu liturgical convention. However, Krishna also wears the Gunjamani mala, a red and black garland. When the poet speaks of his own intense desire for Krishna, he sees him coming in the cloud of dust that accompanies cattle moving along the streets. Krishna has the iconographic conventions that signal his presence—eyes shaped as lotus flowers, a crown in the shape of the crescent moon, a tilak on his forehead made with sandalwood, and the bright Gunjamani mala. He is both cow herder and prince.

This very specific description is vital to understanding the pada. Krishna appears with imagery that not only is in keeping with tradition, but with the full sensory experience of the deity in which the poet's words shape a vision. The vision is not presented as imagination or reflection after the fact but as what the poet sees as he writes. Finally, Paramanand's verse provides an imprimatur—typical of the Astachap poet, verifying this vision and implying that what he has written is based on his own inner experience.

In "Painting Words, Tasting Sound: Visions of Krishna in Paramanand's Sixteenth-Century Devotional Poetry," Whitney Sanford goes further, suggesting that the role of the pada is rooted in synaesthesia, "a process in which one sense is used to apprehend another (or its medium)."[48] In synaesthesia, language becomes vision and sight becomes experience:

> Synaesthesia is a type of the larger category of metaphor, defined as "understanding and experiencing one thing in terms of another." Metaphor provides a conceptual structure for the images in poetry, and each metaphoric image or concept suggests a range of meaning that adds depth and breadth to this realm. When we hear metaphoric language, we bring interpretations to the material that range far beyond the immediate and limited meanings of the words themselves. The devotee integrates the images of the poetry into a system of personal and cultural meaning. These metaphors not only reflect an understanding of the various facets of Krishna's realm, but they also structure the devotee's thoughts and concepts, and therein lies the transformation.[49]

Steeped in metaphor, the synaesthesiatic experience of the padas of the eight Astachap poets transforms sound into sight and literature into experience. The padas are instruments of the alaukika world, lifting the devotee out of the mundane laulika realm and transporting him into the hidden, inner environment of Krishna. They also are intended to so magnify the sight of this inner reality that they create an overwhelming desire for it, ultimately collapsing any level of duality. The process is dialectical but the dialectic itself must collapse in order for the mystical reality to be "seen." The entire experience is transformative—an "experiential and practical means ... to change one's perception of reality."[50]

As Sanford suggests, the experience of synaesthesia is not simplistic. Rather, the padas rely on finely tuned perceptions of the nature of the divine that convey layers of cultural connotations. In practice, these levels of meaning are often sung, incorporating further nuances of meaning provided by the singer.

In Pushtimarg, padas are sung as kirtans using the *Dhrupad* style of North Indian music.[51] In its long history, Dhrupad has had frequent associations with religion. It was developed by a Bengali poet. In the twelfth century CE Jaydev, the author of the *Gita Govinda* (an important influential tract in the history of the bhakti tradition), brought many of his insights about Radha and Krishna to music.[52] While Dhrupad vocalizations can be accompanied by a variety of Indian instruments, they are commonly sung in tandem with a special form of drum called the *mrdangam*. Padas of four stanzas in length are sung, with each stanza being sung in one of four different styles.[53] In Dhrupad, padas may be sung by a master singer and also by a disciple. Together, they engage in a process of unfolding and embellishment in which the strength of the singer's voice is critical in establishing the mood that the pada seeks to invoke. The dialogue between singer, disciple, and mrdangam player is also constructed around a raga, a sequence of notes in Indian classical music that is intended to evoke a mood. Ragas are organized by the season and time of day in which they occur.[54] Dhrupad may evoke the presence of deities and may also contain a word or sound used like a mantra—a repetition that is used to bring about a divine presence.

In the West, the classical expression of *Dhrupad Sangeet* is difficult to maintain, and the complex interactions required to perform this style of North Indian music have become hard to find. However, within Pushtimarg, a cadre of goswamis have worked together in attempting to create a renaissance of this vital tradition. Padas can now routinely be found on the Internet on such rich websites as www.vallabhkankroli.org, which offers information and resources designed for the Pushtimargiya community in diaspora. Such resources are necessary since in transplanted overseas communities, devotees are far removed from the regional centers of the tradition. This, in turn, has created a climate in the West in which the mechanisms of pada and kirtan in the context of darshan are not fully understood. There are few persons in most havelis capable of performing Dhrupad or understanding Braj. The key that allows the darshan to continue to be effective has been the sect's concern with continuing the practice of utilizing trained priests and musicians in their havelis.

The association between pada and song is so strong that havelis go to great lengths to be sure musicians are on hand. If that is not possible, the mukhiya or Vaishnavas with musical training may be recruited. Although there is no requirement that particular padas be sung during each darshan, padas must still fit the mood of the day, the particular darshan that is being performed, and the season of the year.

Padas may also be sung in the home during the private moments of seva. Instructions on how to perform the complex rituals are often passed down through family members. In some instances in the West where Pushtimargiyas have married persons from outside the tradition, elder members of the family may instruct in-laws in the rituals that they have learned, often drawing on practices derived from the gaddi in which they were born. As part of this regimen some devotees also insist that the padas addressed to the deity be sung instead of read.[55]

Similarly, Sanford reports that at the Radharaman haveli in Vrindaban,

> there is no prescribed liturgy or present order of poems; the poems are sung depending on the inspiration of the singers or, perhaps, in response to a request from the audience.... In the absence of musicians, devotees themselves sing— most devotees have accumulated a vast repertoire of these poems through hearing them repeatedly. Anyone who knows the poems can sing them, and visitors can join the musicians to offer song to Krishna.[56]

As the method of interpreting padas is through singing them, the context for the padas is always seva.[57] While seva may be loosely understood as service or even as love for god, its meaning is steeped in surrender in the context of the daily rituals necessary for the maintenance of the deity's well-being. In most havelis in the United States this level of meaning is not just theoretical; it is quite visual and immediate. To the observer of a darshan, it is manifested when male devotees prostrate themselves on the carpeted floor of the haveli before the swarup of Krishna.

The foundation of the synaesthasic experience utilizes the trifold presence of *raj* (emotion), *bhog* (food) and *srinagar* (decorations placed on the deity),[58] which, together, form an intersection between the ordinary and the transformative. In this sense the daily routine of Shri Nathji is the most ordinary of events. After sleeping the night, the infant Krishna is awakened with sound. He is bathed, dressed, and fed. He is entertained not just with music that pleases the ear but also with sounds that evoke visions of his inner realm. Yet, within the ordinary is the possibility of the extraordinary. Knowing this, devotees frequently view the deity, hoping to get that brief, life-changing glimpse of ultimate reality.

PART TWO
EARLY HISTORY

The following two chapters explore the early history of the Vallabha Sampradaya in India. They are written in a different "voice" from part 1, focusing on the support system that institutionalized Vallabha's theology into a viable bhakti sampradaya. As part one explored the sampradaya's spiritual traditions, so part two looks at the history that brought myths to life. Part three (chapters 5, 6, and 7) focuses on the Vallabha Sampradaya in the American Hindu diaspora.

This section also acknowledges that myths and historical data are different ways of knowing with diverse epistemological backgrounds. Karen Armstrong concludes that in traditional societies a myth

> was an event which, in some sense, had happened once, but which also happened all the time. Because of our strictly chronological view of history, we have no word for such an occurrence, but mythology is an art form that points beyond history to what is timeless in human existence, helping us to get beyond the chaotic flux or random events, and glimpse the core of reality.[1]

Myths establish order and define the relationship between past and present.[2] They provide important measures of human identity and give narrative voice to the innermost human concerns. Frequently archetypal, myths connect deeply seated images with expressions of ultimate reality. Their significance is not tied to factual information but instead to paradigms that have broader implications beyond the particular events that they describe.[3]

However, because myth and history have had such different orientations, they have popularly been seen as at odds with each other:

> Myth and history are generally considered antithetical modes of explanation. Writers of each tend to distrust the data of the other. Many historians of the modern period see their task as one of removing all traces of myth from the historical record. Many students of myth consider history to have less explanatory power than traditional narratives.[4]

Because of these difficulties, hermeneutical problems often arise when the context of myth is also an historical event. As a result, careful attention is necessary both in exploring the sampradaya's central myths and in analyzing the historical circumstances that produced them.

One of the most important myths in the Pushtimarg tradition is the journey of Shri Nathji from Mathura to Mewar, described in chapter 4. The story is etiological, narrating the genesis of the sect's movement into a broader geographical arena, and can be understood in mythological terms. Viewed as a sacred journey, the cart bearing the deity is reported to have stopped, becoming stuck in the mud. For attendant priests, this was a sign that Krishna wished to remain in that place. When the cart became immobilized, it also conveyed a broader meaning: that the transcendent was manifest in the mundane and that the journey toward liberation was successful. The story also demonstrated the protective power of Krishna, who was understood to offer his devotees refuge from oppression in the same way that he had sheltered them from the onslaughts of Indra by raising Mount Govardhan as a canopy.

However, as the following pages will also demonstrate, this narrative can also be interpreted historically, revealing a system of royal patronage that the Vallabha Sampradaya had already experienced in Mathura and now sought to continue in the Rajput Hindu states. Patronage was an accepted means of sectarian support and was well known in Hindu temple traditions. In Mughal India, dominated by competing religious traditions and the ambiguity of tolerance and authority, patronage was a visible demonstration of respect for religion. Chapter 3 establishes the role of the Vallabha Sampradaya in soliciting Mughal support through *farmans* issued by the emperor, Akbar. Chapter 4 shows the ongoing patronage of Rajput princes that the sect acquired in the seventeenth and eighteenth centuries.

Pushtimargiya theological tradition contains numerous other examples of ways in which historical context and circumstance helped create larger, more powerful symbolic meanings. For instance, the reliance of the sampradaya on darshan drew from the context of authority in the Mughal period. The *darbars* of the emperors, in Agra and Fatephur Sikri, allowed the public to publicly venerate the emperor and also gave the emperor an opportunity to view his subjects. In the same way Krishna was viewed in a reciprocal process of darshan eight times a day. Similarly, the practice of worshiping in havelis was built on Mughal images of the home, combining symbols of privacy and opulence that defined Pushtimargiya temples as the province of the goswami who managed them.

In the same manner the innermost traditions of seva, darshan, and bhava drew their symbolic power from the wider Krishna cult in a period of competing Hindu and Muslim alliances. The ideology of a trickster deity whose childhood was an essential part of an agrarian lifestyle had been described in the *Bhagavata Purana* and had become part of the spirit of Vaishnavism. But undergirding the nature of the Krishna of myth was a pan–Hindu mode of support that relied on caste-defined loyalties and traditions, patronage, and the extended family.

These examples also demonstrate that in the Indian context, myth and history have been more intertwined than in the secular West, where myth has ceased to function. Peter Heehs argues that myth and history are so interconnected in India that it is not always possible to separate them. A more fruitful approach lies in working toward a "dialectical resolution."[5]

Pushtimargiya literature is immersed in this dialectic of the confluence of myth and history, often increasing the perceived authority of the sect. Emperors and princes are frequently presented among the devout, worshiping Shri Nathji. The Astachap poet Khumbandas presents the emperor Man Singh of Jaipur in the context of worship attending a darshan:

> As the sixth *darshan* period was beginning, Raja Man Singh was conducted into the shrine. There, magnificent *seva* of Shri Nathji was in progress. Shri Nathji had been sprinkled with rose water, and water was flowing all through his shrine from sanctuary to entryway. When he had had *darshan,* Raja Man sijngh threw himself down in homage before Shri Nathhji. He had arrived miserable with the heat, but now he felt cool and refreshed. Having beheld the holy face of Shri Nathji, he was filled with joy and exclaimed, "I have seen in person the consummate Brahman Krishna who is the Moon of Brindaban and the Lord of Gobardhan. Today I have actually seen what before I had only heard of in the *Bhagavata Purana.* This is a day of great blessing." And he whispered to himself, "At this sixth *darshan* period the Lord sits majestically in state."[6]

Within the tradition, there is neither an argument nor a perceived incongruity between myth and history. Narrative histories such as Kanthmani Shastri's *Kāṅkrolī kā Itihās* are important sectarian sources that also provide abundant historical detail about patronage and the complex relationships between the Mughal and Rajput courts and the Vallabhkul.[7] Myth provides the stories in which the miraculous was perceived to unfold. At the same time, history documents the processes that shaped perception of events. One form of knowledge did not deny the other. Rather, both were necessary to understand the centrality of tradition.

Historians of religion have also recognized the symbiotic nature of Pushtimargiya myth and history. Writing about the culture of Braj that produced the Ban-Yatra pilgrimage, David Haberman suggests that the patronage of Mughal rulers was not inconsistent with the myths of the Krishna cult, concluding,

> for the most part the Ban-Yatra is a product of the sixteenth century, but it has continued in a vital way to the present day due to the support of the material cul-

ture of Braj, which has come from a variety of patronage sources.... Examination of the historical events which produced the culture of Braj, however, reveals something else: it helps us understand how the various kinds of stories told in this region are related. We do not find here a hard line of distinction between history and myth. Historical figures reveal myth though their lives and actions, and mythical stories determine historical perspectives and developments.[8]

The following two chapters help the reader to further understand the dialectical relationship between myth and patronage in the seventeenth and eighteenth centuries, exploring patronage as a process that enabled the Vallabha Sampradaya to successfully position itself in Rajasthan and the Gujarat.

3

Krishna's Many Mansions
Mughal Patronage and Expansion

> *This time the order has been given that wherever the cows of Vitthalray, the doubtless well wisher, the wearer of the sacred thread, may be there they should be allowed to graze. In any kind of land Khalsa or Jagir, anyone should not cause them distress, and should not bother them.*
> —Grant from the Emperor Akbar to Vitthalnath, 1638 CE

For many religions, the institutionalization of tradition is often dependent on acquiring social, economic, and political support. The descendants of Vallabhacharya achieved this by encouraging multiple sources of royal patronage. Beginning with the grants received from Mughal emperors, and continuing with the support of Hindu maharajas and maharanas, the sampradaya used patronage to construct a strong regional base in Rajasthan and the Gujarat. Five hundred years later this regional strength enabled Pushtimarg to easily enter the Hindu diaspora.

As a means of preserving wealth, patronage is a well-documented part of the history of classical Hinduism where, using exquisite patterns of sculpture and art, temple construction was untenable without royal support. Patronage is well known in South India. Between the fourth and ninth centuries, the Gupta and Pallava dynasties supported the construction of temples and subsidized Hindu art and culture. Later, in the fifteenth century, three dynasties of rulers in the state of Vijayanagar subsidized Hindu art and architecture. The relationship between religion and the exercise of power was symbiotic:

> The transactions between kings, temple deities, priests and sectarian leaders point to a relationship of mutual interdependence. The priests made offerings to and performed services for the gods; the deities preserved protected and awarded material benefits to the temples, priests and sectarian leaders.[1]

While patronage is a normative part of the history of many religions, this lens has rarely been applied to bhakti, which has been studied through rich patterns of poetry and literature. Yet bhakti sects demonstrate a continuation, rather than a variation, of traditional Hindu patterns of expansion. This chapter offers that perspective, demonstrating how Mughal patronage facilitated the early development of the Vallabha Sampradaya.

Establishing Royal Patronage as a Means of Support

The spiritual heir to the position of acharya and defender of Pushtimarg was Vallabha's son and first goswami of the sect, Vitthalnath, who created the organizational structure of the movement.[2] He established a mechanism for the spread of the sect beyond Braj, developed its doctrines and, most significantly, interpreted this new religion to rulers of the day, increasing the sect's membership, wealth, and prestige.

Vitthalnath journeyed on major pilgrimages to support the image of a rapidly expanding sect. He founded temples and shrines, and garnered sources of income. He established temples in Ahmadabad and Mumbai and attracted numerous converts from the mercantile Vaishnava communities in the region. These converts became the basis of its caste-affiliated following.

Most significantly, as Vitthalnath expanded the geography of the sect, he carried the image of goswami into the Mughal courts, thereby initiating an ongoing process of royal patronage. Numerous grants were issued in his name, providing grazing land for his cattle and the protection of the empire for the sect. Gradually his name became associated with the authority of the empire. Sectarian accounts report that he had several audiences with the eclectic emperor, Akbar, and with a wide variety of Rajput nobility. Reportedly, on returning from a pilgrimage to Adel (or Arial), Vitthalnath is said to have arrived in Bandhava (or Banda), where he was invited to the darbar of Maharaja Ramchandra of Bundlekhand.[3] Ramchand, who maintained an independent kingdom until 1569 when he surrendered to Akbar, undoubtedly appeared to Vitthalnath as a likely supporter of a growing Hindu sampradaya.

Vitthalnath also initiated a process of dynastical control in which patrilineal descendents of his father established gaddis. In most cases these became centers of royal support and patronage. Each gaddi was maintained by the senior goswami, who cared for one of the nidhi swarups. Through this process havelis pointed to the regal splendor of the deity and at the same time to the aristocratic position of the goswami as a member of Vallabha's lineage. Serving as both temple and private residence for the sect's leadership, the havelis

3. Krishna's Many Mansions: Mughal Patronage and Expansion

became virtual palaces, magnifying the image of the resident deity and increasing the regional authority of the sect. In the tradition of classical Hinduism the gaddis became "temple landlords," controlling taxation and rent from nearby villages in the same manner as had classical Hindu temples for centuries.

In time, as this process continued, the goswamis became removed from the day-to-day administration of the havelis under their care. This was accomplished through the creation of the office of temple manager or *adhikara*, a designation first used by Vallabha. Adhikaras were responsibile for securing contributions from members of the sect in each region, supplying the haveli with the goods it needed in order to function, controlling all labor in the temple, and selecting priests.[4]

In all of these actions, Vitthalnath established the practical means for economic maintenance of his sampradaya by re-establishing classical Hindu patterns of royal support as the means for propagating his sect. Under his tutelage goswamis freely associated with heads of state and became recipients of Mughal grants. Later, under the leadership of his seven sons, these associations brought the sect into court life in the Rajput states of Mewar, Kishangarh, and Jaipur. In turn, these royal associations helped inspire schools of art that contributed to the spread of Pushtimarg throughout Rajasthan and the Gujarat. All of this substantially increased the property holdings of each gaddi. The gaddis controlled vast estates and directed the lives of countless tenants and subordinate officials.

None of this would have been possible without the inherited position of the goswami as a composite of teacher (acharya) and holy man. As a result of this elevated status, many were able to gain entry into palace life in Rajput states and to become members of the aristocracy. Welcomed as devotees of a sectarian tradition that had accrued significant political and cultural power, they were often seen as an economic asset to whatever area they inhabited.

The goswamis also became patriarchal figures. Much as had happened with Vallabha and Vitthalnath before them, their roles were enhanced with accretions of myth and legend. As caretakers of tradition they were seen as a natural part of a movement based on the constant and ever-present intervention of deity in human affairs. The sect they created, as a result of this cumulative process, grew rapidly. The expansion evolved from the support Vitthalnath received from the Mughal emperor, Akbar.

According to legend Akbar married a Hindu Rajput and became increasingly sensitized to the bhakti movement. As a result he abolished the tax (*jizya*) on Hindus and initiated a series of grants both to the Gaudiya Vaishnavas (who followed Chaitanya) and the Pushtimargiyas who followed Vallabha.

This support helped establish Braj as the physical repository of Krishna lore, with the result that "by 1580 at least seven temples in the region of Braj had received imperial land grants."[5]

Through Akbar's initiative the Vallabha Sampradaya was the recipient of eight Mughal land grants in the late sixteenth and early seventeenth centuries, the most important of which are discussed here. These grants gave the sect tax-free use of land it had previously acquired, a share in local commerce, grazing rights for its cattle, and perhaps most important, the favor and patronage of the Mughal aristocracy. These were a type of support known as madad-i-ma'ash, given to religious or cultural figures.

Mughal grants included a variety of other forms. Farmans were issued at the discretion of the emperor and included *madad-i-ma'ash* grants.[6] Farmans often included *parwanas*—summaries of the specific land assignments directing the proper officials to carry them out. In addition, *sanads* were orders issued with the authority of the empire but not necessarily by the emperor himself. *Jagirs* were land grants given to persons of power. *Jagidars* (the holders of jagirs) shared in the taxation collected on the property and were also required to raise militias for the defense of the land.

Madad-i-ma'ash grants often had four component parts: (1) a statement of the conditions of the grant and the land assignment made; (2) a direction to the officers of the empire to carry out the conditions of the grant; (3) an exhortation for loyalty and continued prayers for the duration of the empire; and (4) an implicit assumption contained in the language of the document that the recipient of the grant would live and work on the assigned land. This relatively simple pattern differs from jagirs and other military grants of the period that required service in the militia to compensate for the privileges and assignments of land granted.[7]

The use of the madad-i-ma'ash system represented an attempt by the Mughal Empire to elicit the support of religious and charismatic leaders who had significant influence among the peasantry. Accordingly, Hindus and Muslims alike became recipients of the grants. The important consideration for the empire was not the particular doctrinal or theological position a sect championed but the cultural and political power its leadership actively maintained. In return for the gift of madad-i-ma'ash all that was asked was the loyalty of the recipient and his prayers for the continued duration of the empire. Such a demand, however, should not be underestimated. State support of religious institutions provided a practical way of maintaining both communication with and some control over an often-unsettled population.

Akbar inherited the madad-i-ma'ash system but quickly reformed it, attempting to eliminate abuses.[8] He also initiated a policy of giving madad-i-

3. Krishna's Many Mansions: Mughal Patronage and Expansion 77

ma'ash awards to non–Muslims. For example, a *Shaivite* shrine in Jakhbar in the Punjab received a grant in 1581 and a sizable amount of land.⁹

Grantees were often cultic figureheads or sectarian leaders with influence over thousands of devotees. Their usefulness to the government in gathering the loyalty of such sizeable portions of the population cannot be overlooked. For instance, grants supported the members of large *dargahs,* tombs of Sufi saints that frequently exerted significant cultural and religious influence over the Muslim population.

Undoubtedly, with many of these considerations in mind, Akbar issued the first Mughal grant to Vitthalnath (frequently referred to as Vitthaldas or Vitthalray in the grants) in September 1577:

> Royal Farman One ... in connection with the inhabitants of Gokul. The farman of the great hero Jalaludhin Mahammad Akbar Badshah, he is sovereign.
> Badshah the protector of the entire world and other government officials will not bother Vitthaldas, who undoubtedly wishes us well and who lives in the small town of Gokul, nor his companions and servants; to him and to his retinue, he will not demand anything from them. Let them stay worry free in their own place so that he continuously prays to God for our ever-increasing fame and progress.
> This is the order that has been written, government officials must follow what is written in this document.
> Written in the second month, the 23rd day, the year 985, Sukravar 13 of September, the Christian year 1577, Vikram Samvat 1634.[10]

This farman is similar to other madad-i-ma'ash grants of the period and was issued directly to the goswami. Often madad-i-ma'ash grants were given to the heads of religious institutions with no mention of the cult that supported them. In this case the sect is referred to by references to "the inhabitants of Gokul" and "Vitthaldas and his retinue."[11] Further, the document commands the officials of the empire to obey; undoubtedly a parwana would be issued later naming these administrators who would see that the instructions of the farman were carried out.

While the grant does not give the sect land, it bestows the protection of the empire on properties the sampradaya clearly already owned. It also stands out because of its specific hope that Vitthalnath, a Hindu leader, would pray for the empire and its ruler, Akbar. The language of the grant suggests that the emperor wished Vitthalnath to remain "worry free"[12] both in terms of taxation and requests from government officials so that he might "pray to God for our ever increasing fame and progress."[13] Later grants issued in the name of other members of the royal family support the conclusion that Vitthalnath had indeed carried the religion of Sri Nathji to the Mughal courts, where, as sectarian legend concludes, he had several audiences with Akbar.

The specific circumstances surrounding the issue of the first Mughal farmans to the Vallabha Sampradaya are unusual. While Akbar undoubtedly expressed a personal interest in Pushtimarg, historical, political, and social conditions made a grant to a Hindu sect in Mathura politically expedient.

The Vallabha Sampradaya was situated in Gokul, a small village adjacent to the larger city of Mathura. Mathura was a holy city with a large Vaishnava population and an annual influx of pilgrims who visited the places the *Bhagavata Purana* had made famous. The possibility of an open revolt by such a Hindu population in a Muslim empire could not be ignored by any ruler. Further, Mathura's strategic position between the larger city of Delhi and the capital, Agra, made control of its populations essential. Hence, Akbar reportedly made pilgrimages to the shrines and temples of Mathura and Vrindaban. While such pilgrimages may have had religious and devotional components, given the emperor's mystical and eclectic bent, the pragmatic calculus is important. Visible devotion to Hindu religious traditions in the center of Braj—the very heart of the growing Krishna-centered bhakti movement—had political implications that cannot be ignored.

An additional source of motivation for a Mughal grant to a Hindu sect came from an incident in May 1577. A Brahmin appropriated building materials intended for a mosque and used them to construct a temple. Upset when caught, he proceeded to curse the prophet Mohamed. The incident is described in biased language by Al-Badaoni, a well-known opponent of Akbar, who often criticized the emperor for his liberal and eclectic religious policies. Reflecting escalating tensions between Hindu and Muslim populations in the region, Al-Badaoni wrote,

> When the Emperor (Akbar) halted at Fathpur, Qazi Abdu-r-Rahim the Qazi of Mathura laid a complaint before the Shaikh, to the effect that a wealthy and stiff-necked brahmin of that place had carried off the materials which he, the Qazi had collected for the construction of a masjid [mosque] and had built of them an idol-temple, and that, when the Qazi had attempted to prevent him, he had, in the presence of witnesses, opened his foul mouth to curse the prophet (on whom be peace), and had shown his contempt for Muslims in various other ways. When the brahmin was called on to appear, he also obeyed the Shaikh's summons.[14]

The author continues, relating the distress that this incident caused among Muslim jurists and also in the Hindu community:

> The Shaikh required the Emperor's sanction to the execution of the brahmin, but, not withstanding his importunity, no open sanction was given, and the Emperor said in private, "Punishments for offenses against the holy law are in the hands of you, the Ulama, what do you require of me?" The brahmin and the ladies of the Imperial haran busied themselves in interceding for this release but the Shaikh's known opinions stood in the way. At last, when the Shaikh's impor-

tunity exceeded all bounds, the Emperor said, "You have received your answer, it is that which I have already given you." No sooner had the Shaikh reached his lodging than he issued orders for the execution of the brahmin.[15]

The ordered execution of a Brahmin caused ripples throughout the Mughal bureaucracy and among Muslim jurists (the *Ulama*). The *Shaikh* on whose orders the execution was finally carried out lost both prestige and power. Al-Badaoni reports that after censure by Akbar he "withdrew himself from company and avoided it, concerning himself principally with his own claims to superiority and the repudiation of former decisions in legal matters, whether modern or ancient. He never went to Court." He died six years later, having lived the remainder of his life in self-imposed exile.[16]

The execution undoubtedly caused unrest among the Hindu population in Mathura. It had the potential for fueling an open revolt. Hence, in September, four months after this incident, Akbar issued a second grant to the Vallabha Sampradaya. Little doubt remains that the timing of the farman was not an accident. Madad-i-ma'ash was a tool that could be used at the emperor's discretion. Surely this was an instance when it became an invaluable way of disassociating the empire from a situation that had been both politically unwise and dangerous. This time, Akbar's order was also more open-ended, giving the sect unlimited access to land and acknowledging its growth:

Royal Farman 2—(in connection with cow grazing) The great farman of the Emperor Jalaludhin Mohammad Akbar, he is sovereign, God is great.

This time the order has been given that wherever the cows of Vitthalray, the doubtless well wisher, the wearer of the sacred thread, may be there they should be allowed to graze. In any kind of land Kahasa or Jagir, anyone should not cause them distress, and should not bother them; they should be allowed to graze. In connection with this Vitthalray in Gokul should live free from worry. No one should act against this order because all are obliged to follow this order and execute it.

This has been written, in the third month of the journey, the year 989, Thursday 9, the Christian year 1581, Vikram Samvat 1638.[17]

Unlike the first grant, twelve years earlier, this one does not refer to any specific tract or to any particular village. Instead, it simply states that the cows of Vitthalnath were free to graze in any location. However, what can first appear to be an insignificant consideration is actually quite important. The implication is that where the cows of Vitthalnath went, he had the authority to go as well. By extension, this authority applies to the sect itself, whose adherents not only owned cows themselves, but also venerated the exploits of a deity who was directly associated with cattle. As a result of this unlimited grazing privilege the sampradaya now had the assurance that wherever it wished to spread its doctrine, it would be given the full protection of the empire. The grant ordered that even crown properties and those held by military officers (*kahlsa* and *jagir*) were not excluded from the order. Thus by granting a wealthy landowner grazing rights for his cattle and protection for his followers, the empire committed itself to supporting a Vaishnava bhakti sect. The commitment was unconditional and open-ended.

A third grant quickly followed on October 8, 1581, CE. Like those before, it was issued to Vitthalnath (Vitthalray), but this time the grantor was Hamida Banu, Akbar's mother:

> Royal Farman 3a (in connection with cow grazing). The order of Hamida Banu. She is eminent.
> Let it be known to the bright administrators of Mahavan that have entered into the government of Agra the capital of the Empire, and also to others, according to the farman of the great and just Emperor—the cows of Vitthalray, the wearer of the sacred thread, that wherever Vitthalray's cows may be in any kind of land Khalsa or Jagir, there they may not be restricted from grazing and not bothered. In connection with this matter Vitthalray shall live free from worry. All officials are obliged to follow this order and not to act against it.
> This is written on the 10th day of the month of Ramazan the year 989, Sunday October 8, the Christian year 1581, Vikram Samvat 1638.[18]

This farman was followed several months later by a parwana that solidified the farman and made it even more specific:

> Royal Farman 3a (in connection with the grazing of cows).
> The farman of the disciple of Akbar, Commander Bahadur Khan.
> It should be known to present and future officials of the pargana of Od that in Savi and other villages there is a pasture for cows and oxen, therefore no one should obstruct them and harass them on the pretext of supervising, taxation or counting. The reason is that this village has wisely been made a grant. According to this great order all must behave and each year a new pargana must not be demanded.
> Written on the 33rd day of the 11th month of Al Haram, the year 997, 1 December of the Christian year 1588, Vikram Samvat 1645.[19]

Several possibilities may explain Hamida Banu's name on the farman. First, this may be an indication that the royal family was moved by Pushtimarg and sought to support the sect. Or, second, it may indicate a desire on the part of the empire to reaffirm the issue of the earlier grant in a way that suggested the widest possible support. In either case, the total effect of farman and parwana combined is a proclamation of broad-based support for Vitthalnath and an imprimatur that gave the empire's blessing to its expansion.

The potential economic benefit to the sect from these documents should not be overlooked. With unlimited grazing rights, a large herd of cows could easily be sustained. In an agricultural economy where the cow was highly prized

3. Krishna's Many Mansions: Mughal Patronage and Expansion   81

for its milk production and for its other by-products (including dung for fuel and cleaning, and *ghee* or clarified butter, used in most forms of puja) the cow was a measure of wealth.

Other farmans followed. In 1593 Akbar granted Vitthalnath additional rights to property already purchased by the goswami:

> From Emperor Akbar to Gosain Vitthalray.
> Informs that the land purchased by Vitthalray from the owners in Mauza Jatipura and situated in the pargana near Govardhannath temple, where he intends to build garden, cow sheds and karkhanas, is rent free and that all officers have been instructed to take notice of it.[20]

Much like the earlier farmans this document indicates that the land in question had already been acquired by Vitthalnath. The property, in the outskirts of Jatipura, was situated near the Govardhannath temple. These additional lands were now provided rent free to the goswami and could be utilized for the construction of additional cow sheds, gardens, and karkhanas (workshops).

Yet another farman, issued on June 5 of 1589 CE, formally acknowledged the empire's recognition that the Vallabha Sampradaya controlled the village of Gokul:

> From Emperor Akbar to Gosain Vitthalray.
> Regarding grant of the Mauza of Gokul together with the Guzar Ghat to Gosain Vitthalray, tax free in perpetuity to meet the expenses of the Thakurdwara; all the officers were instructed to take note of it.[21]

This farman is more specific than its predecessors about the actual land in Gokul that was owned outright by the Vallabha Sampradaya. It provided this ownership "in perpetuity." The ownership of Gokul was no small matter. Situated in the heartland of Braj, Gokul was widely recognized and revered as the village of Krishna's childhood.

During this same period, Vitthalnath increasingly acquired the image of royalty. Alan Entwistle reports, "Some portraits of Vitthalnath show him wearing the Mughal court dress that was worn only by people of high status—a privilege that is supposed to have been granted to him by Akbar."[22] Mughal patronage of the Vallabha Sampradaya had been fully established within Braj, not only elevating Vitthalnath to the level of aristocracy, but also granting him unlimited access to grazing privileges throughout the empire. These grants served to propel the sect into continued expansion.

Akbar's support of the sect was so firmly cemented in place that his successors also felt obligated to continue the support. The 1593 series of farmans was followed by three others between 1633 and 1643 CE. All were issued by Shah Jahan.[23] A notable change also occurred, one that gave the sampradaya tax exemption, the rent-free use of land, and the right to deed its property to the descendents of Vitthalnath.

The first in this series of farmans was issued on October 9, 1633:

> From Emperor Shah Jahan to Gosain Vitthalray.
> The *Mauza* (outskirts or neighborhood) of Gokul has been granted free of tax from ancient times to the children of Vitthalray to cover the expenses of *Thakurdwara:* instructs all officers not to alter or change this arrangement.[24]

Ten years later the farman of 1643 continued the support of the sect by Shah Jahan, restating the emperor's basic assumptions:

> From Emperor Shah Jahan to Gosain Vitthalray.
> Declaring that Vitthalray is one of the well wishers of the Mughal Kingdom, and a resident of Gokul; instructs all the officers that no one should molest or disturb him and his property.[25]

It was during this same period that Vitthalnath devised a system of patrilineal inheritance that would empower each of his seven sons to carry the mantle of the tradition as custodians of the nidhi swarups. Legends about each deity implied "that they were either acquired by Vallabha through his wife and mother, or were donated by disciples or commissioned from them by Vallabha or Vitthalnath."[26] With each son established as an independent source of authority, the regional development of the sect was empowered. All that was needed was the ability to pass on the property the sect had already acquired to these seven *balaks* (sons). This right was soon granted by Shah Jahan.

Twenty-five years later, in the early spring of 1658, Shah Jahan issued two additional farmans to the Vallabha Sampradaya. These established the sect as a major land owner within the region, controlling desirable amounts of grazing property near Mathura:

> Farman 13 March 1658. From Emperor Shah Jahan to the temple authorities of Govardhannath.
> Informing that the cows belonging to the temple of Govardhannath in the village Gokulpur are allowed to graze on the land in villages in Bachhagon and Bachha; instructs all the officers that this should not be prohibited on the ground of grazing fees.[27]
> Farman 30 April 1658. From Emperor Shah Jahan to Gosain Girdharilal.
> Regarding grant of pargana of Mahaban to Girdharilal and his children by way of charity; instructs all the officers to take notice of it.[28]

The first of these later farmans extended the grazing rights of the sect's cattle from the village of Gopalpur some eight miles from Mathura to the villages of Baccha and Bachhagaon. Bachhagaon is described as a large area with significant grazing lands. By 1880, it included 3,694 acres and was widely recognized as part of the Braj heartland. By that same year 45 temples from different bhakti traditions had been erected there.

The second farman is more important than the first. Granted to Gosain Girdharilal, Vitthalnath's grandson, this document authorizes the gift of the entire administrative district (pargana) of Mahaban to the goswami and to his children. Mahaban was one of the most important districts in the Mathura area and was assessed at substantial value. In the early twentieth century a gazetteer concluded that "in 1556 (it) comprised an area of 290,703 bighas (an amount of land that varied from 1/3 to over 1 acre) assessed at a revenue of 6,784,780 dams (a copper coin in the Mughal Empire); while it furnished a force of 2,000 infantry and 200 horse."[29]

By the time of these farmans, the sampradaya was experiencing internal conflict concerning power and privilege within the sect. These conflicts revolved around the question of succession to the title of goswami. The early history of the sect was mired by increasing competition between descendants of Vallabhacharya as "conflicts began to arise when a senior goswami died without heir and a successor had to be chosen from another branch of the family."[30] In 1622, the swarup of Shri Balkrishnaji was seized in a dispute that erupted over primogeniture and inheritance; it was taken along with another image to Rajnagar (Ahmadabad). The resident goswami, Brajray, petitioned the Mughal court for possession of the deities. As a result, Aurangzeb issued an order granting him custody of the swarup. As if that wasn't enough, with the assistance of Mughal troops Brajray seized the deity from another goswami, Brajbhushan, and forcibly removed it to Surat in 1670, where he established his own gaddi, which his followers consider the sixth gaddi.[31] This dispute and the use of the Mughal courts to resolve it created a prolonged rivalry and disparate claims for the sixth gaddi in Surat, extending the geographical domain of the sect.

These concerns often surrounded the question of custody over the swarups. Eventually, the disputes became so difficult that the empire chose to intervene. Such patterns of conflict not only are indicative of the difficulties that arise when succession is governed by primogeniture but also are not uncommon in patronage systems where dynastical lineage traditions have symbiotic associations with government. In the case of Hindu traditions such as Pushtimarg, where possession of the title of goswami meant a close connection with the continued transfer of wealth from Rajput states to the sect, these conflicts continued through the formative period of the sect's life in the sixteenth and seventeenth centuries.

The disputes, coupled with rivalry with Bengali Vaishnavas, reveal the tensions that accompanied the early expansion of the sect. From the initial grants to the sect in 1577 to the expanded grants given by Shah Jahan, the Vallabha Sampradaya had achieved a level of prosperity that elevated its leadership to the level of aristocracy. Having been given the right to expand the sect as they wished, the goswamis soon acquired the village of Gokul and, in time, the entire district of Mahaban within which it was situated. Thus by 1658 not only were the sect's cattle allowed to graze any place as dictated in earlier farmans; they were also specifically authorized to utilize the lands of Bachha and Bachhagaon and the district of Mahaban, which the goswamis now owned tax-free and outright. These provisions were granted not only to the goswamis but also to their children, assuring the hereditary control of the sect.

As the holdings of the sampradaya increased, the sect received additional income from the markets within the villages it controlled. The parwana of March 7, 1704, verifies this:

> From Mukramat Khan to Gosain Girdharilal.
> Regarding grant of grain market (Mandvi) of Mauza Gokul to Gosain Girdharilal; instructs all the officers to take notice of it.[32]

By the time of this farman the Vallabha Sampradaya not only had expanded its ownership of primary grazing properties but also had ventured into direct control of major sources of grain production, which was a significant aspect of the local agricultural economy. The control of the goswamis was absolute, both economically and culturally. They accrued the taxes and rent from tenant farmers and dominated the socio-religious environment, maintaining their role as keepers and defenders of tradition. They managed large herds of cattle and influenced local commerce. They reaped the benefit of a continuing stream of contributions, accrued through each of the gaddis or seats of the tradition that had been dispersed throughout Rajasthan and the Gujarat. All of this was legitimized by a steady stream of Mughal grants.

The sect acquired other sources of income in traditions that have continued into the present day. As the faith attracted wealthy devotees through a tradition developed to support large festivals and special darshans, sponsors of these events were termed *manorathis* and participated in the accumulation of wealth in the havelis by providing lavish gifts and donations.[33] These traditions centered on the preparation and distribution of large quantities of food first offered to the deity and then to devotees. In return, gifts were seen as extensions of seva, increasing the purity of the donors. The ability to sustain such generosity continued as the sect expanded, and simultaneously attracted adherents.

These avenues of support were augmented by patronage in the Hindu strongholds of Rajasthan. The next chapter argues that during a period of

3. Krishna's Many Mansions: Mughal Patronage and Expansion 85

oppression under Aurangzeb's tyrannical governance, a move to the independent Hindu kingdom of Mewar was prudent. However, the transition was also occasioned by the possibility of continued patronage from Rajput princes. Evidence suggests that both Mughal and Rajput systems of patronage were so well established that following the death of Aurangzeb, Mughal patronage of the Vallabha Sampradaya resumed, and continued through the late eighteenth century. Each successive emperor continued to provide royal gifts, thus insuring that the hereditary model of sectarian governance established by Vitthalnath would survive intact. In 1768, Emperor Shah Alam even decreed that it was not necessary for goswamis to ask for fresh deeds every year.[34]

By reinforcing the economic position of the resident goswamis and establishing Vitthalnath and his seven sons as aristocracy, the Mughal grants prepared the sect for a greatly expanded system of patronage in other Rajput states. In Mewar, Kishangarh, Bundi, and other independent Rajput kingdoms, the Vallabha Sampradaya was lavishly supported by royal gifts. It developed schools of art and secured a regional history, sustaining a system of governance and local control that endured into the nineteenth and twentieth centuries.

These advantages directly impacted the expansion of the sect in the diaspora 400 years later. The sampradaya has looked to the Vallabhkul—the dynasty of Vallabhacharya that supported seven gaddis or seats of the tradition, as continuing sources of authority. Each gaddi, while connected to the sampradaya through the ritualistic authority of Nathdwara where Shri Nathji resides, possesses the right to expand its own purview, to erect its own havelis, and to nurture its devotees abroad.

4

Of Maharajas and Maharanas
Patronage and the Development of Regional Autonomy

When he had darshan, Raja Man Singh threw himself down in homage before Shri Nathji. He had arrived miserable with the heat, but now he felt cool and refreshed. Having beheld the holy face of Shri Nathji, he was filled with joy and exclaimed, "I have seen in person the consummate Brahman Krishna who is the Moon of Brindaban and the Lord of Govardhan."[1]

—Attributed to Khumbhandas (16th century)
in the *Chaurasi Vaishnavan ki Varta*

The Sacred Journey and the Establishment of Nathdwara as a Pilgrimage Center

This chapter shows how the Vallabha Sampradaya used the metaphor of the sacred journey and the dynamics of royal patronage to expand. With the full support of generations of the maharanas of Mewar, the sampradaya established a spiritual center in Nathdwara and gained influence in other Hindu kingdoms including Kishangarh, Bundi, and Kota. The outward journey not only was a movement away from Braj but also became a means of enthroning Krishna with increasing opulence as the descendants of Vallabha (who became identified both as goswamis and maharajas) established autonomous regional centers.

The narrative of the movement of the Vallabha Sampradaya to Mewar state in 1669 is filled with images of the heroic journey.[2] Sectarian sources such as the *Dwarkadhisji ki Prakatya* suggest that following Aurangzeb's edict for the destruction of Hindu temples, the leaders of the sampradaya sought sanctuary for the central swarup of Shri Nathji and another image, Shri Navanitapriyaji—Krishna as a butter stealer.[3] Both icons were temporarily hidden in a private home in Agra. They were then taken to the Rajput kingdom of Kota and later to the states of Kishangarh and Jodhpur. Eventually, protected by a small band of Pushtimargiya devotees and priests, the images were carried to Mewar. Led by the priest Damodar Lal, the small band carefully placed the swarup in a cart. Skirting the Aravalli Mountains, whose arid peaks are a prominent feature of the landscape of Rajasthan, the group moved toward Mewar. Finally, 48 kilometers northeast of Udaipur, the cart bearing the deity became stuck near the tiny village of Sinhar (also referred to as Sinhad or Siarh).[4] The leadership interpreted this event as the deity's desire to remain in place; they renamed the village Nathdwara, "the portal of Shri Nath," and established it as a pilgrimage center.

The narrative serves two purposes. First, as an etiological myth (a myth of origins) that equates divine will with the foundation of a sacred city, it legitimizes the creation of sacred space, transforming a tiny village into a divine portal. Second, and perhaps more significant, the narrative built on the metaphor of movement that had already been established in the tradition when Vallabha transported the image of Shri Nathji from Mount Govardhan to Gokul.

While this metaphor had achieved dominance in painting, depicting Krishna as an adult in the company of his consort, Radha, it also emerged in images of the child god. Always moving, Krishna never remained in one place. This image is found in the poetry of Surdas:

>Dark one, stop, don't go away.
>I'm doing it for you, my cowherd boy—
>Listen to me, my lovely little lad—
>I'm filling the vessels full as they'll go
>With all six tastes of food.
>Why go off where others live?
>Why make such elaborate plans
>To get the milk and curd and ghee
>And butter they too have to give?[5]

The metaphor carries with it an implicit assumption that has characterized pilgrimage and sacred space in Pushtimarg. Once a center of sacred space has been defined, it can be expanded or relocated. In turn, a single sacred center can become multiple centers, creating a vast web of interconnecting geography. From this perspective, the center of worship of Shri Nathji was shifted by Vallabha from Mount Govardhan to Gokul. Taking advantage of economic opportunity and attempting to free the sect from a location in the very heart of Mughal domination, the center of sacred space was again shifted to Nathdwara. Later, in the sixteenth and seventeenth centuries, new centers were again created as the seven sons of Vitthalnath moved their swarups into Rajasthan and the Gujarat. Through these combined movements, each motivated by different circumstances and needs, the sampradaya created a broadly defined sacred geography. This pattern, much in keeping spatial transposition, asserts that one region can incorporate the sanctity of another.[6]

Mewar in the Seventeenth Century and the Establishment of Patronage as a Royal Practice

The small Rajput state of Mewar was a symbol of Hindu independence in the seventeenth, eighteenth, and nineteenth centuries. Mewar resisted both Mughal imperialism and British control.[7] This image was cultivated in a well-touted lineage of the maharanas of Mewar, who claimed descent from Rama and drew on a mythologized history that captured the spirit of the hero of the *Ramayana*.[8] The mythology of the Sisodia clan of Rajput princes particularly drew strength from maharana Pratap Singh (1572–1597 CE), whose resistance to Mughal imperialism and defense of Mewar during the battle of Haldighati in 1576 became legendary.[9] The battle, which was not a victory for either side, became a symbol of defiance as the maharanas thwarted the advance of Akbar's troops.[10] Although Mewar ultimately surrendered to Jahangir in 1615, the prowess of maharana Pratap continued as a point of pride.

Even after 1615, the ruling maharanas of Mewar continued to bolster their image with rhetoric drawn from Hindu tradition, retaining a public image of resistance and independence. An example of this public face was its official deity, an incarnation of Shiva named Eklingji, who was understood to protect and preserve the kingdom. Epic poems of the period such as *Ekling Mahatmya* reflect the influence of the Shavite cult of Ekling, which became a unifying force in Mewar. Since the maharana acted on behalf of the god, his military campaigns took on an aura of the just war. In this sense Mewar was a theocracy that, under the leadership of its maharanas and their tutelary god Ekling, maintained the symbolism of an independent Hindu kingdom long after its government was forced to acknowledge its allegiance to the Mughal Empire.

Mewar was affected by Hindu traditions with even greater appeal among the masses. According to legend, Mira Bai, the poet saint of the devotional tradition, was the daughter-in-law of maharana Sangram Singh of Mewar.

While her actual lineage and historical circumstance are more obscure, her popularity is undisputed.[11] Mira Bai's poetry was closely linked to the growing popularity of Krishna in Rajput states.

The Move to Nathdwara and the Underlying Dynamics of Patronage

While Aurangzeb's iconoclasm may have provided impetus for the sect's move, the transformation of a small village into a Vatican-like center of pilgrimage cannot be seen entirely as a defensive reaction. In a context of deteriorating relationships between Hindus and Muslims in Mathura, the move had been anticipated.

In 1669, the year of the Vallabha Sampradaya's move, the Jats, an influential Hindu agricultural caste group in Mathura and Gokul, rebelled against Aurangzeb. The revolt had undoubtedly been provoked through the iconoclastic policies dating from the 1661 destruction of a Hindu temple and the construction of a mosque in its place by the empire's official, Abdul Nabi.[12] Abdul Nabi was killed during the revolt, which was followed by additional waves of persecution. In that same year, fueled by the unrest, Aurangzeb issued his famous general order of April 9, 1669, ordering the demolition of Hindu temples and forbidding public worship.[13]

Tensions escalated when a Muslim officer who was sent in 1671 to destroy temples in the pilgrimage city of Ujjain was killed in a riot.[14] In addition, there are recorded cases of the demolition of temples being postponed or "neglected" as priests paid Mughal officers to keep their sanctuaries standing.

In this climate of oppression the Vallabha Sampradaya's sectarian expansion would be difficult. A move became prudent. The ultimate decision to transfer the center of the sect to another location was the result of cultivating a relationship with the maharanas of Mewar that had begun with the early pilgrimages of Jagat Singh to Mathura and Vrindaban. As early as 1658, maharana Jagat Singh embarked on extensive pilgrimages to temples in the Braj-speaking parts of Rajasthan. On one such trip he was even portrayed as the disciple and devotee of Sri Nathji.[15] Pushtimarg had become a popular religion of choice in Mewar, a practice that was continued by Raj Singh.

Both regents understood the economic benefits that accrued from a bhakti sect to Mewar. Since bhakti was a populist movement replete with growing centers of tradition such as Mathura and Vrindaban, its ability to generate revenue was clear. Pilgrimage centers produced income for shop owners and temple managers. Akin to the benefits of tourism in the modern world, pilgrimage produced a ready supply of devotees all of whom relied on the local economies to meet their needs.

For the sampradaya, the move to Mewar also afforded a number of advantages. As an insular state that had resisted Mughal control and retained an aura of its original independence, Mewar provided a protected atmosphere for a bhakti sect. Jagat Singh was intent on managing the brief peace and maintaining the delicate balance of relations with the Mughal Empire. As early as 1633, he had sent presents to vassals of Shah Jahan in an attempt to secure the fragile peace. As a result of these initiatives his 26-year reign was a time of "uninterrupted tranquility."[16]

Jagat Singh used the interlude of peace to complete large-scale public works projects that were visible symbols of the culture of harmony that he intended to create. The Raj Samand dam was completed by 1652. Other dams followed, and large lake construction projects were initiated in 1662. During a time of famine he strengthened the state's public image so that at times it rivaled the pomp of the Mughal Empire itself. He became a patron of the arts. His policies were continued by his successor, Raj Singh.[17]

The security and tranquility that Mewar offered in 1669 was a window of opportunity in a tense political environment. Within ten years, harmony between the empire and the Sisodia rulers ended. Aurangzeb invaded neighboring Marwar, and Mewar attempted to come to its aid. Near the end of the century resistance to Mughal oppression also increased, strengthening the security of Hindus in the state. When Aurangzeb sought to impose the jizya tax, required by religious law (*Sharia*) for all non–Muslims, it was resisted.

Had the move of the Vallabha Sampradaya to Mewar only been a reaction to the threat of Mughal persecution it is doubtful the sect would have been so quickly received in a Hindu state that was trying to maintain a delicate balance of power with a new emperor. The act of harboring a runaway Hindu sampradaya would have strained the fragile peace between Agra and Udaipur. Perhaps the strongest evidence that the move to Mewar was motivated by more than an attempt to seek sanctuary are the series of grants given to the sect well before its move to Mewar in 1669. In 1665 maharana Raj Singh decreed that the village of Asotiya be given to two goswamis, Pranvallabhaji and Giridharilal. Introduced with the proper acclamations to Rama, Ganesh, and the state deity Ekling, the grant had already established the sampradaya as a landowner a few miles from the village of Sinhar, which would later become Nathdwara. The economic and sociological benefits of a bhakti revival that had the potential to transform a handful of insignificant and economically unproductive villages into a major Vaishnava pilgrimage center were not likely overlooked.

During this period of initial contact between the sect and the Mewar nobility, bhakti was far more than just a popular Hindu religion. It was a source of art and artisans, drawing the loyalty and devotion of thousands of pilgrims who flocked to any location associated with Krishna. Places associated with the bhakti movement often grew as centers of Hindu culture. Festivals filled such holy cities to their bursting points. Bhakti brought fame and income to the locale.

While a strong tie existed between the maharana and the priesthood of Eklingji, Mewar had not benefitted economically from its official god. The deity attracted few pilgrims from outside the state, inspired little art, and while producing a comradery among the Rajput soldiers, offered Mewar little else. Thus, in the sixteenth and seventeenth centuries the Sisodia rulers of Mewar gave their patron deity no more attention than necessary. They participated in the annual festival of Ekling and utilized the seal of the god and his salutation on royal orders and letters. Few paintings or records of the period reflect an interest of the rulers in spreading the cult of Elking either numerically or geographically. Rather, their attention was often diverted to other, more popular forms of Hinduism, and specifically to Vaishnavism.

Both Jagat Singh and his successor, Raj Singh, let it be known that they had adopted Pushtimarg as their personal religion. They made pilgrimages to the sect's temples. They welcomed goswamis as dignitaries, respecting their office. They personally participated in darshan. In return, the fruits of the bhakti movement—painters and the devotees who purchased their work, pilgrims and the merchants who provided for their needs, temples and the service industries that maintained the images—came to Mewar. There was little risk in supporting a sampradaya that had already received the patronage of the Mughal Empire, in a state that was attempting to revive its independence and autonomy.

The Mewar Grants

Within two years of the move to Mewar in 1669, the goswamis built a temporary shrine in Asotiya for the image of Shri Dwarkashish, one of the swarupas associated with Shri Nathji. A more permanent temple was constructed on the shore of the Raj Samand Lake, in Kankroli, in a visible affirmation of support of the state. When the deity was installed the royal court sent presents of soldiers, servants, elephants, and horses, thus publically giving the blessings of the state to the deity.

In subsequent years the sect began to acquire additional property in the vicinity of Asotiya. Securing villages near Kankroli, the site of the permanent temple of Dwarkadhish, the goswamis developed baronial estates much in the manner of Mewar nobility. Nathdwara and Kankroli became central seats of Pushtimargiya spiritual and economic power. Twenty-one villages situated in different parts of Mewar, held rent free, were given to the sect as *muafi* grants from the maharana. Thirty villages were given to the Tilkayat, the senior goswami of Nathdwara and the spiritual head of the sect.[18] As with the Mughal madad-i-ma'ash grants, these charitable donations of land exempted the recipient from paying taxes.[19] The Tilkayat of Nathdwara was given 30 villages.

The sect received additional grants from the state between 1695 and 1701 affirming the continued support of the monarchy. The first, issued in 1695, ordered that the villages of Asotiya and Rajnagar be given to goswami Brajbhusanji. The grant also specified that the goswami would live in a haveli on the shore of the royal lake, Raj Samand, in a visible union of Pushtimarg with one of the more formidable symbols of the Mewar nobility. The symbolism of a unified "church and state" was reinforced when the permanent installation of the swarup was made to coincide with the inauguration of the Raj Samand dam. Provincial chiefs and estate owners all came to an event that promised to be the single most important ceremony in eighteenth century Mewar. Later, stone tablets placed near the dam told the tale. Poets, in the Mewari epics, wrote of it. To the public who witnessed the simultaneous events, the monarchy became inexorably linked with the blessings of Dwarkadhish, who had made Mewar his new home.

A second order issued in 1696 CE reconfirmed the gift of the village of Rajnagar. A third document, six years later (1701) records the gift of yet another large haveli to Goswami Brajbhusanji as the personal donation of the Maharana[20]:

The Victory of Shri Ram

The Grace of Shri Ganesh　　　　　　　　　　　　　　　　The Grace of Shri Ekling
Friends

Maharajadhiraj Maharana Shri Amarsinghji commands to Gusai Brajbhusanji his one haveli east west 81 (eighty-one) gaj, north south 71 (seventy-one) gaj, accumulating 5751 gaj (five thousand seven hundred fifty-one) ...
Pancoli Damodardas, Pancoli Gordhandas having written it. Samvat 1757, the month of Magaser, the 8th day.[21]

By 1737, with the continued support of the Mewar nobility, the goswamis had gained absolute control of the village of Siarh, which they renamed *Nathdwara* ("Portal of Shri Nathji"). A document issued by the maharana confirmed the gift, which was originally given by the chief of the province of Dilwara:

4. Of Maharajas and Maharanas

Maharana Sri Gujjut [sic] Singh Commanding:

The village of Siarh in the hills, of one thousand rupees yearly rent, having been chosen by Nathji (the god) for his residence, and given up by Rinna Raghude, I have confirmed it. The Gosaen [sic] and his heirs shall enjoy it forever.
Samvat 1793 AD 1737[22]

Under the criteria of muafi grants, the revenues from the properties granted could be collected by the new owner and utilized for any purpose that he saw fit.

After 1750, the land given to the Vallabha Sampradaya by the maharanas of Mewar had substantially increased. A grant given in 1778–1779 broadened the control of the sect.[23] British agent James Tod described the grant as including "a list of thirty-four entire towns and villages ... besides various parcels of arable land, from twenty to one hundred and fifty bighas, in forty-six more villages."[24] The sect's economic position was secure.

As Nathdwara evolved as a pilgrimage center within the developing Pushtimargiya tradition, the Mewar nobility also began to grant it increasing shares in the commerce and economic benefits that were the by-product of the bhakti movement. By 1809, these benefits were substantial and were summarized in an edict of Maharana Bhim Singh:

Sri Maharana Bhim Singji Commanding

To the towns of Sri-ji, or to the (personal) lands of the Gosaen-ji no molestation shall be offered. No warrants or exactions shall be issued or levied upon them. All complaints, suits or matters, in which justice is required, originating in Nathdwara, shall be settled there; none shall interfere therein, and the decisions of the Gosaen-ji I shall invariable confirm. The town and transit duties (of Nathdwara and villages pertaining thereto), the assay (purkhaye) fees from the public markets, duties on precious metals (kasoti), all brokerage (dulali) and dues collected at the four gates; all contributions and taxes of whatever kind, are presented as an offering to Sri-ji; let the income thereof be placed in Sri-ji's coffers.

All the products of foreign countries imported by the Vaisnavas whether domestic or foreign, and intended for consumption at Nathdwara, shall be exempt from duties. The right of sanctuary (sirma) of Sri-ji, both in the town and in all his other villages, will be maintained: the Almighty will take cognizance of any innovation. Wherefore, let all chiefs, farmers of duties, beware of molesting the goods of Nathji (the God), and wherever such may halt, let guards be provided for their security. If of my blood, or if my servants, this warrant shall be obeyed for ever and ever. Whoever resumes this grant will be a caterpillar in hell during 60,000 years.

By command—through the chief butler (parairi) Eklingdas: written by Surut Sing, son of Nathji Pancholi, Mah-su 1st, Samvat 1865; AD 1809.[25]

Warning of the dire karmic punishments that would result from any act of disrespect to Shri Nathji, the grant clearly expressed the growing economic dominance of the Vallabha Sampradaya in Mewar—a process accomplished in 138 years from the time the cart carrying the deity had become stuck in the mud near the tiny village that would become Nathdwara. Transit duties, fees from public markets, duties on precious metals, gate fees (monies collected on entrance to the walled city), contributions and taxes, were all now considered the rightful property of the god. Further, the sect was permitted to import goods it needed duty-free. Provincial chiefs were required to protect the god's caravans as they travelled through their districts. Finally, this document, as the two before it, was issued to the goswamis and their descendants in perpetuity, thus endowing Nathdwara with inalienable rights and privileges. The ability of the goswamis to extract duties on goods produced in the marketplace was an important part of their regular income.

In the Gujarat, where fees of this nature were responsible for an even larger percentage of the goswamis' income, strict regulations were adopted for their collection. Caste groups including *Bhatia, Bania,* and *Lohana* merchants were required to sign agreements affecting almost every item they sold.[26] One quarter *anna* per 100 rupees of sale was to be collected on all types of cloth. One anna per every thousand rupees of transaction was to be gathered on bills of exchange and drafts. Pearls and jewels, grain of every type, and foodstuffs including ghee, oil and rice were all taxed. Raw materials such as iron, rope, gold, and silver were assessed at different levels depending on their worth and the unit of measurement. Services by insurance brokers, agency brokers, and cloth merchants also had duties levied upon them. All this wealth accrued to the Vallabha Sampradaya.

The goswamis' ultimate authority in Nathdwara transcended the established regulations for commerce in the state. From the taxes brought upon commodities in the market to the fees collected from pilgrims as they passed through the city gates, no possible source of revenue was left untouched. Within this cumulative system of patronage, the small village of Sirah was transformed into a virtual Vatican with total control over its domain reinforced by the authority of the crown. In time this control produced a culture of patronage in which the sect's influence in the arts prospered.

This pattern of patronage increasingly attracted nobility in other states. By 1685, the sect had successfully negotiated the gift of two villages in Sadri, a province located near the southern border of Mewar. These grants resulted from the conversions of the *Rajrana* of Sadri, who became a devotee of Shri Dwarkadhishji in 1685. Controlled by the *Jhala Rajput* clan, Sadri had ancestral ties with the most important provinces in the state and was widely considered a political prize.[27]

In time, goswamis residing in Nathdwara began to accumulate property in Rajasthan and the Gujarat. Avenues of patronage similar to those in Mewar were employed. Large estates were acquired in Baroda, Bharatpur, Karauli, Kota, Partabgarh, and Ajmer. Income from these estates was substantial.

The image of personal piety and royal patronage continued well into the nineteenth century and was popularized through the arts. A temple hanging (*pichhavai*) produced in Nathdwara about 1830 depicts Shri Nathji receiving darshan. His attendants include a Tailangana Brahmin and maharana Raj Singh, a visible reaffirmation of the maharana's support for his sampradaya.

Patronage and the Arts

As the Vallabha Sampradaya acquired continuing royal favor, it also used its position to develop schools of art. Pichhavais, miniature paintings and other objects of art lifted the influence of Shri Nathji. In time the Nathdwara School of art gained a reputation that spread across Mewar and into other regions of Rajasthan. The Mewar court in Udaipur even established regulations that required resident artists in Nathdwara to "join those attached to the Udaipur court whenever the Maharana required their assistance on one of his various projects."[28] Pushtimargiya artists exerted a noticeable influence among several schools of Vaishnava art in the adjacent states of Kishangarh, Bundi, and Jaipur. Paintings produced in Bundi in the seventeenth century expanded the theme as rulers and members of the court commissioned renderings of Krishna, similar to those in Mewar.

Pushtimargiya art also spread through royal marriages. After 1660, when a Bundi princess married Prince Raj Singh of Mewar, artists from Udaipur migrated to Bundi. A resurgence of Bundi art followed. These painters, inspired in the style of Mewar, depicted Krishna enthroned.

However, evidence abounds that Pushtimargiya art was produced in Bundi well ahead of the marriage, demonstrating receptivity to Pushtimarg. Pichhavais were temple art, and miniature paintings were used by devotees. Some show a close alignment between religion and the state. For example, a drawing produced between 1635 and 1640 shows a noble seated on a swing surrounded by female attendants; described as "Hindola Raga," the miniature depicts the prince giving darshan, clearly demonstrating the growing royal favor of the sect.[29] Further, maharana Chattar Sal (1631–1659), under whose reign the Bundi resurgence of art began, sponsored such paintings, often portraying himself as a great lover using the well-established aura of Krishna to enhance his own persona.

The influence of the Nathdwara School of art in Bundi is also evident in the use of dominant colors and in the repetition of themes. In both Nathdwara and Bundi, earlier Mughal themes were replaced by Krishna, who occupied the center of the artist's attention. The deity often appears as a prince who looks to the enchanted, forested realm of Braj. Unlike earlier miniatures depicting the dark god, these paintings show the sophisticated palaces and courts in settings of undeniable luxury and elegance.

The evolution of Vallabhacharya art in the courts of Kishangarh is even more revealing than in Bundi. Between AD 1735 and 1748 a series of Vaishnava miniature paintings were executed in this small Rajput state. In these, the concept of Krishna enthroned was magnified even beyond what had already been produced in Mewar and Bundi.

A major influence that brought Pushtimargiya art to Kishangarh was the conversion of the son of maharaja Raj Singh, Savant Singh, to the faith. Savant Singh, born in 1699 CE, became well known after his adoption of Pushtimarg for taking the name Nagari Das. He was recognized as a major seventeenth century Braj poet who wrote of religious as well as romantic themes. Das' poetry inspired a school of art, for which Kishangarh has been known since its re-discovery by historians in the nineteenth century. The primary executer of these works was Nihal Chand, who, residing at the court, utilized the palace as the setting for his portrayal of Krishna.

The Kishangarh School was also influenced by maharaja Sadar Singh, who commissioned most of the Kishangarh art from 1748 to 1764 CE. Following his rule, Pushtimarg became favored by Kishangarh regents who continued to openly patronize the Vallabha Sampradaya and its art. Savant Sing eventually retired to Braj in a further affirmation of his devotion to Krishna.

Pushtimarg influenced art in other locations. In Jaipur, for example, a haveli was constructed in the city palace. In Kota and Jodhpur, Pushtimargiya art increasingly became a visible affirmation of the union of royal piety with the proliferation of a Vaishnava bhakti sect.

The End of Patronage

Not only was the temple given royal support; income from villages deeded to the deity also provided a sustained revenue. In Nathdwara, patronage continued through the eighteenth and nineteenth centuries. Income was secured from rental fees, from forests, and grazing charges as well as from the use and sale of land.[30] Other gaddis also enjoyed similar patterns of royal support.

However, by the end of the eighteenth century, stability in Mewar was shattered by recurrent raids of Maratha warriors.[31] In 1802, conflict had resulted in removal of Shri Nathji from Nathdwara to a place of refuge in Nathdwara.³² In 1818, seeking to gain more control over the region, the British entered into an alliance with Mewar, hoping to create independent princely states loyal to the East India Company. As part of this alliance, British officials helped the state re-establish traditional forms of land tenure and patronage.

Yet Mewar remained physically and financially in ruins, suffering not only from the Maratha raids but from clan rivalry. Government agent James Todd reported, "Udaipur, which formerly reckoned fifty thousand houses within the walls, had not now three thousand occupied, the rest were in ruin, the rafters being taken for firewood."³³ Attempting to restore order, the British deployed solders as a visible presence, including an encampment at Nathdwara.

While such difficult times were dramatic and temporarily reduced the flow of revenue, throughout the nineteenth century Nathdwara continued to receive income from villages, cultivated land, forests, and pilgrimage. When patronage formally ended in 1947 with the dissolution of the ruling power of the maharana, Nathdwara had already become one of the wealthiest temples in India, second only to Tirupathi.

However, in Nathdwara and the other gaddis, the ability of the Vallabha Sampradaya to utilize the fruits of this long history of patronage came under increasing scrutiny in a climate of moral reform. Emanating from the nineteenth century Hindu Renaissance, the opulence of wealthy temples became an increasing national concern. The nineteenth century Hindu Renaissance was both a reaction to British colonialism and the beginning of an Indian independence movement. It was influenced by the history of Christian missions in India that saw Hinduism as corrupt. As early as 1828 in Bengal, Hindu leaders including Ram Mohan Roy met to discuss reform, naming their coalition the Brahmo Samaj. Denigrating icon worship, the proliferation of sects, caste, and "superstition," the Samaj initiated a call for social reform in India based on Christian principles. Other movements followed.

In the Gujarat another sectarian tradition, the *Swaminarayan Sanstha*, also sought its own level of reform, targeting what it perceived as corrupt Hindu practices. Orientalist writers including Monier-Williams used this theme to challenge what they understood as the corruption within Vaishnavism, challenging the practices of Pushtimarg. However, as Raymond Brady Williams demonstrates, these accusations were misguided and without foundation since there had been close affinity between the two traditions:

> However, the major adversaries of Sahajanand were not the disciples of Vallabhacharya. Nowhere in the literature is it mentioned that Sahajanand criticized the followers of Vallabhacharya or the Maharajas. On the contrary, he adopted

the pattern of temple worship, fasts, and observances of festivals as prescribed by Vitthalanath, the son of Vallabhacharya, and ordered in the *Shikshapatri* that his followers should continue to follow these practices.[34]

Nevertheless, by the mid-nineteenth century, damage to the sampradaya's reputation had been done. In Bombay, negative public opinion was advanced through the tirades of an editor, Karsondas Mulji, who was employed by a weekly paper, the *Satya Prakash*. Mulji's attacks were focused on the goswamis themselves, challenging them with allegations of corruption, sexual impropriety, and graft. Festivals such as Chappan Bhog (an accumulation of 56 types of food that are offered to Shri Nathji) became a flash point for Mulji's allegations.[35]

Responding to this public condemnation, goswami Jadunathji Maharaj brought suit arguing that Mulji "falsely, wickedly, willfully, designedly and maliciously" maligned the sect.[36] The suit not only alleged slander but challenged the use of religious opinion as the mechanism for public humiliation.

Mulji mounted a strong defense and was vindicated in an emotional trial that garnered outpourings of public opinion. The allegations became lost in a sea of controversy that presented an increasingly bleak impression of Pushtimarg. Negative public opinion lasted well into the twentieth century. As late as 1935, Mulji's biographer further escalated the debate with a tirade of assaults on the sect, more than 70 years after the case had ended.[37]

In the last quarter of the nineteenth century these difficulties were compounded by an internal disagreement over financial control within the sampradaya. Goswami Girdhari Lal was accused of taking financial advantage of the weakened condition of Mewar when its underage maharana, Sajjan Singh, was unable to rule.[38] When the government acted with the full support of the British Raj, it attached a number of villages that had supported Nathdwara, encouraging the senior goswami (the Tilkayat) to subordinate himself to the maharana. The Tilkayat refused and quickly became the subject of an armed intervention. The officiating political agent, British Major Gunning, and members of the Mewar Regency Council, accompanied by a detachment of Mewar Bhil Corps, proceeded to Nathdwara. The Tilkayat was arrested and sent to Udaipur while the management of the temple was seized. As a result of this dramatic intervention, the affairs of the Srinathji temple in Nathdwara came under governmental control, ending the continuous pattern of patronage that had lasted almost 300 years. This action also paved the way in Post colonial India for the intervention of government in religious affairs.

In the 1950s a number of Indian states passed legislation that gave them increasing authority over Hindu religious endowments.[39] In Nathdwara, a temple board was created to manage the vast assets of the temple under the authority of the Nathdwara Temple Act of 1959 (Act 13). In the same year, the Nathdwara Inquiry Commission issued its *Report*, which addressed the difficult concerns about the ownership of the assets of the Nathdwara temple and the degree to which the goswamis could participate in its control.[40]

All of these conditions left the Vallabha Sampradaya in a difficult position. Unable to receive the donations from regents who had openly supported the sect, limited in its use of monies derived from villages, and stripped of the historical control that the goswamis had developed, the sect was threatened with loss of support. Compounding this difficulty, in 1959 the Nathdwara Inquiry Commission ruled that the wealth of the temple belonged to the deity with stringent requirements placed on the Tilkayat. The report concluded that "the Nathdwara Temple is in the nature of a public temple and the properties belonging to the Idol [sic] are trust properties which the Tilkayat could not claim as his own."[41] The Tilkayat was left as a functionary who was responsible to the state.

Later, in 1973, another temple act defined the amount of support the Tilkayat could receive. He was allowed a monthly allowance of 5,000 Rupees "for the maintenance of the dignity of his office,"[42] 6,000 rupees for travel outside Nathdwara, 3,000 rupees for the *Braj Yatra* (pilgrimage), 1,000 rupees per month for secretarial staff, 5,000 per year for maintenance of his residence in Nathdwara, and 500 per month for the maintenance of his car.[43] The total stipend (excluding additional funds given to his family) of 32,000 rupees equaled $4,156 (using the 1973 dollars-to-rupees ratio of 7.7). While this amount would have been adequate for running a small business during the same period, it paled in comparison to the net assets of the temple which, by 2011, had reached over two billion rupees.[44]

The next chapter shows how, after the termination of patronage and the migration of Pushtimargiyas from Ahmedabad, Vadodara, Mumbai, and other regions to the West, the sect began to move into the diaspora. While havelis in India continued to invest their wealth and to receive gifts from devotees, this pattern of out-migration foreshadowed the globalization of the faith.

Part Three
Pushtimarg in America

As patronage supported expansion of the Vallabha Sampradaya from the sixteenth through nineteenth centuries, so globalization has shaped Pushtimarg in the modern world. Part Three introduces the reader to the latter stage of this process, describing the development of havelis in North America. Chapter 5 demonstrates how the same entrepreneurial emphasis that has empowered Pushtimarg in modern India equips lay leaders in the United States to expand their religious tradition. Chapter 6 explores the role of Pushtimarg in a denominational society where it co-exists with other forms of American Hinduism. Finally, chapter 7 examines some of the challenges that Pushtimargiyas experience when transplanting their faith to North America.

5

Vaishnavism Without Borders
Shri Nathji and the Journey Abroad

O Kanh, why do you go far away to play?—Surdas[1]

The preceding two chapters have shown how beginning with the Great Mughals and continuing for more than 300 years, the Vallabha Sampradaya received patronage from emperors and princes. This process, coupled with the creation of a dynastical system of inheritance, spread the sect in Rajasthan and the Gujarat, producing a regionalized structure with little centralized control. While Nathdwara became the undisputed source of spiritual authority, the gaddis maintained autonomy. Within this structure goswamis developed havelis and directed the expansion of the sampradaya in a process well attested by sectarian sources.[2] However, in the late twentieth century, as economic and demographic changes transformed urban India, lay populations of Pushtimargiyas took increasing responsibility in developing their temple tradition.

Beginning with a case study of Ahmedabad, the chapter explores the way that economic and demographic changes produced a highly educated, urban middle class. Using the skills they acquired in India, expatriate entrepreneurs became architects of the sect's presence in the United States. Finally, the chapter explores alternative models of haveli development outside the United States, where devotees have employed more traditional patterns of growth as illustrated by the Shrinathji haveli in Toronto.

Following the First Generation of Pushtimargiyas from India: A Case Study of Ahmedabad

American Pushtimarg cannot be fully understood apart from recent demographic changes in India that have given lay entrepreneurs a greater role in the tradition. In the seventeenth through nineteenth centuries, when patronage was the dominant mode of support, the sampradaya was primarily defined by caste and village loyalties. With increased urban growth and the rapid expansion of the Indian middle class in the second half of the twentieth century, the sect's base of support began to change, thus mirroring changes in urban India throughout the country.

A visitor to New Delhi in the 1970s would still have seen much of the old India, built on a British model and incorporating the infrastructure of the Raj. Rotaries defined the flow of traffic and the center of urban life. The heart of New Delhi was Connaught Place, which in the colonial period had been the primary center of commerce. Animals roamed the streets. Pollution was rampant, fueled by congestion and the inefficiency of an array of cars, motor rickshaws, and scooters.

Today, Delhi's metropolitan area has expanded, leaving little evidence of this earlier period. New Delhi boasts high-rise office buildings, a state-of-the-art subway system, and an ultramodern international airport. While air pollution is still a problem, it has been greatly reduced by the use of bottled natural gas to fuel public buses and motor rickshaws.

As New Delhi and Mumbai became the largest metropolitan areas in India, six smaller cities were also transformed. In Kolkata, Chennai, Hyderabad, Bangalore, Pune, and Ahmedabad,[3] industrial growth was facilitated by the presence of transnational corporations. This accelerated expansion of the middle class and fueled patterns of out-migration. This was particularly the case in Ahmedabad, which has become a pivotal city for Pushtimargiya migration to the United States.

Ahmedabad was a traditional North Indian city with origins in the fifteenth century Gujarati Sultanate. In the British period, the city was a center of the textile industry. Cotton mills dominated, employing a labor force that constituted half of the city's population.[4] Mill owners became wealthy industrialists while the labor force, recruited from the lowest rungs of the caste system, had little political clout. As a traditional walled city, Ahmedabad retained the character of Mughal India, with large populations of Hindus, Jains, and Muslims.

The combination of a traditional industry and a burgeoning low caste labor force attracted Gandhi, who used the city to launch his reforms. Ahmedabad became identified with general strikes and increasing resistance to British imperialism. Both Ambedkar, the leader of an untouchable movement, and Gandhi used Ahmedabad as a center for labor reforms as mill owners and workers became locked in a struggle intensified by the growing nationalist movement.[5] The struggle also produced a renewed pride in Gujarati heritage that ultimately lead to the creation of the Gujarat as a state, separate from the Bombay Presidency, that segregated Marathi from Gujarati-speaking populations.[6]

The increasing population of the city, coupled with the wealth that had been generated by the mills, accelerated the growth of the middle class, which evolved cooperative housing ventures and

> provided an important legal mechanism to facilitate this middle-class residential expansion…. Government regulations making land purchase, materials purchase, construction costs, and taxes less expensive for cooperative societies fostered this extraordinary growth. The greatest number of them were located in three wards on the western side of the city Naranpura, Usmanpura, and Ellisbridge; in one middle-class ward in Maninagar, in the east; and in Rakhial, a working-class area situated among the mills.[7]

Although the composition of the rising middle class was diverse, it included traditional populations of "Patels, Brahmans, and Vanias."[8] Within these groups, *Patels* and *Vanias* were mid-level caste groups that had traditionally been affiliated with the Vallabha Sampradaya.

By the 1980s, Ahmedabad's Pushtimargiya population had swelled. Many younger male Vaishnavas had moved to the city looking for employment. By 2001, the percentage of urban populations in the Gujarat had increased by 22 percent.[9] Ahmedabad achieved the greatest growth in the state, followed by Surat and Vadodara, both historically tied to Pushtimarg. Vadodara (Baroda) held significance as the headquarters of the sixth gaddi, while Surat became the official residence of the nidhi swarup of Shri Balkrishnaji. Together, Vadodara, Surat, and Ahmedabad became a significant center of the faith, which had also expanded in other metropolitan areas including Mumbai.

An increasing literacy rate further helped expand the city's growing middle class. Ahmedabad achieved the highest rate in Gujarat state when its percentage of literacy climbed to 79.69 percent in 2001.[10] This dramatic rise was influenced by the rapid expansion of Gujarat University into the rural areas. The number of affiliated colleges jumped from 31 to 235 as the student population increased to over 162,000 by 1971.[11] In addition, accessibility to education also increased as more campuses were opened and as the medium of instruction shifted from English to Gujarati.[12]

As Ahmedabad increasingly attracted a young, highly literate middle class population, its core economy began to experience dramatic change that created the conditions for entrepreneurship. Cotton mills, the city's principal employer since British India, declined in importance during the second half of the twentieth century. A managerial class of businessmen and investors began to replace the mill owners. Many of the new industrialists were not local, as the city also began to attract new industries and a growing cadre of transnational corporations.[13] By 2000, the diamond polishing industry expanded, employing between 100,000 and 150,000 workers.[14] The chemical and pharmaceutical industries developed strong corporate communities in a diversified economy that included biotechnological and energy producing firms, and rising healthcare industries.

Ahmedabad's expanding middle class quickly seized the opportunity for development. For instance, Nirma soap was created, "successfully challenging the giant multinationals, Hindustan Lever and Proctor and Gamble."[15] Karsanbhai Patel, who developed Nirma, also founded a number of management institutions including the Nirma Institute of Management, the Nirma Institute of Technology, and the Nirma Institute of Diploma Studies. Together, these educational institutions helped elevate the already growing entrepreneurial tradition within Ahmedabad's expanding middle class.[16] Still other training grounds for new entrepreneurs emerged, including the Ahmedabad Management Association. Even the textile industry was reborn in a new form, manufacturing synthetic cloth as the industrial firm Ambani expanded:

> In 1978, Ambani launched a nationwide advertising campaign that made Vimal, the brand name of Reliance's synthetic fabric, a household word. He built an India-wide distribution network to match, and "by 1983, on the eve of its entry into petrochemicals, Reliance had become India's largest composite textile mill, sprawling over 180,000 sq. meters, producing three million square meters of fabric per month, and employing 10,000 workers." From this base, Ambani proceeded to build the largest industrial empire in India. In his other industries—his polyester yarn plant at Patalgana, near Mumbai, and petrochemicals near Jamnagar and at Hazira, near Surat—Ambani demonstrated his belief that Indian manufacturing could and should be world class."[17]

Ahmedabad's highly competitive entrepreneurs sought increasing opportunities. Many looked to the Gujarat's long history of out-migration as a way of maximizing their interests as high-level jobs became increasingly difficult to find in Ahmedabad.

Yet rapid economic development and urbanization were not problem free. Ahmedabad was racked by communal violence. Attacks on Muslims became a regular part of the cultural landscape, fueled by a rise in a fundamentalist form of Hinduism called *hindutva*.[18] In 1992, the destruction of a mosque in Ayodhya provoked a renewed cycle of communal violence. Massacres of Muslim families in Ahmedabad in 2002 followed, precipitating some of the worst clashes between Hindus and Muslims in modern Indian history. These attacks and their aftermath made Ahmedabad into an increasingly segregated city, setting the stage for increasing migration.

Throughout the boom period, the Pushtimargiya population continued to grow, accelerated by the increasing prosperity of the traditional Vaishya communities that had always been part of the sect. The number of havelis in Ahmedabad reached 32 by 2012. Of these, one source estimates that 18 are relatively recent.[19] At the same time the traditional pattern of creating havelis also began to change as more lay Vaishnavas began to take an active, entrepreneurial role in founding temples.[20]

Pushtimargiyas also expanded their religious infrastructure with renewed patterns of pilgrimage. As transportation networks expanded, travel times to sites of religious importance began to shrink. Vadodara and Surat became more accessible. The Ahmedabad Vadodara Expressway collapsed the distance into less than a two-hour drive. Similarly, Surat could easily be reached in only a few hours.

As metropolitan Ahmedabad, Vadodara, and Surat have become increasingly interconnected, so traditional Vaishnava pilgrimage sites also became more easily accessible. Following the government of India's accession of control of Nathdwara, the pilgrimage industry began to develop the holy city. Nathdwara increased in popularity, second only to traditional pilgrim venues such as Tirupathi in South India. During its expansion, the city not only maintained its traditional pilgrim rest areas (*dharmshalas*) but also began to offer a wide variety of accommodations ranging from more traditional pilgrim venues to the highest level of tourist facilities, which carried names connoting Pushtimarg opulence. An example is the Shree Ji Holiday Resort, advertised as "expensive but quite worth it."[21] Hotels, villas, bed and breakfasts, and other venues increasingly blurred the distinction between pilgrim and tourist. The construction of high-end hotels in Nathdwara not only reflects this merging of religious and secular travel but also shows the rising class status of Pushtimargiyas.

Tour companies began to offer tours from Ahmedabad not only to Nathdwara but also to other sites in the Gujarat that have particular significance for Pushtimargiyas, including Dwarka, home of the Dwarkadhish temple. They also began to assist devotees in reaching baithaks near Ahmedabad, Vadodara, and Surat.

The implications of this pattern of tourism for the diaspora were especially significant. With the growth of metropolitan Ahmedabad and the dynamic increase of a business-oriented middle class, Pushtimargiya leaders became well equipped to develop new temples in the West, appealing to the same educated, upwardly mobile population. Already skilled in international business, shipping, and the development of new enterprises, Vaishnava leaders were amply prepared to expand havelis in the diaspora that replicated the India-centric experience. American havelis offered easy and regular accessibility to holy sites that in India could only be visited occasionally.

American Havelis and the Role of Gujarati Immigrant Entrepreneurs

The following pages will demonstrate how Gujaratis fit into a well-established American tradition of immigrant entrepreneurs.[22] As astute organizers with significant international connections and associations, immigrant entrepreneurs have skills in accumulating social capital. Social capital reflects the benefits that may be accrued from patterns of cooperation and trust, bonding people together and creating "norms of reciprocity."[23] The economic gain that results from social capital is considerable, as generations of entrepreneurs have discovered when developing ethnically owned businesses. In temples as in businesses, organizers experience a level of trust and knowledge of each other's villages, caste affiliations, and shared friendships in India.

For immigrant ethnic groups, social capital helps sustain and support members in times of need. Money may be loaned without contract or collateral.[24] Financial advice is freely given. Opportunities for employment

Fig. 5. A sign in Hindi in front of the Vraj temple.

are found through extensive ethnic networks that operate beyond borders. In short, as one member of the Gujarati business community observed, "Everybody thinks like a family."[25]

As South Asians, Gujaratis share a background in which the extended family is dominant. Aunts, uncles, and even distant cousins are considered intimate members of the family. The role of the extended family helps Gujaratis to enter a variety of businesses, including fast food franchises and the lodging industry, with impressive results. Researchers discovered that in Texas in 1999, 35 percent of independent hotels and over 50 percent of motels not affiliated with national chains were owned by Gujaratis. Gujaratis also controlled 50 percent of properties affiliated with Days Inn, Econolodge, Comfort Inn, and Super 8.[26] In these businesses, economic assets are often pooled, permitting family members to invest in mutually beneficial projects. At the same time this system can provide a ready source of employment.

Gujaratis are also connected by intricate global networks that are valuable in constructing a labor force and in seeking employment. The network can become a rotating credit association, providing help to persons in need. It exists through frequent face-to-face contact and a cadre of shared values that reify the social capital it produces. In America, the network has spawned Gujarati associations, which can be found in many metropolitan areas. It has also produced large matrimonial conventions in which planners help their sons and daughters to find mates.

For Gujaratis, as for other immigrant populations of South Asians, caste also functions as a way of bonding individuals and generating social capital. As discussed earlier in the text, caste is a function of endogamous groups, or jatis, that share a level of ritual purity.[27] Although caste is not viable in the United States, the affinity between jati clusters can be a valuable asset in business relationships. Jati identification is complex and invisible to observers outside the community. Jati affiliation is coded in surnames. Gujaratis are aware, for example, that the common name Patel connotes a mid-level Vaishya identification and that some Patels have a higher position than others.[28]

As a result of these abilities, Gujarati Vaishnavas have erected havelis in rapid order. In less than three decades they have created temples across the United States, primarily in metropolitan areas with large Gujarati populations. They have secured mortgages and often paid them off in a few short years. In more than one instance the havelis have grown so quickly that they have rapidly outgrown their facilities.

Vraj: The Official Presence of Shri Nathji in the Western Hemisphere

The Vraj temple in rural Pennsylvania (fig. 5) evolved as the spiritual headquarters of Pushtimarg in North America through a dedicated group of entrepreneurs. The initial vision for the project was seeded by Govindbhai Shah, a humanitarian and Pushtimargiya devotee known for social outreach in the Gujarat. Shah envisioned a Pushtimargiya temple in the West. His dream was soon adopted by a group of creative entrepreneurs including Pramod Amin, a successful businessman whose biography reflects his entrepreneurial skills. The industry describes his rise to success:

> In 1971, Pramod C. Amin arrived in Richmond by Greyhound bus with $20 in his pocket and a degree in civil engineering looking for an engineering job. The native of Baroda, India found his engineering job and had hoped to save enough money to go back home. However, after working for 8 years, he wanted to work for himself. P.C. and his brother-in-law B.N. Shah purchased a struggling motel in Lumberton, North Carolina and with vision, high standards of guest service, and sheer hard work and determination a successful company was born.[29]

Utilizing the skills that had made him successful in the lodging industry, Amin consolidated the leadership of Vraj into a highly effective group of entrepreneurs with backgrounds in real estate, business, and the media. Their work was supported by visits to the United States of two members of the Vallabhkulgoswamis Mathureshwarji and Indirabetiji. Both goswamis reinforced grass roots efforts to launch Pushtimarg in the United States, also providing assistance to devotees in Houston, New York, New Jersey, and other locations. In short order a plan was developed for the transformation of an older resort into Vraj—the spiritual headquarters of the Vallabha Sampradaya in the West.

Originally constructed on a 300-acre site near Stone Mountain in 1924 by Jacob and Maud Boltz, the property had been developed in the 1930s. The site included "a large picnic area with pavilions, childrens [sic] playground, a building for refreshments, grille, dance hall, a beautiful lake for boating and a wooded area for hiking."[30] The resort prospered through the late 1950s and continued to be run by the Boltz family until 1975, after which it was sold to the Kripalu Yoga Ashram Retreat under the tutelage of Yogi Amrit Desai. Kripalu sold the center to the developers of Vraj in 1987 when the *ashram* moved to Massachusetts.

The compound provided easy access to expanding Pushtimargiya populations in New York City and New Jersey. By the early 1990s visitors to the former Stony Mountain Manor campus noticed significant changes. The large, central building in the compound had been transformed into a haveli. Using an open area on the ground floor, an altar had been established.

Festivals were soon developed that brought an authentic Indian character to the facility. During large festivals, the building was filled to capacity. During Annakut, a principal Pushtimargiya festival celebrating the emergence of Krishna from Mount Govardhan, the floor was covered with trays of sweets.

The Vraj temple was financed by Vaishnavas in the United States in a manner that conformed to American denominational practices. In order to retain a non-profit, tax-exempt status, a system of governance was created. The temple leadership organized an administrative structure including a steering committee, a board of trustees with an executive committee that would manage the work. In keeping with the Vallabha Sampradaya's history of support from the aristocracy, the sect's fundraising efforts began to concentrate on large donors. Categories of "Regent" contributions were created in a reference to the earlier, Indian pattern of patronage:

Great Grand Benefactor ($100,001 and up)
Grand Benefactor ($75,000 and up)
Benefactor ($51,000 and up)
Sponsor ($25,000 and up)

Fig. 6. At the dedication of the Vraj temple, devotees parade toward the new haveli.

This pattern of development, which relied on affluent Pushtimargiyas in the United States, soon became popular in other havelis across the nation.

As plans for utilization of the campus developed, the leadership envisioned a new haveli. Utilizing the skills of Atul Parikh, a respected Indian architect with abilities in temple design, the plan was ambitious. It included renovating a pond, erecting a two-story stone haveli that would incorporate a smaller temple inside, and extensive use of marble and stone combined with red sandstone *zarukas* or window sculptures. The latter proved to be one of the most difficult parts of the construction. Zarukas were crafted near Jaipur and shipped to the United States—a time-consuming process that resulted in damage to the stone. Once in Pennsylvania, the builders discovered that the massive weight of the sculptures needed additional support.

Amin's effort was supported by a cadre of successful Gujarati businessmen from all over the United States who formed a 33-member board of trustees. The first stage of their work culminated in 2002 with the dedication of the new haveli (fig. 6). During a three-week period, from May 25 to June 16, 2002, a crowd of 18,000–22,000 persons assembled for the dedication of the temple.[31] The persons who attended were a mixture of Gujaratis from the United States and Canada, international guests, and dignitaries. Visiting goswamis accompanied the Tilkayat of Nathdwara, who gave his blessings. Leading a vast procession of devotees in a Rolls Royce, the Tilkayat escorted an image of Shri Nathji to the new haveli. To mark the symbolism of the occasion, three helicopters landed simultaneously on an adjacent field carrying priests from temples in New York, New Jersey, and Houston, demonstrating support.

The dedication also marked the first time that the Tilkayat of Nathdwara had authorized the construction of a haveli in the West, establishing Vraj as the spiritual headquarters of the Vallabha Sampradaya in the Western world. The event also firmly rooted Vraj as a pilgrimage center, independent of any local congregation. The event was also significant in officially recognizing Vraj as sacred ground, confirming its linkages with Vaishnava mythology and recreating the mystical landscape of Braj on American soil.

In anticipation of this transformation, the buildings at Vraj had been given Pushtimargiya names. The pond outside the newly constructed haveli was identified as *Chandra Sarovar* ("the moon lake")—replicating a prominent baithak in Pushtimargiya mythology.[32] Land around the temple was referred to using names from the Indian Braj, equating the magical homeland of Krishna with a tract in the heartland of Pennsylvania.

In the midst of these dramatic events, Vraj took on the appearance of an Indian village. Outside the newly constructed haveli vendors sold jewelry, saris, icons, and ritual accoutrements. Visitors could wait in line for Gujarati dinners, sample Indian sweets, and attend performances of classical Indian dance in an auditorium that seated over 1,000 people. Hundreds of pilgrims waited for prasad, carrying the blessings of the deity. A sea of people was everywhere.

Following the dedication, progress on the building continued. However, despite initial success in fundraising, progress seemed to stall in the mid-nineties. However, by the twentieth anniversary of the haveli in 2010, new momentum was apparent as the level of contributions increased. The Chandra Samovar was finished. A shrine to the river goddess, Shri Yamunaji, significant in Pushtimargiya tradition, was erected on its shore. The sandstone window ornaments were finished and plans were made for the erection of an upscale residence for visiting pilgrims which was completed in 2013. In addition, a smaller model of Mount Govardhan was created behind the new haveli. There, with shoes removed, devotees could now circumambulate the holy mountain much as they would in Rajasthan.

As Vraj has experienced a number of physical changes, so developers of the haveli also had to contend with a number of cultural changes. In India, havelis are supplied with milk and foodstuffs through traditional avenues of village support. In America, these relationships do not exist. Havelis in India are run using labor from extended families with histories of service to the temple. In the United States, specialized jobs are filled by immigrants often recruited from India.

As the spiritual headquarters of the Vallabha Sampradaya in North America, Vraj has pioneered the difficult task of bringing mukhiyas and kirtankars to the United States, and has also assisted other havelis in locating these ritual specialists. It has helped to seed other institutions, contributing $8,400 to new havelis and sending representatives to festivals and dedications of the new institutions. Vraj has also attempted to create sources of unity within the diverse American Pushtimarg community. This was apparent in the Global Vaishnav Convention in 2009, which coincided with the 20th anniversary celebration of Vraj.[33] Havelis from New Jersey, Illinois, Texas, Arizona, California, and Toronto participated. Nine goswamis including the Tilkayat of Nathdwara attended. In addition, Vaishnavas from Kenya, Australia, New Zealand, Great Britain, and other parts of Europe became part of the event, which sought to consolidate the Vaishnava diaspora and to affirm the ties between Vraj and the evolving centers of Pushtimargiya tradition in North America.

The Texas Nathdwara

Like Vraj, the Texas Nathdwara (Vallabh Priti Seva Samaj) was developed by a talented organizer, Suresh Patel. In 1984, Patel, his father, Shantilal, and their families convened local Vaishnavas at a residence. The group decided to seek authorization to perform seva. Overtures were made to two visiting goswamis, who both took active roles in a planning process that culminated in the construction of a haveli and the installation of a swarup in 2005.

As indicated by its adopted name, the Texas Nathdwara attempted to make an important connection with Nathdwara, while at the same time using Texas imagery of size, grandeur, and independence. The effort was a collaborative project including local businessmen and professionals in cooperation with the Baroda-Surat gaddi.[34]

Houston was an appropriate site for a haveli. The metropolitan area has experienced rapid growth and includes a sizable Gujarati community of more than 20,000 persons, including large numbers of Swaminarayan and Pushtimargiya devotees. The project was conceived in a way that would combine several facilities into one, including a haveli, an educational center, and a place for senior citizens.

Following the early organizing meetings in 1984, goswami Mathureshwarji suggested that the Vaishnavas "have a formal organization and perform formal seva at one place."[35] Following this, a prominent Vaishnava offered her home for a temporary haveli. Goswami Indirabetiji authorized the project and located a swarup.[36] This shows how enterprising Gujarati businessmen worked collaboratively with goswamis crafting a facility specifically designed for the diaspora. The initial energy for the project and the entrepreneurial skill to develop it came from the laity, who looked to visiting goswamis as consultants. When goswami Mathureshwarji formally suggested that a haveli be created, the project was legitimized. Acting as a broker between the Indian origins of the faith and the American organizers, goswami Indirabetiji located a swarup in India and sent it to Houston.

An important adaptation of tradition occurred when, in lieu of a trained mukhiya, a prominent Vaishnava laywoman was authorized and trained to perform the daily sevas. Later, when her daughter became president of the growing Vaishnava community, both goswami Indirabetiji and goswami Mathureshwarji agreed with the American Gujarati developers that a tract of land should be acquired for a more formal structure. Knowledge of the Houston real estate market was provided by American devotees who brought their entrepreneurial skills to bear on the project. Before property could be secured a 5,000-square-foot office building had been purchased, which became the community's first free-standing haveli.

As Houston's Pushtimargiya population grew, the leadership created additional administrative structure. Goswami Indirabetiji authorized the formation of a temple committee to meet the needs of developing a more complex site.

She educated leaders about the basic requirements of havelis and helped them prepare a floor plan. Subsequently, when bylaws were written, three goswamis, including Indirabetiji, blessed them and recommended their approval. A board of trustees was appointed, and plans for the new haveli began.

The planning process became an exercise by Gujarati developers to preserve tradition but at the same time to craft an innovative structure that would meet the needs of American clientele. Planners selected property in Sugar Land that offered a number of advantages. Zoning requirements were minimal, and non–Christian institutions were able to erect substantial structures with minimal interference from the community. A large Vietnamese Buddhist temple had been erected a short distance from the haveli.

In time, three goswamis became affiliated with the project (Indirabetiji, Mathureshwarji, and Drumilkumarji), strengthening ties with the sixth gaddi. Their detailed involvement in the effort not only affirmed the ability of individual gaddis to establish a presence in the diaspora, but also showed how globalization of the Vallabhkul dynasty made this possible. For example, goswami Mathureshwarji had already been the prime mover behind a number of projects in Africa, India, and the United States. Using his global popularity and success, he stretched the influence of the sixth gaddi to the West.[37]

The vision became the "Texas Nathdwara," which included a nandalay (the traditional term for a haveli), a community center, and a retirement facility. The plan emphasized flexibility. Not only could the large 23,000-square-foot auditorium be used for demonstrations of classical dance and music; it could also accommodate large banquets and events. Classroom space was provided for a wide range of subjects including language, music, cooking, health science, and religion. This offered the second generation access to Hindu culture, using teachers recruited from the Pushtimargiya community.[38]

The total facility incorporated elements of Indian design into an American plan. The haveli was envisioned as a 12,000-square-foot structure with imported marble and granite lotus designs on the floor. Two sliding doors, weighing over 1,000 pounds and sculpted with Indian designs, provided access to the haveli. A residence for the mukhiya completed the religious structure. A *parikrama* or walkway around the circumference of the haveli allowed devotees to circumambulate the swarup.

In a pattern similar to the financial plan at Vraj, the Texas developers instituted a hierarchical system of fundraising, targeting wealthy members of the haveli. By the time of the project's completion four "Grand Benefactors" had donated $100,000 to $250,000 each; seventeen "Benefactors" had given $25,000 to $100,000 each, and thirty-three "Patrons" had given $10,000 to $25,000 each.[39] Once the financial stability of the venture had been secured,

5. Vaishnavism Without Borders

Fig. 7. Celebrating Chappan Bhog at the 20th anniversary of the Texas Nathdwara in Houston, 2010 (courtesy Suresh Patel [VPSS]).

the haveli adapted a democratic form of fundraising. Four hundred persons were recruited to donate up to $10. Others gave gifts in kind to help furnish the haveli. Still others were encouraged to loan money to the project. Finally, in keeping with Pushtimargiya tradition, the Texas Nathdwara incorporated the manorath plan as a way of underwriting the costs of daily operations.[40]

By the time of the 20th anniversary of the Texas Nathdwara in 2010 (fig. 7), the plan for the retirement community had not been realized. However, the haveli, the community center, and school had been completed. The Vallabh Vidya Mandir now offered 18 courses and had created a course called "Texas Nathdwara Management Workshop," "with intent to develop future leaders who can operate and manage the organization."[41] By actively incorporating the second generation into the plan for the haveli, the project began to approach the broader issue of assimilation systemically.

In 2010, at the 20th anniversary of the temple, success of the project was reported in a way consistent with American business and religious practices. Almost $750,000 had been paid on the initial mortgage of $994,000.[42] Equity in the project had also dramatically increased, with a projected net worth of $8 million.[43] New programs were developed to help reduce the remaining debt. The haveli had secured $1,739,000 of loans through its mem-

Fig. 8. Vaishnav Samaj of Midwest, Addison, Illinois.

bership and had converted $260,000 of that into donations. The leadership now proposed that if 275 families could enact loans of $5,000 each, the balance of the mortgage could be paid. As an incentive, the association offered one percent above the current CD rate. Additional levels of support were sought for the physical plant including an "Inner Dome and Courtyard Fountain" project to complete the architectural design. This plan for financial development incorporated a remarkable blend of Pushtimargiya tradition, economic knowledge, and entrepreneurial skill that would establish the Texas Nathdwara as an American institution. The sixth gaddi maintained an active level of involvement with the project, extending the arm of the gaddi into the American diaspora and utilizing the advice of three influential goswamis. In every step of this process the haveli appealed to American entrepreneurial spirit, offering its membership numerous incentives to invest in the project.

The Vaishnav Samaj of Midwest

Yet another example of entrepreneurial spirit was developed in Addison, Illinois, where devotees relied on the initiative of a group of successful businessmen in order to construct the first haveli in the Chicago metropolitan area (fig. 8). In the late 1980s a group of Pushtimargiya businessmen in Chicago began to discuss the need for a haveli.⁴⁴ Together, they formed an association and helped support the purchase of land in a western suburb, Addison.

When their successors took office the project was reinvigorated. The new eleven-member board was comprised of successful businessmen. Each contributed a minimum of $100,000 to the project, enabling the association to quickly raise a million dollars. With this in hand the leadership secured a $4 million loan. A foundation was laid immediately and work commenced on the structure. The haveli was completed and dedicated on Memorial Day weekend in 2007.

Since 2007 the Vaishnav Samaj of Midwest has developed a mailing list of 2,000 families and expects to reach additional Vaishnavas in greater Chicago. Leaders calculate that as many as 8,000 Gujaratis reside in metropolitan Chicago and contiguous urban cities such as Gary, Indiana.⁴⁵ The haveli is already too small for large events. Crowds spill over frequently, necessitating the use of large tents. As a partial remedy to this problem the haveli was able to purchase an adjacent property and will use the land to create additional parking.

Throughout the construction phase the leadership was aware that the physical structure was only part of the challenges the new institution faced. The greatest difficulty would be recruiting a mukhiya from India. The haveli began to work with goswami Indirabetiji, who assisted in the search. She suggested a candidate who had conducted seva in one of her havelis, and a review process was started. In keeping with effective business practices, a resume was prepared and the leadership agreed that the individual had promise.

Another important part of the process was convincing immigration authorities in the United States that the candidate should be allowed entry. Securing a visa and green card are often fraught with obstacles since immigration officials are often unaware of the distinctive nature of Pushtimarg and the role of mukhiyas in the tradition. Defined by lineage and caste, they are a skilled body of Brahmin priests who must be knowledgeable in patterns of seva. Well-trained mukhiyas do this skillfully, imparting a rhythmic beauty to the rituals, which become sources of pride.

The candidate was particularly attractive: his father and uncle were both priests. Further, he was a native of Sanchor and had grown up in the rich cultural environment that has produced mukhiyas for generations. When he was a boy, following the death of his father, his uncle had taught him the complex rituals. Following this he served for ten years near Vadodara and then in Vadodara itself, where he trained under goswami Indirabetiji.⁴⁶

The haveli secured letters from two other gaddis in India who supported the effort to bring the mukhiya to America. They received support from a local congressman, which was helpful in persuading immigration authorities to allow the priest into the country. For American havelis, the difficulties caused by the extensive delays that are often part of the immigration and visa process also created an additional need. Seva is a daily practice, and havelis must conduct a regular cycle of darshans every day. In order to accommodate the delay another mukhiha was secured on loan so that the regimen of darshans could be completed.

Once a permanent mukhiya was identified, the haveli began to concentrate on membership. The leadership was particularly concerned about youth who fail to bond with the institution. They instituted an educational program called *Tavasmi* (developed in the United States), trained teachers, and began to offer programs for the second generation. The new haveli also began to make decisions about the cycle of festivals that it would perform during the liturgical year.

The Chicago leadership decided to celebrate six major Pushtimargiya festivals including Krishna's birthday (*Janmastimi*), *Diwali* and *Annakut* (both celebrated at the Hindu New Year), the anniversary of the haveli called *Patutsav* (celebrated on Memorial Day weekend), Vallabha's birthday (celebrated in April), *Holi*, and Vitthalnath's birthday in December. This cycle of festivals includes Pushti-specific traditions that are attached to a number of pan–Hindu festivals such as Diwali and Holi. The Chicago haveli also celebrates lunar festivals including *Saratpunima*. Observed on the fifteenth day of the full moon, the festival is marked with stories of Krishna's play with the gopis. Devotees also recognize *Agiaras,* a local festival in the Gujarat, in which once in a fifteen-day period they are asked to do something special for god. Still other festivals have been organized around the liturgical year.

The complex festival life of the Vaishnav Samaj of Midwest affords devotees close contact with Indian culture. For first generation members, the temple reinforces their heritage. Festivals also draw the second generation, who accompany their families; this assists in their acculturation. They are also significant in recruiting Vaishnavas from greater Chicago.

The Shreenathji Temple of Phoenix

In another adaptation of entrepreneurial tradition, a retired Air Force physician in Phoenix organized an effort to create a haveli with ties to the sixth gaddi (fig. 9). Dr. Dave, the son of a mukhiya, designed a plan that would allow land to be purchased jointly by Pushtimargiyas and a local Jain community.[47] Dr. Hari Dave had grown up in India and had family ties with the

5. Vaishnavism Without Borders

Fig. 9. Shreenathji Temple, Phoenix, Arizona.

Surat gaddi in the villages of Amreli, Kandiwali, and Champaranya, where he felt spiritually supported by goswami Dwarkeshlalji. Dave's father also had become the first mukhiya to serve a haveli in the United States at the New York haveli.

In 1993, Dave and other leaders initiated religious discussions (satsang) in homes, organizing the Vaishnava Samaj of Phoenix.[48] By that time Hinduism had become well-established in Arizona. Hindu temples first began to appear in Phoenix after 2000, and the building process rapidly escalated after that, creating a diversified presence including South Indian temple traditions, ISKCON, and a Swaminarayan temple.

Joining together, the Pushtimargiya leaders and the Jains bought eight acres of land in South Phoenix, splitting the purchase into two equal tracts. The planners envisioned that the gentrification of poorer neighborhoods near the temple would continue. Once land was obtained for both communities, zoning approval was quickly granted.

Drawing on Dave's relationship with the Surat gaddi, goswami Dwarkeshlalji became the haveli's spiritual benefactor.[49] Eight other balaks were also recruited including goswamis Yogeshkumarji, Mathureshwarji, Indirabetiji, Drumilkumarji, Vrajrajkumarji, Rajkumarji, Chandrikabetiji, and Pritirajabetiji.[50] In 2003 a board of trustees was formed. A temple development body followed three years later. Fifty families donated funds for the project. A dedication ceremony for the property (*Purshottam Yagna*) was held in May 2007, and a more formal dedication the following year. Construction on the temple started in April 2009 and was completed in six months.

As plans for the temple developed, the leadership employed a full range of

Fig. 10. Vallabhdham, Newington, Connecticut.

international connections. Massive sculpted brass doors were acquired from India. A Gujarati businessman with connections in China secured marble that was used for exterior decoration. Finally, through the efforts of the haveli's spiritual benefactor, the swarup of Shri Nathji was obtained and installed (see cover).

Vallabhdham, Newington, Connecticut

Located in a former synagogue in Newington, Connecticut, in the same space that for 39 years housed the sacred scrolls of Judaism, a tapestry of Krishna as Shri Nathji now hangs. Part of metropolitan Hartford, Vallabhdham ("the place of Vallabha," fig. 10) was conceived in 2003 by a Gujarati entrepreneur and businessman, Rajeev DeSai, who provided the initial momentum for organization and development of the temple. DeSai helped organize satsangs in private homes. In 2010 the Vaishnava leaders purchased a former synagogue and preparations were made to transform the space into a haveli.

Newington is strategically located, within reach of both greater Hartford and Springfield, and accessible from Boston and northern New England. The haveli regularly draws Vaishnavas from a wide area, filling its parking lots and maximizing its space during festivals. Purchase of the synagogue offered an advantage since the building was already equipped with classrooms, worship space, and a large kitchen. Newington has also seen a growing South Asian population, evident in the Indian-owned businesses in the area.

In a reflection of the continuing globalization of Pushtimarg and the

Fig. 11. A model of Govardhan hill at Vallahhdham showing Shri Nathji and Vallabha embracing.

business networks of its leaders, planners decided to use modular technology and container shipping to transform the building from a synagogue to a haveli. Wood was obtained from Burma, while in India artisans cut and carved panels to fit each wall. The overall vision was unique—Vallabhdham was to become the first haveli with a carved wood interior in the United States. Upon completion in India, the panels will be sent in a container to the United States. Members talk about the process that will transform the stark brick walls into a warm environment filled with traditional carving. A model of Shri Nathji inside Mount Govardhan has been positioned in front of the inner doors to the sanctuary, marking the transition that is to come (fig. 11).

Acting on the developer's personal ties with the sixth gaddi, the Newington temple has relied on a spiritual relationship with a single goswami. Shri Dwarkeshlalji serves the Shree Kalyanrayji Mandir in Vadodara. He has a similar relationship with the Shreenathji Temple in Phoenix. Perhaps because of this affinity, when Vallabhdham needed a mukhiya, the Phoenix temple offered assistance and loaned one of its priests to Vallabhdham. Such continuing relationships among havelis that look to the same spiritual benefactor is one model of religious development that both strengthens the role of individual goswamis in India and offers advantages in the United States, where sister institutions can assist each other even at a great distance.

Like other havelis in the United States and Canada, the Newington temple depends on volunteers, many of whom are first generation immigrants who continue traditions once found only in India. During an evening darshan, members provide the music, singing padas to the accompaniment of *tabla* and harmonium. The resident mukhiya addresses the painting of Shri Nathji with the same devotion that he will offer a stone swarup after it is completed in India and installed. As the songs fill the air, two women carefully construct garlands (malas) of rose petals in an art form rarely seen outside India. Using long needles attached to thread, they fold the petals into consistent sizes in a fresh mala made to honor the deity. Following the darshan, members gather in the kitchen to cook meals for a large festival that will take place over the weekend. Preparing traditional Gujarati foods, volunteers work on into the night, assisted by the mukhiya.

In Newington, Vaishnava leaders have replicated many elements of the regional expression of the faith they experienced in India in Ahmedabad and Vadodara. Continuing the relationship with goswami Dwarkeshlalji that began in India creates continuity. These relationships also apply to the mukhiya, whose family in India is well known to temple leaders. Swarups that are carefully maintained in homes also provide deep connections with parents and grandparents. Together, these continuing traditions and relationships create a globalized religion in which American devotees conceive of their haveli as an extension of experiences in India. For them, to be Pushtimargiya remains much the same in India or in Newington, Connecticut.

Some Reflections on American Havelis

It is clear in this discussion of examples of American havelis that worship facilities for Pushtimargiyas in the United States have benefitted from the skills of entrepreneurs. Using talents that have led them to successful careers in a variety of fields including international business, these leaders have envisioned unique structures, motivating volunteers, raising capital, and developing plans for construction. In a process akin to that of corporate developers who often recount the beginnings of their businesses in private residences and even in garages, these entrepreneurs have rapidly built temples across the United States.

However, there are also Indian precedents for their efforts. In the nineteenth century in Ujjain, a Pushtimargiya temple was created through the efforts of a wealthy benefactor. The temple was initiated when a couple dis-

5. Vaishnavism Without Borders

covered a black stone in their well that they interpreted as Shri Nathji. Peter Bennett describes what happened next:

> During the nineteenth and early twentieth centuries, Shri Nathji remained the domestic deity of a family of Audicha Brahmans who ran their household as a private temple, allowing Pushti Margi neighbors to attend daily. At some stage the temple was moved from Kartik Chauk to its present Dhaba Road site. About fifty years ago, both deity and temple were dedicated to the Maharaja at Indore who delegated the responsibility for the supervision of the temple to a Managing Committee.[51]

The temple was envisioned after a theophany and was first organized at the home of a wealthy benefactor. Subsequently, when local Pushtimargiyas began to worship there, the temple became part of the second gaddi. Later, in the twentieth century when patronage had ended, the haveli was dedicated to the maharaja of Mysore, who established its system of governance. Even in the absence of patronage, interest from former royalty continued.

In the United States, havelis are not organized because of theopanies and cannot be blessed by the government. But like the Ujjain temple, they have been developed by wealthy benefactors. Well outside the purview of any gaddi, they have sought a variety of patterns of affiliation, often resulting from the benefactor's own history and ties. At the same time they have also benefitted from the increasing globalization of the Vallabhkul, evident after Indian independence. Following the migration of Pushtimargiyas to Great Britian, Kenya, Australia, and Dubai, goswamis began to redefine their purview, taking on a new, global role.[52] Expatriate Pushtimargiya communities sought increased visits from goswamis who fulfilled the role of gurus, which mukhiyas could not.[53] Goswamis increasingly traveled to distant lands to meet the needs of their devotees.

This has been the case with goswami Indirabetiji (fig. 12), known to her devotees as "Jiji."[54] She is the daughter of goswami Mathureshwarji of the sixth gaddi in Surat, a prestigious leader who founded schools, established havelis, trusts, and charitable organizations. As a woman in a patriarchal tradition, Indirabetiji is unique and is known for charisma, global outreach, and social service. Frequently called on to provide public discourses in the United States, she is an inspirational figure who maintains exhaustive travel schedules. Easily found in the social media, she regularly travels to London, Toronto, and throughout the United States. She has helped support havelis in Pennsylvania, Texas, Illinois, New York, Arizona and other states, assisting temples to find mukhiyas, musicians, and swarups. She has created numerous programs in India and the United States, extending the outreach of the sixth gaddi to the West.

Born in 1939, goswami Indirabetiji has developed a strong record of scholarship. She holds a master's degree in Sanskrit and is known for study of the

Fig. 12. Goswami Indirabetiji welcomed at the celebration of Chappan Bhog at the Texas Nathdwara in Houston in 2010 (courtesy Suresh Patel [VPSS]).

Vedas, Upanishads, and other Hindu scriptures. She has written a number of books and has become the motivating force for havelis globally. She has also been an active leader in social welfare movements in India, constructing health care facilities, literacy camps and organizing relief work in the wake of natural disasters. When flash floods devastated Morvi in the Gujarat in 1979, she sponsored efforts to provide food, shelter, clothing, and education. Following the earthquake in Lutur, Maharashtra, in 1994, she is credited with completely rehabilitating two villages. After the earthquake in 2001 in Kitch and later, in 2005, after the tsunami in Tamilnadu, she provided relief, supplying 60 fishermen with boats to replace the ones that were lost.

Goswamis such as Indirabetiji fulfill six primary functions abroad that make the boundaries of nation-states seem irrelevant. Their journeys are not as much from India to the United States as from gaddi to havelis, connecting transnational communities to tradition. First, they used their office to help establish and legitimate havelis overseas. Recognizing that American devotees were free to cultivate the support of a single gaddi, or a combination of gaddis, they compete for the American market. They continue relationships with families who have left India in a process that is evident in havelis in Toronto, Phoenix, and other North American cities.[55]

Goswamis have exhibited a second role, helping havelis in North America to establish new programs, attracting participants through their presence. An example of this programmatic function is the Vallabh Youth Organization (VYO) created by goswami Vrajrajkumarji. Born in 1986, Vrajrajkumarji is the eighteenth descendant of Vallabhacharya and has achieved a following with Pushtimargiya youth in the diaspora. He has recorded a Gujarati and an English version of a highly romanticized song, "Oh My Krishna," which has become popular among youth.[56] In 1999, Vrajrajkumarji developed the concept of a Pushtimargiya organization dedicated to young adults, formally launching the Vallabh Youth Organization in 2009.[57] The VYO was established to "bring about awakening amongst youth in cities, villages & abroad to realize the aim of global youth awakening."[58] As part of this vision, VYOs set goals of establishing spiritual centers, organizing seminars, encouraging creativity, as well as providing food for needy families in India.[59] The organization was subsequently established in a number of Indian cities including Ahmedabad, Surendranagar, Nadiad, Dahod, Haloi, Goldhra, Mumbai, Chennai, Yavatmal, and Nagpur. When it was brought to the United States it became a way of organizing Pushtimargiya devotees, often leading to the formation of havelis. VYO chapters and events are now found among large concentrations of American Pushtimargiyas, where the organization sponsors youth camps and helps acculturate recent arrivals. A VYO chapter was started in June 2011 in Scranton, Pennsylvania.[60] The organization is composed of first generation Pushtimargiyas and draws as many as 50 persons for its monthly meetings, which have also been used to help integrate new arrivals from India.

In Charlotte, North Carolina, the VYO became part of an effort to establish a new haveli, leading to a ground-breaking ceremony on July 31, 2011. Goswami Vrajrakumarji has also helped organize VYOs in Tampa and in Richmond. He has worked with youth in Daytona Beach and has been instrumental in the formation of a VYO in the greater Detroit area.[61] In Boston, a VYO was formed as a legal entity to help provide a base for Pushtimargiyas in New England.[62] As a result of this effort the Shrinathji Haveli was established in Lowell.

In a third programmatic function, goswamis have become instrumental in establishing social service programs in India. The relief work of goswami Dwarkeshlalji, goswami Indirabetiji and others has aligned them with the work of international religious leaders, increasing their visibility and attracting devotees. Amplifying their role as spiritual leaders, the NGOs and foundations that they have created have helped establish Pushtimarg as a global presence. For example, at the Shree Kalyan haveli in Vadodara, India, goswami Dwarkeshlalji has established a number of foundations and charitable trusts including these:

- The Shree Vallabh Vihar Educational and Charitable Trust, which provides computer education programs for devotees.
- The Shree Kalyanraiji Sarvajanik Charitable Trust of Varodara, which preserved Pushtimargiya manuscripts and provides scholarships for students.
- The Shri Pushti Prabha Memorial Trust, which offers scholarships, computer education and health care.
- The Shri Vallabh Vadil Vihar Trust, which organizes medical care in remote locations through medical camps.
- The Shree Savotam Charitable Trust, which has worked in children's education.
- The Shree Vallabhacharya Mahaprabhuji Navnidhi Charitable Trust, which has helped modernize a hospital in Bahadarpur near Vadodara.

The goswami has also supported the Vadodara Society for the Prevention of Cruelty to Animals, and the Shree Kalyanraiji Sarvajanik Charitable Trust in Rajasthan, which seeks to restore Vaishnava temples.[63]

In a fourth role, goswamis have become global brokers, helping new havelis in North America to find ritual specialists from India. Visiting goswamis routinely help North American temples to locate priests. They are instrumental in finding swarups. They offer counsel on designs for havelis and may voice opinions about plans for construction. They are also welcome visitors for devotees who have known them in India, forging links between members of the extended family at home and abroad.

The changing role of the goswamis is part of a wider process that is breaking down the distinction between Gujaratis in India and the United States. This distinguishes diasporan migrations from earlier patterns of immigration. Unlike earlier population movements, "the homeland, [is] not as something simply left behind, but ... a place of attachment in a contrapuntal modernity."[64] Studies of Gujarati communities in England have even concluded that "migrants in Britain and their relatives in Gujarat should therefore not be viewed as separate communities but should be considered in the same unit of analysis."[65]

In a fifth function, goswamis stretch the authority of the gaddis abroad. Maintaining standards of purity as in India, their presence abroad requires havelis to maintain standards. Traveling in traditional attire, members of the dynasty stay in the homes of devotees where purity is preserved. Preparations for the visit of a goswami are extensive. The home must be free from ritual contamination. The goswasmi enters the home as family members chant; flower petals may be strewn on the floor and bare floors are covered. Visits are symbols of prestige for the host families and carry the imprimatur of the lineage into distant lands.

The sixth role of the traveling goswami, overseeing initiations, is a traditional function but has been adapted to the needs of devotees 7,000 miles away. Historically, goswamis have provided the only path to initiation in Pushtimarg, which authorizes the devotee to perform seva. The rite of initiation, Brahmsamband, is usually administered following a recommendation of leaders in a haveli.

In the diaspora, unlike the homeland, the goswami is a visitor who carries Brahmsambandh to the Pushtimargiya community. As a result, initiation comes to accommodate a variety of realities such as travel arrangements, visa requirements, and other fluid realities that can alter the date of the rite.[66] This has created demanding schedules, particularly during the summer, when the more popular goswamis may visit several countries and multiple havelis.

After receiving Brahmsambandh the goswami becomes a personal guru. In the diaspora this relationship is also dependent on travel schedules and can only be realized through periodic visits. Because goswamis may provide restrictions on how the seva is to be performed, they are in constant demand by initiates who seek to further their own spiritual insight.

Preserving Pushtimarg in the Diaspora Through Festivals

For Pushtimargiyas, the *utsava* or festival is one of the primary ways in which the ethnic community preserves Hindu culture. Utsavas not only support sectarian traditions but also are celebrated for observances of lunar holidays as well as pan–Hindu events. For the immigrant community they are an important means of reinforcing community bonds, combining traditions of food, music, and dance (fig. 13). For sectarian organizers and entrepreneurs they are also a way of maximizing social capital, creating linkages between generations through firsthand experience. In the Gujarati diaspora they provide a way for people who may live in different regions in the United States to connect, often reuniting friends from India. They are important sources of revenue and are frequently used to help sustain contributions from donors.

Festivals celebrated in North American havelis are of six types: those that are specific to Pushtimarg, festivals that are pan–Vaishnava, seasonal festivals, pan–Hindu, festivals that are part of the Hindu lunar calendar, and regional festivals.[67] The number and variation of festivals is so complex that Pushtimargiya families and havelis rely on the first generation to set parameters for what will

PUSHTI SPECIFIC	PAN VAISHNAV	SEASONAL	PAN HINDU	EKADASHI (two per month)	REGIONAL
Bangala Manorath (can be offered around the year)	Janmastami and Nanda Mahottsav	Hindola (month long festival during the monsoon season)	Bali-Prati-Pada	24 Ekadashis in a year year	Ghoomar
Palana Manorath (can be offered around the year)	Ram Navmi	Sanji (during fortnight of the ancestors)	Samvatsar (Indian New Year in the Summer)	Prabodhini, Utpatti	Teej
Hindola (month long festival during the monsoon season)	Narsimha Jayantiyanti	Khel (40 days during spring)	Diwali and associated festivals	Mokshada, Safalaafala	Kasumba-Chhath
Sanji (during fortnight of the ancestors)	Vaman Dwadashi	Water related Summer festivals (dependant on weather)	Labh-Panchamichami	Putrada, Shitala	Thakurani Teej
Khel (40 days during spring)	Tulsi Vivah	Holi-and Dand-ropan	Yama-dwitiya	Jaya, Vijaya	Hariyali Amas
Patotsavas (lots - celebrates the day(s) when Thakorjis were installed in a particular haveli)	Maha Raas (Sharad Purnima)	Chandan Yatra and various cooling, summer festivals	Makar Sankranti	Amalki (Kunj), Paap Mochani	
Birthdays of sects leaders and balaks (numerous)	Ratha Yatra		Ganga-Deshra	Kamda, Varuthini	
Pavitra Ekadashi and Dwadashi	Saan Yatra		Raksha-bandhan	Mohini, Apara	
Gopastami	Radhastami		Dev Diwali	Nirjala, Yogini	
Chappan Bhog (though it can be offered at any time of the year - there are set times through the year aswell)	Yamunaji-Dashami		Vasant Panchami	Dev Shayani, Kamika	
Bagicha-nom	Snan-Yatra		Holastaka	Putrada (Pavitra), Aja	
Bagicha-trayodashi	Chandan-yatra		Holi	Kamala/Padmini	
Ranga Panchami			Duleti/ Dol	Parivartini, Indirandira	
Nav-manorath			Akshaya-Trutiya	Panshakunsha Rama	
Nag-Panchami – to celebrate sighting of ShriNathji's hand			Navratri as Nav-Vilas		
Kevda-Teej			Vijaya-Dashami (after Navratri		
Hatadi (during Diwali)			Eclipse		
Annakut (New Year)					
Various flower and water related manoraths during the summer season					
Navratri as Nav-Vilas					

Fig. 13. Common festivals in Pushtimarg (courtesy Bhagwat Shah).

be observed. Many havelis also celebrate anniversaries of their founding, which are called *Patutsavas*. These occasions (which may be recognized every decade or even annually) provide a means for the institution to mark its growth. This vast array of interconnecting festivals blurs the distinctions between religion and culture, creating a fabric of traditions transported around the world.

5. *Vaishnavism Without Borders*

A Patutsava (anniversary festival) held at the Texas Nathdwara in 2010 demonstrates the ways in which traditions are often combined, maximizing Indian heritage and at the same time creating unity in the diaspora. Celebrated during an eight-day period from July 23 to 31, the 20th anniversary of the founding of the Texas Nathdwara was combined with the celebration of Chappan Bhog—a traditional Pushtimargiya festival in which 56 kinds of food are offered to Krishna (fig. 14).[68] The event fulfilled a number of functions. It created a series of intergenerational opportunities for families, consolidated recognition both in the United States and in India, engendered further opportunities for funding, and solidified the faith community. Categories of donations were created as part of the event, maximizing its use as a source of revenue. Copies of miniature paintings from the schools of art associated with Pushtimarg were made available and used as a way to raise additional support.

Extending the reach of the Patutsava beyond Houston, the planning committee invited representatives from other havelis. The occasion also became an opportunity for renewing friendships. The evening meal created opportunities for old friends to meet, transforming the site into an Indian village. As the speaker system carried the sounds of Dhrupad Sangeet into the evening,

Fig. 14. Chappan Bhog at the Texas Nathdwara (courtesy Suresh Patel [VPSS]).

the smells of Gujarati food filled the air as older attendees shared stories of their youth and reminisced with friends.

Adapting to the Diaspora Through Educational Programs

As festivals became a way of preserving culture, so havelis in the United States have also looked to education to help bond their youth to the faith. Hindu temples in America have a long history of creating *Bal Vihar* programs for their youth, which are modeled on American Sunday schools. Yet, for most, education is not only concerned with the transmission of doctrine, but with a host of programs fostering cultural identity.

Pushtimargiyas developed a similar approach through a program called Tavasmi ("I Am Yours"), which focuses on Vallabha's teaching, seva, and a broad outline of the faith. Tavasmi helps children to become ready for Bramsambandh and functions, much like curricula that help prepare Christian children for confirmation or Jewish children for Bar and Bat Mitzva. Tavasmi has spread rapidly, and classes have rapidly become part of the life of most American havelis. Teachers are recruited from the membership, and sessions are designed to fit the complicated schedules of American families.

Because of the culture gap between first and second generation Pushtimargiya Americans, Tavasmi does not emphasize linguistic traditions such as Gujarati or Braj Bhasha. Regional differences between the gaddis also receive minimal attention. Instead, Tavasmi offers a more homogenized approach to the faith. Seva is described in a uniform way and does include the inherent diversity that arises in family practices but also through the counsel of different goswamis.

In all of these aspects, Tavasmi has been created to preserve the essential teachings of the faith and to help minimize the loss of older children from the faith. American Pushtimargiyas are experiencing the same type of attrition that is common in other American denominational traditions. While churches and synagogues work hard to retain children, once initiated, many drift away. College is an important benchmark in this process—few children return to the religious institutions of their parents after leaving home. For Pushtimargiyas, the problem can be even more severe. Doctrine can be compromised by intermarriage and by the absorption of American values. This will be discussed in the next chapter, which explores challenges Pushtimargiyas face in diaspora, including assimilation.

Traditional Models: The Shrinathji Haveli, Toronto

While many Gujaratis have become globalized in India, developing havelis in metropolitan areas with large Pushtimargiya populations, more traditional patterns of haveli development remain. This model has also been exported and can be found in such diverse locations as Melbourne, Australia, and Toronto, Canada. The following discussion explores the Shrinathji Haveli in Toronto, which is typical of a traditional model of development.

On most any morning in Toronto it is easy to find signs of the city's diversity. A Punjabi Sikh walks on a main street with a manicured beard and turban, reading the *Times of India*. A variety of languages are commonly spoken in Toronto, including Chinese, Italian, Punjabi, Tagalog, and Portuguese.[69] Beyond these dominant tongues, a visitor encounters a vast array in the city where 31 percent of the population claims a native language other than English or French.[70] There are increasing signs of diversity. Ethnic restaurants abound. The spires of mosques are evident, as are the sounds of daily worship in over 50 Hindu temples in the metropolitan area. Within this diverse mix of peoples, more than 100,000 Gujaratis make Toronto their home. They support a Jain center, a Swaminarayan temple, and a Pushtimargiya haveli.[71]

In a residential section of the city, Canadian Pushtimargiyas worship Krishna in the Shrinathji haveli. The temple, which was built from a former church, was developed through the direct involvement of goswami Dhrumilkumarji, who first met with a group of expatriate devotees in 2004 to discuss planning a festival. Unlike American havelis, which have often relied on entrepreneurs, Canadian devotees looked to Drumilkumarji for a vision of what they might achieve. A small group of devotees was recruited, forming the Pushtimarg Vaishnava Samaj. Members began to look for a place where darshans could be conducted. A vacant church was located near the heart of the downtown and plans were made to secure a swarup. On November 12, 2005, the haveli was formally dedicated by goswami Drumilkumarji, the temple's spiritual benefactor.

While it is difficult to speculate why the Toronto haveli did not adopt the practice of relying on a lay developer, the traditional nature of the Pushtimargiya community may help explain the decision. Toronto Vaishnavas chose a model of organization that was closely allied with tradition, in which goswamis directed development.

The Shrinathji temple has maintained an orthodox approach to the faith with close ties to India. This may also reflect the multi-ethnic nature of Toronto itself, where contact with India moves in a number of directions. It is not unusual, for example, to encounter visitors from India in the haveli in

Fig. 15. A child dances at a festival at the Shreenathji Temple, Phoenix, Arizona (courtesy Shreenathji Haveli).

the same way that international visitors abound in the city. The multi-ethnic nature of Toronto also reflects Canadian immigration policy, which is more open than that of the United States.

The haveli's traditional orientation is demonstrated in a number of ways. Members frequently gather for satsang in homes, discussing a wide range of topics. Older members retain approaches to seva that they learned in pre-Independence India and share them in close relationships among extended families. Patterns of ritual purity and pollution are strictly adhered to.

There are also differences among the second generation when compared with havelis in the United States. Young adults comment on their Pushtimargiya identity and exhibit few signs of struggle in adopting their parent's religion. There are few classes on the general nature of Hinduism or on wider aspects of Indian culture, typical in American havelis. Instead, the Toronto temple conducts classes often focused on seva, kirtan, and protocols within Pushtimarg, demonstrating the ties of youth to the tradition.

The Shrinathji haveli is the first to be constructed in Canada. It claims a membership of 1,500 families, frequently drawing 1,200 persons during festivals.[72] Served by a resident priest, the temple has been assisted by the Vraj temple in Pennsylvania, which sent a priest on loan to Toronto before a permanent mukhiya was located. The effort to establish a haveli in Toronto also received assistance from the Vallabh Youth Organization and its organizer, goswami Vrajrajkumarji. In addition, a number of other goswamis assisted the Canadian organization.

Festivals are important to the haveli and often provide an opportunity for goswami Drumilkumarji to meet the community regularly. The temple celebrates a wide variety of gatherings every month, including a significant number of Pushtimargiya festivals as well as seasonal gatherings and observations in the Hindu lunar year (fig. 15). Goswami Drumilkumarji often visits the temple during these periods, offering Brahmsanbandh. Local Vaishnavas open their homes during these periods, providing the visiting goswami with consistent standards of purity and decorum. The temple has also attracted a wide range of other visiting goswamis.

The small former church building and parking lot are often filled to capacity during festivals and darshans on the weekend. Because multiculturalism is so widely accepted in Toronto, ethnic institutions such as the Shrinathji haveli easily co-exist with other South Asian groups. Members actively assist new immigrants and understand that work as part of the mission of the haveli.

6

Fitting Pushtimarg into American Hinduism

"(Dark One)—Why go off where others live?"—Surdas[1]

This chapter puts Pushtimarg in context, exploring how it fits within the developing fabric of American Hinduism. A number of interpretations have been applied to this diverse, evolving group of transplanted traditions. Prema Kurien has distinguished between popular and official forms of Hinduism in cases such as grass roots organizations being supported by national organizations such as the Vishwa Hindu Parishad.[2] Vasudha Narayanan has described a range of formal and informal groups that have opened temples, practiced American adaptations of tradition such as satsang, organized cultural events, and established a virtual presence.[3] Raymond Brady Williams has explored the role of adaptive strategies in forming national, ethnic, ecumenical, hierarchical, and individual expressions.[4] Others looked to the appeal of gurus who have brought their traditions west.[5]

Drawing on these resources, the chapter looks at a number of forces that have brought Hinduism to the West, including nineteenth century religious movements, immigrant traditions in the early twentieth century, gurus, post–1965 immigrant traditions, and the American denominational context. The chapter argues that while connected to the diverse fabric of popular Hinduism, North Indian bhakti sects such as the Gaudiya Sampradaya, the Swaminarayan movement, and the Vallabha Samradaya represent yet another phase in the development of American Hinduism. Their presence in America has been conditioned by demographic changes in India, the period during which they arrived, and the receptivity of Americans to their practices.

Indian Antecedents: Creating an Image of a Transportable Hinduism

In the nineteenth century, sectarian movements in the Hindu Renaissance reacted to British imperialism in India by creating reductionist images of the faith. These simplified forms of Hinduism, bereft of the nuances of culture, also made it transportable, opening the possibility of movement abroad. Reductionist imagery, which narrowly redefined Hinduism in terms of philosophy and text, remained popular in American intellectual circles for more than a century. By the mid-nineteenth century such literary notables as Ralph Waldo Emerson and Henry David Thoreau had even adopted the *Bhagavad Gita* as part of the canon of Western literature, singling it out from the vast corpus of Hindu scripture. Yet, for the Orientalists who studied the *Gita* and the transcendentalists who wrote about it, the Hindu cultural matrix was absent, as were expressions of animism, the complex traditions of caste, and the dynamics of village diversity.

The Hindu Renaissance

When the young, charismatic Swami Vivekananda assumed the podium at the 1893 World Parliament of Religions in Chicago, he stunned Americans by implying that Hinduism had been destined to come to the West:

> The star arose in the East; it traveled steadily toward the West, sometimes dimmed and sometimes effulgent, till it made a circuit of the world, and now it is again rising on the very horizon of the East, the borders of the Tasifu, a thousand-fold more effulgent than it ever was before. Hail Columbia, motherland of liberty! It has been given to thee, who never dipped her hand in her neighbor's blood, who never found out that shortest way of becoming rich by robbing one's neighbors, it has been given to thee to march on at the vanguard of civilization with the flag of harmony.[6]

A disciple of the Hindu mystic Ramakrishna, Vivekananda had arrived penniless in Boston. Befriended by a benefactor, he made his way to the assembled gathering of the parliament not only steeped in the tradition of his guru, but also well aware of Western assumptions about religion. He saw himself as the very instrument through which an American Hinduism would be born. Vivekananda positioned himself as a seed that "is put in the ground, and earth and air and water are place around it. Does the seed become the earth, or the air, or the water? No. It becomes a plant; it develops after the law of its own growth, assimilates the air, the earth and the water, converts them into plant substance and grows a plant."[7]

Vivekananda's interpretation of Hinduism fit well within the Hindu Renaissance, redefining the faith in Western, Orientalist terms. Some groups, such as the Brahmo Samaj, jettisoned Hindu tradition, replicating Christian theology. Others, such as Swami Dayananda's *Arya Samaj,* advocated a form of Hinduism centered in scripture, borrowing a religious paradigm from the West. Both employed reductionist language, stripping Hinduism of caste and culture.

Vivekananda reduced the broad spectrum of Hindu philosophy and praxis to a series of simplified ideas that quickly engaged his audience. The ancient traditions of yoga were supplanted by a single form of meditation—which he dubbed "raja yoga."[8] Similarly, the spectrum of Hindu philosophies was reduced to an emphasis on a single school—*Vedanta*. Vivekananda empowered the very images of Hinduism that the West had rejected:

> I remember, when a boy, a Christian man was preaching to a crowd in India. Among other sweet things he was telling the people that if he gave a blow to their idol with his stick, what could it do? One of his hearers sharply answered, "If I abuse your God what can he do?" "You would be punished," said the preacher, "when you die." "So my idol will punish you when you die," said the villager.[9]

In the same address he recast Hinduism as an amalgam of images of unity, tolerance, and equality—all of which resonated with Americans. In other papers delivered in cities across the country, Vivekananda echoed many of the same themes in an attempt to appeal to intellectuals and intentionally shaping the beginnings of an American Hinduism.

Vivekananda was not alone in this attempt to bring Hinduism to the West. Keshab Chander Sen, who assumed a leadership role in the *Brahmo Samaj* in the 1860s, had quietly begun the same task 30 years earlier. Sen had been attracted to the reforms of Ram Mohan Roy, who emphasized the affinity of Hinduism with Christianity. Following this attempt at reform, Sen had abandoned the use of the sacred thread, worn by the upper three classes (*varnas*) of the caste system, and also attempted to arrange inter-caste marriages, defying his culture. Going further than Vivekananda would have dared, Sen completely disavowed icon worship and affirmed British presence in India. In his flurry for reform, Sen also demonstrated that Hinduism could be repackaged in a way that facilitated its growth in the West.

Unlike Vivekananda, Sen did not attempt to organize devotees or to create an institutional presence. Instead, he looked to Christian intellectuals in Britain with whom his ideas could be shared. Using colonial stereotypes of Hindus to his advantage, he strove to create sensation and affinity:

The Christian World, a digest of the activities of all the major branches of Nonconformity, described the interest Keshab generated thus: "No one who has ever landed on our shores has created more interest in himself and his work amongst all classes of religionists in this country than our Hindoo visitor.... At more than one of our May meetings his reception has been—I can use no other words—a perfect ovation."[10]

By visiting England, Sen helped prepare the West for a seamless interpretation of Hinduism, bereft of cultural trappings, and easily compatible with a colonial view of civilization.

Early Immigrant Traditions

Beginning in the late nineteenth century and continuing to World War I, Indian immigrants made the arduous journey to the United States. Coming by steamship, many sought jobs in mining and agriculture. However, reacting to the continued presence of the growing diversity of Asian peoples, most of whom were on the West Coast, federal and state governments began to restrict the flow. Beginning in 1882, the United States Congress passed a series of Chinese Exclusion Acts, aimed at eliminating migration from China.[11] This followed attempts to recruit Chinese to work in the mines after the discovery of gold in Sutter's Creek, California, in 1848, and later to help create a transcontinental railroad after the Civil War.

In 1913, Hindus and Sikhs formed the *Ghadr* party in California in an attempt to ward off further discrimination. Led by the charismatic Har Dayal, the party published a newspaper by the same name, which called for an end to the mistreatment of Indians and also advocated the termination of British imperialism in India.[12] However, Har Dayal was unable to halt nativist sentiments, which had been given legal voice in 1913 when California passed the Alien Land Law prohibiting persons who were not citizens from owning land. Similar laws were passed in other states.

The federal government moved in the same direction. Passing the Immigration Act of 1921, the government upheld restrictions that became law in 1917, creating a barred zone from which immigrants could not be admitted to the United States. This exclusionist policy was tested in a Supreme Court decision on February 19, 1923, that affirmed the use of restrictions based on race in excluding Asian Indians from entry to the United States. The decision, *The United States v. Bhagat Singh Thind,* was supported by Justice Sutherland, who declared that Indians were neither white persons nor Caucasians. Thind had argued that as an Indian, he was Aryan and should be identified as Caucasian.

A year later, in 1924, the congress passed the Johnson Reed Act (the Immigration Act of 1924), which ended migration to the United States from Asia. In California, where many Sikhs and Hindus had become farmers, conditions became increasingly difficult. The efforts of the Hindu Association and Ghadr dissolved when the coalition of Hindus and Sikhs fell apart. The Johnson Reed Act further cemented a national policy of exclusion. Most Asian Indian immigrants were unable to afford the cost of return to India. Many men who remained in the country were unable, because of the federal legislation, to bring their families to join them.

Because of these conditions Hinduism in America ceased to develop. Apart from Vedanta Centers, developed after Vivekananda's tour of the country, Hinduism had little public presence. However, among American intellectuals, interest in Hindu ideas that had been championed at the parliament continued.

The First Appearance of Gurus in the West

In 1946, Paramahansa Yogananda followed other gurus west, first coming to the United States in 1920. In 1946, he published *Autobiography of a Yogi*, which ignited further interest in Hindu ideas.[13] Yogananda's *Autobiography* was replete with descriptions of mystical experiences that appealed to Western intellectuals.[14] Yogananda described visions and trances, helping readers to vicariously experience the nuances in the spiritual relationship between guru and student (*chaila*). Yogananda had encountered the young Vivekananda in Chicago in 1893, and—acknowledging a strong affinity with him—followed in his footsteps.

Yogananda relied on American perceptions of individualism and free choice. In *Autobiography of a Yogi* and a wide range of other publications, he appealed to essential elements of the American spirit.[15] Exploring Christian theology in biblical commentaries, Yogananda emphasized that all people are the children of God.[16] In magazine articles and numerous publications he persuaded his readers that they could overcome the obstacles that life put before them. He quickly became popular in the West. Expanding Vivekananda's emphasis on tolerance and unity, he presented an open, accessible but reductionist form of Hinduism with little connection to culture, purity and pollution, or the fabric of Indian life.

In keeping with this emphasis Yogananda championed a form of meditation called *Kriya Yoga*, which he believed would appeal to Americans because of its active rather than passive orientation:

The science of *Kriya Yoga,* mentioned so often in these pages, became widely known in modern India through the instrumentality of Lahiri Mahasaya, my guru's guru. The Sanskrit root of *kriya* is *kri,* to do, to act and react; the same root is found in the word *karma,* the natural principle of cause and effect. *Kriya Yoga* is thus "union (*yoga*) with the Infinite through a certain action or rite (*kriya*)." A yogi that faithfully practices the technique is gradually freed from karma or the lawful chain of cause-effect equilibriums.[17]

Attempting to explain the benefits of Kriya Yoga in scientific terms, he described it as an "ancient science" which functioned by oxygenating the blood[18]:

> *Kriya Yoga* is a simple, psychophysiological method by which human blood is decarbonized and recharged with oxygen. The atoms of this extra oxygen are transmuted into life current to rejuvenate the brain and spinal centers. By stopping the accumulation of venous blood, the yogi is able to lessen or prevent the decay of tissues. The advanced yogi transmutes his cells into energy.[19]

This "scientific" explanation gave Yogananda a mission that he interpreted as a mandate. Adapting the aura of an evangelical, he came to the West as a missionary, actualizing his father's plea to "go then to that far Western land; spread there the creedless teachings of *Kriya Yoga.*"[20] In England he met with mystic Therese Neumann, demonstrating his willingness to accept Western mystics as authentic.[21] In the United States, he inspired the creation of the Self Realization Fellowship which offered Americans grass roots involvement with yogic practices.[22]

Later, the reductionist imagery of the Hindu Renaissance was also perpetuated by Gandhi, who championed non-violence, selflessness, and innocence. Touted by Yogananda, Gandhi's popularity soared in the West and soon outshone his following in India. In the United States the Gandhian image was so strong that many Americans even perceived him to be Christian. As Vivekananda and Sen popularized a truncated form of Hinduism, so the evolving image of Gandhi in the United States continued on the same tack—reducing Hinduism to a series of highly transportable principles and images.

Early interpreters of Hinduism such as Vivekananda, Sen, and Gandhi were also missionaries to the West, seeking to construct a more tolerant image of Hinduism among the very people who had sent their own missionaries to India. Unlike later Hindu immigrants who sought to redefine Hinduism for Hindus in diaspora, these early reformers interacted with a Western audience that had little understanding of or empathy for Hindu culture.

Because of their efforts, the perception of a highly transportable, non-violent form of Hinduism that was tolerant of diversity and stripped of culture remained in American intellectual circles throughout the first half of the twentieth century. At the same time popular accounts of Indian culture widely published in America, such as Kathryn Mayo's *Mother India*[23] and the movie *Gunga Din*,[24] exploited the image of Asian Indians. For those Hindus who had emigrated to America before the harsh immigration laws passed after World War I, public expression of their tradition became difficult. However, following the reversal of U.S. immigration policy in 1965 and the migration of thousands of Hindus to the United States, cultural expressions of Hinduism became part of the American religious landscape.

Immigrants and the Evolution of an American Temple Tradition

Following the passage of the first amendment to the Immigration and Nationality Act in 1965, Hindu immigrants began to create a visible change in the American religious landscape. By 1970 the Indian population had risen to 51,000 and within ten years it had grown to over 206,000 immigrants.[25] Many of these first arrivals were students who enrolled in American colleges and universities, hoping to improve their chances for employment in India. Often stereotyped as part of a "brain drain," some remained in the United States, creating the beginnings of a temple tradition. As temples grew a variety of forms emerged. Some borrowed from the American denominational milieu, creating "ecumenical" institutions that attempted to accommodate a diverse Hindu clientele.[26] Others erected more specific institutions that conformed in architecture and practice to northern and southern styles of Hinduism. At the same time gurus became increasingly visible components of the transmission of tradition.[27]

Together, these components of a growing American Hinduism created a shift in emphasis. Earlier forms of the tradition championed by Vivekananda, Sen and others had sought to reinterpret Hinduism for the West. By the early 1970s Indians had reached a critical mass in the United States and now targeted their interpretations of Hinduism in diaspora for the ethnic community. While the tolerance that leaders of the Hindu Renaissance had helped establish in the West was helpful, the process of redefining American Hinduism now had a different purpose.

SOUTH INDIAN TEMPLES

On July 4, 1977, a guru, Sri La Sri Pandrimalai, dedicated a temple in Flushing, New York, erected by the Hindu Temple Society of North America.[28]

The effort of the Temple Society marked the attempt of the Indian community to provide for its religious needs with no attempt to attract Western converts. In architectural form the structure was a rendition of classical South Indian architecture, but functionally the temple attempted to serve a variety of populations in what would later be understood as a form of "ecumenical" Hinduism, described in the next section. Dubbed "The Hindu Temple," the structure boasted an ornate, carved *gopurm* or gateway, typical of South Indian temple construction. The temple had been sponsored by the government of the southern Indian state of Andra Pradesh and the Tirumala Tirupathi Devasthanam, one of the largest and most highly revered South Indian temples.[29]

Efforts to build a South Indian temple in the New York metropolitan area had begun seven years earlier. One hundred fifty workmen in Andra Pradesh sculpted large granite blocks for the *vimana,* the tower built above the *garbha griha* or inner sanctuary. Each block was carefully identified and loaded on board a cargo ship, the *Vishwa Apurva,* carrying the name of the god Vishnu, identified as the "Lord of the Universe." Traditional craftsmen, shilpis, followed to begin work.

For the Indian craftsmen, working in a major Western city presented numerous challenges. They had never seen winter before and were ill equipped for the difficulties of working in freezing temperatures. The New York infrastructure also presented a host of challenges. Even though the shilpis followed traditional patterns of their craft, honed for centuries in South India, building inspectors advised them that the temple construction would have to conform to strict codes. Costs were also surprising. When the granite blocks arrived in the New York harbor, temple administrators discovered that it would cost an additional $17,000 to transport them to the site of the construction in Flushing.[30]

Despite the difficulties in adapting to the West, temple leaders persisted, installing shrines within the temple and identifying the sacred space with *yantras*, or sacred designs. The yantras remained in place for five years, insuring that the inner space would be pure for the resident deities. The temple was also renamed the Sri Maha Vallabha Ganapati Devasthanam in honor of the god Ganesh, associated with beginnings. The use of a traditional Sanskrit name demonstrated the evolution of the tradition and the developing context of a growing South Asian minority for whom such patterns of name recognition were important.

However, while the Ganesh temple was identified with South Indian tradition, it resisted more narrowly defined sectarian interests, attempting to establish a broader base. Reaching out to both Vaishnava and *Shaiva* Hindu populations, the temple claimed two levels of identity. In its architecture and style of worship, it was South Indian. However, at the same time it also became "ecumenical" in an overlapping pattern of identities. As fresh arrivals of Hindu immigrants became affiliated with the temple, two groups began to vie for control. The more orthodox resisted any form of democratic control. Others looked at the Ganesh temple as a congregational tradition governed by a voting membership. The battle became even more complicated when workers filed a class action lawsuit claiming that they had been discriminated against during the construction of the temple, claiming that

> the temple's cooks and priests, who were brought over from India under religious worker visas, were forced to work long hours without overtime pay.... The lawsuit also accuses the temple of obtaining religious worker visas for its cooks under the pretext that they would only be performing religious duties such as preparing cooked offerings and food for religious festivals.[31]

Ultimately, siding with the faction that sought democratic control, the Supreme Court of the State of New York called for elections, dismissing the trustees who resisted change.

These internal disputes in America's oldest Hindu temple suggested that Hindu temples were subject to the same forces that have influenced mainstream denominational traditions. The temple was caught between attempts of its founders to replicate South Indian orthodoxy and American understandings of religion based on self-governing voluntary societies.

Other Southern Indian temples followed, defining their mission in more sectarian ways and resisting the factionalism that had plagued the Ganesh temple. In Penn Hills, Pennsylvania, a magnificent replica of the famous Shri Venkateswara temple in Tirupati was erected. Organized and developed by the Shri Vaishnava community, the temple retained strict patterns of ritual orthodoxy but also adapted its pattern of governance to the American milieu. Other examples followed. In Bridgewater, New Jersey, another variation of the Shri Venkateswara temple opened to service the burgeoning Indian population in central New Jersey.

"Ecumenical" Temples

As Hindu temple societies attempted to fit into the American religious landscape, other examples of Hindu ecumenism became evident. In Allentown, Pennsylvania, the Hindu Temple Society of the Lehigh Valley opened a temple next door to a Baptist church. Hoping to avoid conflict, the temple was constructed to appear as a large house, bearing no sign in front or any other obvious characteristic that would identify it as Hindu. Drawing on the name of Gandhi's ashram in India, Shantiniketan ("Abode of Peace"), the temple used ecumenism not only to house different regional expressions of Hinduism, but also to provide a religious center for local populations of Jains and Sikhs.

In mid-sized communities where no single Hindu temple tradition was of sufficient size to finance a religious institution, ecumenical temples like *Shantiniketan* increasingly became a viable alternative to sectarian traditions, assuring Hindus of a solid membership base. Raymond Williams observes how this evolving American tradition differed from the parent faith:

> An ecumenical Hinduism is developing in the United States that unites deities, rituals, sacred texts, and people in temples and programs in ways that would not be found together in India. In temples and centers created on an ecumenical model, emphasis is placed upon all–India Hindu "great tradition," on devotion to major deities, and upon some elements of the Sanskrit tradition in an adapted "Sanskritization."[32]

Ecumenical Hindu temples frequently copied classical patterns of architecture, attempting to represent mainstream Hinduism. However, in ritual and programmatic functions, they were often diverse. Many evolved as a curious blend of traditions, incorporating elements of classical South Indian Hinduism with the needs of northern clientele. In some temples, the performance of a generic puja was not enough, as temple organizations grew to include regional and ethnic associations that could continue festival traditions and forms of worship unique to each area.

Gurus and Ashrams

In the 1960s, gurus became visible in American public life. In contrast to mainstream Hinduism, which is rarely evangelical, some gurus sought to proselytize the growing counterculture. Much like the leadership of the Hindu Renaissance, their vision of Hinduism was transportable, frequently reductionist, and tailored for a Western clientele.

The growing American counterculture of the 1960s and 1970s was receptive to the new missionaries from India. Disillusioned with Western values and drawn toward transcendentalism, the American left increasingly sought direct experience of the sacred. In a reversal of nineteenth century European and American missionary traditions, a flood of Hindu gurus emigrated to the West. Building on the Hindu Renaissance, their primary audience was not the evolving Indian population in the United States, but the counterculture who looked to Hindu spirituality as a way of encountering the holy.

One of the more popular examples of this new American form of Hinduism was Maharishi Mahesh Yogi who, as part of a world tour in 1959, brought a form of yoga dubbed Transcendental Meditation to a number of

U.S. cities.³³ Born Mahesh Prasad Varma in a small town in central India, Maharishi pared the complex, life-consuming practices of yoga down to a simplified practice, echoing the reduction interpretations of the Hindu Renaissance. Offering the West a discipline that was without cultural baggage or extensive ritual requirements, he created

> what many would identify as a highly influential Hindu global theological perspective through his Transcendental Meditation Movement. In the West, he has achieved this influence in part by denying the "Hindu-ness" of his teachings, and at least for a time, their religiosity as well. In so doing, he thrust the reach of his Advaita Vedantin interpretations and many standard cultural markers of Hinduism into a global context.³⁴

A stream of gurus quickly followed. Swami Prabhupada, founder of the International Society for Krishna Consciousness, arrived in Boston on March 17, 1965. In 1971, a boy identified as Guru Maharaji-ji borrowed American missionary jargon to establish the Divine Light Mission in the United Kingdom and the United States. At the same time Guru Bhagwan Shree Rajneesh arrived in northern New Jersey, where he created a communal ashram with liberal mores. Establishing the Chidvilas Rajneesh Meditation Center in Montclair, New Jersey, in 1975, his followers gained notoriety and were forced to leave when the community erupted in opposition to the center, branding it as a cult.³⁵ The controversy had been fueled by the guru's flagrant display of wealth coupled with acquisition of one of the most expensive properties in town. When it became evident that community leaders intended to move the conflict into the courts, Rajneesh yielded, opening a new center in Antelope, Oregon, which was renamed Rajneeshpuram. However, difficulties persisted when members of the commune were accused of crimes and Rajneesh was accused of immigration violations and deported. The movement quickly died.

Other less controversial figures established more lasting expressions of Hindu tradition. Among them was Swami Muktananda, who created the *Siddha Yoga Dham* movement, developing 80 meditation centers and five ashrams.³⁶ Siddha yoga combined spiritual practices drawn from Kundalini yoga with an ideology replete with images attractive to a Western audience to whom individualism is paramount. His teachings proclaimed,

> Honor your Self,
> Worship your Self,
> Meditate on your Self,
> God dwells within you as you.³⁷

Synthesizing Hindu and American values, Siddha Yoga Dham offered its participants a retreat from materialism in a way that Americans could easily access.

More recently, Mata Amritanandamayi, known as Amma, the "hugging guru," created an interpretation of Hinduism that was easily transplanted, depending entirely on her presence. Drawing thousands of persons from all walks of life to convention halls and outdoor gatherings, Amma offered a transformative experience centered in a hug—a dominant Western expression of warmth and compassion. Little else was required. Amma's presence remains uncluttered with ritual and freed of cultural constraints, reducing the complex pattern of Hindu praxis to a simple act. Because of this, Amma has become a global traveler, drawing large crowds of the curious and the devout—all intent on experiencing the hug of a guru who is frequently identified as a savior, easily understood in a country where Christians are a majority. This image has been reinforced through Amma's impressive array of charitable acts. Rescuing entire villages from the ravages of natural disasters, funding hospitals and schools, her appeal is a natural continuation of Renaissance piety, bridging East and West. Drawing financial support from India and from supporters in the United States, she bridges both worlds and is easily accessible in both. In India and in the United States devotees can access her North American tour dates on the Internet in a movement that is parallel and complementary to, competing with, and yet different from earlier expressions of Western interests in India.[38]

NORTH INDIAN BHAKTI MOVEMENTS

The development of Krishna centered North Indian bhakti traditions, represents another phase in the evolution of American Hinduism and has been shaped by the presence of Gaudiya Vaishnavism, the Swaminarayan movement, and Pushtimarg. In each tradition, Krishna is central but at the same time metaphorical of a heightened level of devotion and personal religious experience. However, in America the three bhakti traditions have followed very different paths of development. Gaudiya Vaishnavism left its Rajasthani and Bengali origins, becoming a pan–Indian experience that has borrowed from American evangelical models of religion. The Swaminarayan faith deemphasized its ethnic beginnings, creating a worldwide temple tradition borrowing from corporate models of transnational business in which different communities of devotees have become financial backers. Pushtimarg has remained the most traditional of all three movements, retaining its ethnic focus, and defining its havelis as extensions of the Gujarati community in diaspora. In each case, the American identity of the tradition has been shaped by the historical circumstances that accompanied arrival in the United States.

The International Society for Krishna Consciousness (ISKCON)

The American history of ISKCON was shaped by the migration of a Vaishnava monk, Bhaktivedanta Swami Prabhupada, to the United States. Practicing the sixteenth century Gaudiya tradition of Chaitanya, Prabhupada arrived in Boston from Calcutta in 1965—well before the impact of changes in U.S. immigration law had been felt.[39] At 69, he was one of the first representatives of a sectarian Hindu bhakti tradition that most Americans had ever encountered. His visit was seen by scholars not only as the journey of a guru to the United States but also as the beginnings of a fuller, more ritualistic expression of Hinduism in diaspora. Thomas Hopkins concluded:

> What I did not expect, and what really surprised and pleased me, was the degree to which the ritual tradition was also brought over and put into place. That's something that no other movement has succeeded in doing, nor even really tried to do; transplanting a traditional Hindu ritual structure into a Hindu religious movement in America.[40]

Prabhupada came as a missionary to the West during a time of domestic turmoil and culture change. His target audience was Western converts rather than the ethnic Indian community. Convinced of the decadence of American life, and attempting to change it, he expressed his feelings in a lengthy poem, *"Markine Bhavata Dharma"*:

> My dear Lord Kṛṣṇa, You are so kind upon this useless soul, but I do not know why You have brought me here. Now You can do whatever You like with me.
> But I guess You have some business here, otherwise why would You bring me to this terrible place?
> Most of the population here is covered by the material modes of ignorance and passion. Absorbed in material life, they think themselves very happy and satisfied, and therefore they have no taste for the transcendental message of Vāsudeva. I do not know how they will be able to understand it.[41]

Prabhupada used the voice of the Gaudiya tradition to create a utopian vision of an alternative lifestyle that instantly appealed to the evolving American counterculture of the 1960s. However, as the "Krishna Consciousness" movement coalesced, his confrontation with the West changed and he began to immerse Vaishnavism in Western values. Well aware of American individualism and self-determinism, Prabhupada articulated an interpretation of bhakti based on self-help. In an address to the World Health Organization in 1971, he proclaimed,

> So according to Bhagavad-gita [sic], as we are preaching, we are also opening centers, self-help centers. In New Vrindavban, West Virginia, we have already

opened a very big community center. We are going to open in California also, and we have already opened in India.... "Be self-sufficient. Save time for spiritual culture." That is human civilization.⁴²

As ISKCON matured, Prabhupada further adapted his vision, creating an accommodated form of the faith that rejected Western culture and at the same time attempt to partially meld with it. On one hand, Krishna was the North Indian god who was intimate, knowable, and defined by his culture. Yet at the same time, for Prabhupada he was also a culture-despiser who rejected the secular militarism of America in the 1960s.⁴³

Prabhupada's dialectical response to the relationship between culture and religion also elevated the role of Brahmin priests. This allowed him "to place value in the Hindu social system, especially in the ministerial role of Brahmins, and at the same time reject the notion that such classification is based on hereditary caste."⁴⁴

Well aware of the denominational nature of religion in the West, Prabhupada also prepared for the time when the movement would no longer be directed by a living guru. He created a Governing Body Commission that took the place of the guru, providing for a way of achieving consensus and avoiding schism. In so doing, he accepted the American values that supported nonprofit corporations, tailoring Vaishnavism to a vision of democratic life. He

> intended the body to function like the board of directors of a modern corporation. (Incidentally, the name "Governing Body Commission" was the title of the board of directors of the India Railways during the British Raj). At the GBC's first annual meeting in Mayapur, Prabhupada guided the proceedings, "showing how the GBC should strictly follow parliamentary procedure (as set forth in Robert's *Rules of Order*), how proposals should be put forward, discussed, and voted upon ..." Prabhupada envisioned a management structure that would be strong enough to carry the movement forward without him, and yet simple enough to allow members to remain focused on otherworldly pursuits.⁴⁵

Following Prabhupada's death in 1977, ISKCON evolved in other directions. Prabhupada had popularized the Hare Krishna movement among disaffected young adults disillusioned by the Vietnam War. Most of the movement's clientele were outside the South Asian community. While first generation Hindu Americans frequently sent their children to ISKCON's vibrant summer camp program, most avoided closer ties with the movement, which had been stereotyped as a cult. However, as the counterculture waned, immigrants began to affiliate with ISKCON. The organization matured and began to address issues related to leadership and financial support. In time, "the Indian immigrants created a new context in which ISKCON was able to successfully stabilize."⁴⁶

As a symbol of this growth, ISKCON had constructed an elaborate temple called "the Palace of Gold" in Moundsville, West Virginia, originally conceived as a home for Prabhupada. The area was rebranded as New Vrindaban, quickly becoming a tourist attraction. ISKCON seemed to be firmly established in the American religious landscape. However, when the spiritual head of the site, an American-born devotee who had taken the name Kirtananda, was bludgeoned by a devotee, New Vrindavan began to change. Recovering from the attack, Kirtananda formed the separatist Eternal Order of the League of Devotees, elevating his position and control and initiating a dissident tradition. The order established 13 temples throughout the United States.[47] Offended by this separation and aware of allegations of corruption, ISKCON finally expelled Kirtananda in 1987. Subsequently, in 1990, he was indicted by the federal government on corruption charges, including conspiracy to murder two members of the West Virginia commune whose bodies had been discovered on the property. Because of the scandal New Vrindaban was temporarily removed from ISKCON.

After the scandal, the persona of the Hare Krishna movement in the United States began to change again.[48] This process of "selective conversion" was tied to the transnational community and was linked to immigrants who were on "the upper end of the socioeconomic ladder."[49] The emphasis within ISKCON also began to shift from earlier patterns of temple-centered devotion to members' homes, in a natural adaptation of patterns of immigrant communication:

> One important part of this social infrastructure is coming to the temple as often as possible to interact with other devotees while practicing Krishna consciousness in the temple itself. But what is likely the most important aspect of the social infrastructure is the tight network of Indian householder devotees. These devotees go to school, work, and live outside the temple, but they spend much of their free time together in religious classes and programs in each other's homes, especially on the weekends. Each of their homes is adorned with deities and pictures of Krishna and Prabhupad and serves as a temple outside of the main Chicago temple.[50]

The theological emphasis that Prabhupada had established, devaluing the Western, materialistic world, continued. Devotees were urged to retain Krishna Consciousness and to reject worldly gain. At the same time ISKCON ncreasingly withdrew from public scrutiny, developing into a sect that, while still advocating values apart from the American mainstream, was no longer popularly perceived as threatening.

SWAMINARAYAN HINDUISM

Like ISKCON, which inherited a North Indian theological tradition and developed it in a unique period of American history, the transnational experience of the Swaminarayan Sanstha has also been shaped by events in the United States. Drawing not on American converts but on an upwardly mobile immigrant Gujarati population, it has rapidly become part of the religious landscape during a time when the American economy was dominated by transnational cultures and globalization.

The history of the movement in India shaped its emergence in the West. Two "dioceses" in Ahmedabad and Vadtal were initiated by the founder Sahajanand Swami (1780–1832), whom his followers recognize as Swaminarayan, an incarnation of Krishna and the highest form of ultimate reality or parabrahman. Both have established transnational traditions, drawing on the same extended path of emigration that has influenced all Gujarati religions, including Pushtimarg. The Ahmedabad diocese established the International Swaminarayan Satsang Organization (ISSO). Another sect, whose roots had been in the Vadtal diocese, became particularly active globally. The Bochasanwasi Shri Akshar Purushottam Swaminarayan Sanstha (BAPS) was developed from the teachings of a monk, Yagnapurushadas, who left Vadtal in 1906, denying the spiritual authority of the teachers (acharyas) in the tradition. Yagnapurushadas defined another form of the Swaminarayan movement based on the authoritative role of Gunatitanand Swami (1785–1867), a disciple of Swaminarayan, whom he perceived as a manifestation of the highest state of being (*akshar*) and a prototype of spiritual leadership. Gunatitanand was seen as a "God-realized saint" who was able to become the abode of the purest and highest form of ultimate reality (*purushottam*), which was also identified with Swaminarayan. As BAPS developed, gurus were linked to the continuing manifestation and authority of Gunatitanand.

In the twentieth century, the continued role of God-realized saints became increasingly important. A devotee from the Gujarat, Jinadhai, was recognized as the fourth spiritual successor to Gunatitanand. Born in India in 1892, he became a sadhu later in life and was identified as Yogiji Maharaj.[51] Yogiji Maharaj developed an extensive interest in expanding the tradition and was particularly active with young people, whom he increasingly drew into the faith.[52] After his death in 1971, the mantle of leadership was passed to his successor, Narayanswarupdas, who was given the title *Pramukh Swami Maharaj*. This designation again affirmed the perception of a God-realized saint and also bestowed the additional role of administrative president.[53] In keeping with the need for an organizational structure that would be capable of expanding the tradition both in India and abroad, Pramukh Swami encouraged the development of a complex administrative structure that emanated from two trusts in the Gujarat, one dealing with religious affairs and the other with social welfare. The total structure enabled the boards that controlled each trust to manage the entire organization in a way that reached down to the smallest local association or satsang:

> Proposals and decisions emanating from those boards are mediated through a complex organizational scheme which reacts down to the smallest village or group of satsangis meeting at a house. A network of committees reports to a central committee and subdivisions deal with such articles as the children's programme, the youth organization, women's work, publications and examinations. The kotharis (managers) of the larger temples, or sadhus sent out to undertake or to supervise planning work, act as liaison officers between the laity and the centre.[54]

Pramukh Swami began to globalize the faith, taking advantage of the changing world economy. BAPS expanded reaching the United Kingdom and parts of Africa. In 1974, the first BAPS temple in the United States was established in Flushing, New York:

> Property was purchased on Bowne Street in Flushing, New York, for a temple, and in 1974 Pramukh Swami installed images in a temporary shrine in the basement of a house on the site. After raising funds from devotees across the country in the amount of $95,000 for the property and $200,000 for construction, the first Swaminarayan temple in America was consecrated in a large festival by Pramukh Swami on 3 August 1977.[55]

Devotees in Flushing captured the spirit of this global outreach. The central icon in the temple had been painted on a large mirror that had miraculously survived transport from India to Africa and then to England and finally to the United States. They understood this feat as a sign that their religious tradition was destined to come west.

Within ten years other temples were established. The ISSO opened a temple in Weehauken, New Jersey.[56] A BAPS temple was created in Edison. Other BAPS temples were established in North Bergan, Cherry Hill, and Absecon.[57] In an attempt to further expand, leaders sought to acquire property in western New Jersey. Following a proposal to Independence Township (Warren County) in 1985, BAPS leaders sought to turn a 162-acre tract of land into a million-dollar complex including a temple, school, dormitory, and marble temple.[58] When community leaders rebuffed the proposal, stereotyping the sect as a cult, the plan was withdrawn. Six years later, in 1991, as a means of stemming some of the continuing stereotyping and prejudice that Swaminarayan devotees had encountered, Pramukh Swami launched the Cultural Festival of India on the campus of Middlesex County College in Edison, New Jersey.[59] There, 1.2 million visitors from July 12 to August 11 encountered exhibits about Indian culture and religion. A volunteer force of 2,100 persons helped transform the campus into a microcosm of Indian life. Conferences and academic gatherings were part of the festival. Participants could visit an Indian village created on the site, attend performances of traditional Indian dance, and visit reconstructions of Hindu temples.[60]

The Cultural Festival of India helped establish American Hinduism as a living entity. Although participants might not have realized the full import of the Cultural Festival, it also foreshadowed a continuing global transformation of BAPS, which began to take on some of the characteristics of a multinational corporation in which a transnational religion employed global marketing strategies. This was consistent with dramatic changes that were already taking place in the United States and in India as international business and less restrictive patterns of immigration increasingly positioned the United States in global markets. Forces were at work freeing trade barriers and making business across borders more viable. By 1986 the World Bank and the International Monetary Fund had developed policies for trade liberalization.[61] Three years later the fall of the Berlin wall formally marked the end of the Cold War and the emergence of global capitalism as the dominant force. In 1991, India launched a series of market reforms "aimed at transforming a quasi-socialist economy into a more open, market-oriented economy."[62] At the same time the creation of the Internet and the proliferation of free trade agreements transformed the global economic landscape. BAPS increasingly took advantage of these changes, developing scenarios for erection of temples around the world.

One of the most dramatic of the new BAPS temples was a traditional, open air stone Hindu temple, erected in the greater Houston metropolitan area in 2004. Crafted of Italian marble, the temple represented not only classical Hindu architecture but also the evolution of global business practices within BAPS. Once the marble had been secured, it was computer coded, assuring that pieces with differences in color and texture would not appear together. Shipped to India, the stone was carved in traditional patterns of Hindu art, yielding 33,000 pieces in a massive process of engineering and business practices.[63] After the stone was transported to Houston, site managers erected the temple in just 16 months.

As the twentieth century came to an end, BAPS temples had been erected in major metropolitan areas including New York, Chicago, and Los Angeles using the same globalized techniques that had been perfected in Houston. By 2005, with the opening of Akshardham in New Delhi, the largest stone Hindu temple erected in modern times, BAPS had made a complete transformation from its localized beginnings in the Gujarat. Akshardham incorporated advances in global communication, borrowing ideas from theme parks in the West. With the success of Akshardham, Pramukh Swami also began to envision "megatemples" in the West to serve Indian communities concentrated in major metropolitan areas. A larger replica of Akshardham was conceived for a site in Robbinsville, New Jersey.

In keeping with global business practices and innovations in international communication, Pramukh Swami's presence was now easily facilitated through videoconferencing:

> The *shilas*, or sacred stones, sanctified on August 31, 2011 by Pramukh Swami Maharaj in Mumbai, India, had been sent to New Jersey for the final ceremony. This commenced on the morning of 6 October, when Pramukh Swami Maharaj led the Shilanyas ceremony from Mumbai, India via live videoconference, as Pujya Mahant Swami, Pujya Ishwarcharan Swami, swamis and devotees performed the rituals in New Jersey. In subsequent sessions over the next several days, devotees enjoyed Swamishri's performance of the ceremony through playback of the video feed. It was a unique memory for all those present—an interactive Shilanyas ceremony between the devotees and their guru with a few oceans and a few thousand miles in between![64]

As the number of Swaminarayan temples increased around the world, the role of guru also changed. In addition to his spiritual role as guru, Pramukh Swami increasingly became a temple developer, not only authorizing sites for new temples but also building an infrastructure that connected BAPS devotees around the world. BAPS became

> a truly transnational organization. BAPS groups in different countries are connected not just to the headquarters in Gujarat but also to one another. Members living in various parts of the world meet at the major BAPS festivals held in India and in other countries. When Pramukh Swami decides that a new shikarabadda mandir should be built in a particular country, money for the temple is solicited from members throughout the diaspora. When that temple is inaugurated, visitors and donors from all over the world attend the ceremonies.[65]

Some Differences Between ISKCON, BAPS and Pushtimarg in Diaspora

While ISKCON or BAPS have both developed American temples through international religious organizations, havelis are developed in the West primarily through local initiative by local South Asian communities. The process is consistent with the ethnic centers of Gujaratis in the United States and with demographic changes in India that have produced strong immigrant Pushtimarg populations.

Pushtimargiya arrived in the United States in the mid–1980s at the same time that the Swaminarayan movement was developing in the diaspora. The material success of the West, the prestige of its major universities, and the relative ease (when compared with India) of reward for talented entrepreneurs brought devotees from each of the gaddis. Once here, they used entrepreneurial abilities that they had developed in India to shape their American religious institutions.

Unlike either BAPS or ISKCON, Pushtimarg recognizes multiple sources of authority in the diverse community of goswamis. The total body of goswamis, or Vallabhkul, is a large, extended family with a number of branches. While the heads of the seven houses function as gurus and are viewed by Pushtimargiyas as spiritual guides, there is little consensus about how balaks (literally "sons"—a synonym for goswami) become gurus. Since Pushtimarg places great value on heredity and also understands Vallabhacharya as an incarnation of Krishna, the lineage is seen as a corporate embodiment of the divinity. All balaks, whether they choose an active role within the sect or not, carry this imprimatur. However, in India, the organization of the sect is focused on the gaddis, and those balaks who remain visible within the life of the gaddi are seen as gurus.

While havelis have helped each other get started, loaning mukhiyas and even assisting in expenditures, each temple remains independent. Because Pushtimarg recognizes multiple sources of authority in the Vallabhkul, there can be no singular directive that mandates the collective to act in a particular way. Even the voice of the Tilkayat who cares for the swarup of Shrinathji exercises spiritual rather than ecclesiastical control over the confederated tradition.

Unlike the more visible gurus of the 1960s, Pushtimargiya goswamis do not maintain an agenda for changing or transforming Western culture and also do not seek to become part of it. Accordingly, the Vallabhkul does not exercise managerial functions for the whole sampradaya and does not provide any unified policy or program that would bring its disparate parts together. In this sense, it has avoided the trappings of Western models of organizations, emphasizing familial traditions rather than corporate management functions.

Havelis are primarily defined by the presence of a *swarup* rather than the temple tradition. As a result, havelis are not only spiritual centers but also places of pilgrimage. This dynamic frequently results in the presence of diverse populations who visit a haveli, hoping to experience darshan. In larger American havelis such as Vraj, the spiritual seat of Pushtimarg in North America, the crowd attending the darshan on any single day may include a diverse body of devotees, not all of whom are Pushtimargiyas.[66]

The presence of the deity in defining the haveli has also conflated the swarups in the West, focusing primarily on Shri Nathji. While some havelis, such as the Shree Dwarkadhish temple in Parlin, New Jersey, have been organized around other swarups, the overwhelming manifestation of the tradition in the American diaspora is centered on Shri Nathji. This centralization of a single, dominant swarup allows American havelis to represent the broader face of the tradition and to avoid the difficulties that could arise in recruiting Pushtimargiya populations from a wide variety of gaddis. In North America, all of the gaddis are represented and havelis have an "ecumenical" function to meet and integrate devotees from each of the houses.

The American Denominational Context

As the preceding discussion has shown, transplanted Hinduism has adapted to patterns of American religious life. Like other forms of transplanted Hinduism, it has also participated in the well-established milieu of American denominational tradition. Russell E. Richey describes the origins of the system:

> The denomination was an Anglo-American contribution to religious organizational taxonomy and within Christianity the most important institutional development since the Emperor Constantine. It came to characterize American religion and define ways of being religious, as the party came to characterize American government and define ways of participating politically and as the corporation came to characterize American enterprise and define ways of doing business. And like its political and economic counterparts, the denomination emerged gradually, without blueprint, assembled from various existing social patterns, and evolved as American society changed.[67]

A number of characteristics have enabled denominations to become the primary form of religion in America. Representing a pluralistic range of religious traditions, denominations have looked to voluntary support and non-profit identities. The denomination "was 'a voluntary association of like-hearted and like-minded individuals, who are united on the basis of common beliefs for the purpose of accomplishing tangible and defined objectives.' Denominations became the primary of organizing religious communities in America."[68]

Denominations have also created strong linkages between ethnicity and religion.[69] Although patterns of ethnic identity are often diminished as religious groups assimilate over multiple generations, vestiges remain, as has been the case with German and Dutch Reformed churches and Orthodox Judaism. Historically, denominations have also developed systems for acculturating new generations of devotees.⁷⁰ The American Sunday school system, the use of church camps and retreat centers, and denominationally based colleges are all part of this lasting history.

Existing in a competitive marketplace of religions, denominations have spawned local, regional, and national organizational structures. Regional presence has often reflected the dynamics of population growth and ethnic density. Thus, Roman Catholics tended to cluster in urban areas where the Industrial Revolution had produced opportunities for employment. Other groups including

> Congregationalist and Unitarian churches spread across New England, and Lutherans were clustered in the Upper Midwest. Methodism, a national denomination, were especially strong in the Midwest and South. Mormons dominated Utah, extending their presence throughout the nation through aggressive evangelism.... Baptists ... divided into various regional sub denominations with American Baptists in the East and West and ethnic Baptist churches—German Norwegian, Swedish—spread throughout the Midwest.⁷¹

Denominations have also relied on both quantifiable memberships and an entrepreneurial spirit that has enabled them to endow religious institutions, foster colleges and universities in their name, and establish common expectations of religious conformity.

These characteristics of American denominations have created an ebb and flow of new forms in postwar America. Martin Marty has described the difficulties that denominations began to experience after World War II:

> The denomination was being put on trial and its future seen as insecure through all the decades after 1945. The form, while it had some prehistory in England, was largely an American invention, designed to permit the various immigrant and evangelized peoples to be faithful to their traditional creeds, to perpetuate inherited liturgies, to assure the integrity of faiths, and to provide the theological basis for attracting new members, nurturing longer-term members, and directing their mission.⁷²

As traditional denominational structures drew increasing questions about their viability, some researchers began to identify new forms. Scott L. Thumma has described megachurches, which have replicated many of the functions of denominations at a local level.⁷³ Robert Wuthnow has looked at parachurches, "voluntary agencies that drew on the resources of believers in congregations and denominations even as they competed with them."⁷⁴ Others have studied the impact of secularization.⁷⁵

Within this changing religious climate, new arrivals such as the Hindu temple replicate significant elements of the American denominational tradition in a number of ways. Akin to the Protestant and Roman Catholic traditions in the United States, they have attempted to preserve ethnicity. Hindu temples in the United States have begun to develop patterns of entrepreneurship, similar to traditions that have propelled Protestant churches into the American mainstream. They also began to rely on membership as a means for solidifying their base, becoming 501(c)(3), non-profit, tax-exempt institutions. Some temples even established criteria for membership including standards for financial support. Shantiniketan in Allentown, Pennsylvania, began to keep track of its membership in relationship to the number of Indian families in the area, hoping to increase its base through ethnic association.[76]

Like the majority of established forms of religions in the United States, Hindu temples often emphasize congregational identity, creating cultural comfort zones for members of the ethnic community. As non-profit organizations they have created structures that reduce the liability of individuals by adopting conventional practices of locating authority in boards of trustees. Like most American denominations, they employ a variety of systems of management but emphasize participatory traditions. Obtaining 501(c)(3), non-profit, tax-exempt status, they conform to IRS guidelines that have evolved from dominant church-related traditions.[77] However, as Prema Kurien also notes, Hindu temples cannot always meet the requirements that enable them to be perceived as "churches."[78]

Temples are dependent on the same spirit of voluntarism as their counterparts in other forms of American religion. Temples are constructed through the initiatives of local committees. For some heavily globalized forms of the faith such as the Swaminarayan tradition, decisions to construct temples are initiated by international bodies following directives from the presiding guru. But even in these cases, local committees are formed and trustees appointed with significant input from each area.[79] The majority of Hindu temples in the United States depend on a cadre of dedicated volunteers.

Many American temples have become congregational in their orientation. This is a sharp departure from the role of Hindu temples in India, which exist independent of congregations. Instead, temples are erected through donations or patronage for the care of a deity and employ priests (pujaris) for that purpose. While they may attract members of the same community, there is no congregational orientation and no attempt to bind devotees together into a cohesive community.

Like their Christian predecessors in America, Hindu temples emphasize the education of children into the faith. First generation leaders are acutely aware that their children will grow up with American values and will not have the same experience that their parents did in India. While most South Asian families with children work hard to retain ties with the homeland and take their children to India on periodic visits, members of the second generation are rarely accepted as equals in Indian society. As a result, educational institutions (Bal Vihars) attached to temples have become an important way of teaching Hindu values. They have replicated well-established patterns of American religious education. Leaders recruit and train teachers, appoint volunteers as administrators, and build religious education into the mindset of the families that support the temple.

Hindu temples have often depended on the same kind of local initiative that has characterized American religion. Among Southern Baptists, the largest Protestant denomination in the United States, "principled localism" has become a dominant factor in the polity. Southern Baptist churches exhibit independence and self-reliance, while at the same time affirming the theological principles of the faith. From a very different theological and cultural position, Hindu temples exhibit many of the same values. Like their Christian counterparts, Hindu temples have established local identities. They have also evolved national organizations in an official Hindu presence. While groups like the Vishwa Hindu Parishad have given American Hinduism a public voice, the local forms of the tradition are what provide the greatest mix of religious and cultural traditions.

Finally, Hindu temple traditions have begun to develop national organizations, configuring their presence in a way that is familiar within the landscape of American denominationalism. The national presence of religious traditions has had a number of functions. The National Council of Churches represented mainline Protestant traditions in their heyday and performed a variety of coordinating functions among its members. Immigrant faiths evolved national organizations for a number of other purposes. The Anti-Defamation League of B'nai B'rith was formed to redress recurrent anti-Semitism. American Muslims have formed a wide variety of organizations for similar purposes, including the Islamic Society of North America and the Council on American Muslim Relations. While combating prejudice, these national organizations also maintain an important educational role, correcting stereotypes and disseminating information about their faith.

Prema Kurien concludes that Hindu organizations were formed in the United States in a response to the development of Hindu nationalism (hindutva) in the West:

> The demolition of the Babri mosque on December 6, 1992, energized American Hindu nationalist groups and encouraged them to publicize their efforts to a greater extent. The VHPA [Vishwa Hindu Parishad of America] started to emphasize openly the need for Hindu unity and also became more militant and more overtly political.[80]

Kurien suggests that following the Ayodhya incident and the destruction of the Babri mosque, a number of Hindu national organizations were formed, including the Hindu Federation of America (1985) and the Federation of Hindu Associations.[81] Other organizations met a variety of purposes. The Hindu Students Council helped Hindus establish a religious presence on American campuses. The Dharma Association of North America assists disparate elements of the American Hindu community to connect. The Council of Hindu Temples of North America seeks to unite Hindu temples and to officially represent them. While the overall pattern is unique to the Hindu experience in the West, and consistent with the rise of hindutva in the diaspora, it is also consistent with American denominational tradition which, rooted in ethnic experiences of transplanted religions, seeks to establish a national identity in a religiously competitive society.

Fitting Pushtimarg into American Denominationalism

When Pushtimargiyas arrived in the United States in the 1980s and 1990s, they found a different religious environment from the one they had known in India. While, in the wake of the 1965 U.S. immigration reforms, Hinduism was rapidly becoming a visible part of the American religious landscape, the temples represented many traditions. There were no gaddis and an absence of Hindu sacred geography. Using the same entrepreneurial skills that had already helped expand Pushtimarg in India, Vaishnava leaders rapidly became aware that the process of building temples required participation in denominational life, as had other American Hindu temple traditions. The prototype for this pattern of adaptation began with the creation of the Vraj temple in Pennsylvania, which is described in historical detail in chapter 6. As the spiritual seat of Pushtimargiya tradition in the West, Vraj began to model ways in which denominational identity could be created.

The temple recruited a cadre of religious specialists including priests (mukhiyas) and musicians (kirtankars). Quickly adapting to the pervasive pattern of voluntary associations, Vraj began to depend on a large core of volunteers who would help cook for the deity, manufacture his clothes, and prepare the facilities for regular use. Volunteer training programs were initiated and students were particularly encouraged to give their time during open houses, festivals, and other large events. The Vraj campus also began to increase its short-term residential facilities for laity, as festivals became an increasingly important source of popular support.

Like most other religious institutions in the United States, Vraj began planning retreats as a way of reaching youth. In addition to a flourishing summer camp program, college age students attend semi-annual gatherings on the Vraj campus. At a winter retreat in 2013, 40 young adults gathered over a long weekend.[82] The majority of participants had experienced the summer camps and many had also served as counselors. Conversations during the weekend included discussions about the preservation of the Hindu heritage, differences in cultural values, and assimilation.

Religious retreats marked a departure from Hinduism in India. While the larger havelis may administer social welfare programs and develop educational resources, there is little emphasis on acculturating youth. In the United States, where many religions have experienced the loss of young adults, retreats have become a routine way of constructing bonds with religious institutions and instilling religious values.

The expansion of the retreats in the United States as a way of connecting to the tradition is parallel to the growth of tourism in India as a component of pilgrimage. Both experiences are dependent on cultural perceptions about the nature of religion. At Vraj, students who have participated in retreats have become an important part of festivals and retreats. They assist with parking and crowd control, routing devotees through the darshan, which becomes congested. This has become particularly important as Vraj has begun to attract larger crowds on weekends. On New Year's Day 2013, 300 participants attended the noon Raj Bhog. Even larger crowds have become the norm during the summer. Every Saturday in June, July, and August the temple draws 700 persons, and on Sundays it frequently attracts between 1,500 and 1,700 persons.[83] This increase has also encouraged the temple to expand its residential facilities. One of the original houses on the campus was razed in 2012 and is being replaced with a new structure that will include luxurious accommodations. Plans are also underway for renovating other buildings.

In addition to increasing its reliance on volunteers, Vraj has also developed instructional programs that parallel American religious education. In 2012, leaders launched the Pushti Education Institute, which is developing a series of mobile classes.[84] Developing the program in northeastern New Jersey near large concentrations of Pushtimargiyas, the program has arranged classes built around fixed syllabi and examinations in both English and Gujarati for different age groups.

Much like other temples, churches, and synagogues, Vraj has also come to rely on local initiative. Volunteers frequently share their expertise in helping the temple to maintain up-to-date services. Professionals in the Pushtimargiya community have given their services to the temple. For instance, the community devised an innovative plan for its own waste treatment facility, avoiding the difficulties of a traditional septic system. Volunteers have also assisted the temple in long range development to accommodate rapid growth.

New Patterns of Denominational Growth: Regional Centers Without Fixed Memberships

While havelis have adapted to patterns of American denominational life, unlike the majority of churches and many Hindu temples in the United States, they have not emphasized fixed memberships. There are few provisions in the tradition for this practice. Initiation practices follow the traditional Hindu model of diksha, which authorizes devotees to practice seva but is not linked to membership. Although Vraj uses the language of family membership as a means of identifying categories of financial support (ranging from $101,000 to $25,000 as a "Regent," $15,000 to $8,400 as a "Trustee," and $5,000 to $500 as a family member "Supporter"), participation in the ritual life of the community is not dependent on it. There are no congregational meetings, funds are not raised through member pledges, and communication is not limited to a defined constituency. Instead, havelis raise their support through the donations of Pushtimargiyas and income raised from manorathis who sponsor individual darshans.

However, within this traditional framework, some havelis have developed a regional presence, building on American models of retreat centers. The principal example of this integration into American denominational tradition is Vraj, which not only draws adherents from the northeastern United States but also has a national appeal. On a smaller scale, other havelis aspire to a regional presence, which is actualized in festivals that attract devotees from a wide area. Vallabhdham in Newington, Connecticut, draws Vaishnavas from Connecticut and Massachusetts and looks to New England for future growth. In Addison, Illinois, the Vaishnav Samaj of Midwest hopes to attract devotees from the greater Chicago metropolitan area. While these and other regional havelis are unable to offer overnight accommodations like Vraj, they are connected to a growing trend among transplanted Asian religions that has encouraged the development of regional retreat centers.

Since the early 1970s, Hindu, Buddhist, and Jain retreat centers have expanded the Hindu idea of ashram into comfortable settings where Americans can purchase a respite from the rigors of everyday life. Using this model, ashrams and meditation centers have been constructed throughout the country. In Honesdale, Pennsylvania, the Himalayan Institute was founded by Pandit Rajmani Tiginait in 1971. In Stockton, Massachusetts, the Kripalu Center has taught yoga since 1983. In Buckingham, Virginia, the Yogaville Ashram has developed a spiritual center based on the teachings of Swami Satchidananda. Near Dallas, Texas, Siddhayatan was constructed as a retreat center for Hindus and Jains and aspires to develop a North American Meditation Park. Many of these centers, like Yogaville and Kripalu, began as more traditional ashrams but expanded, borrowing from the tourist industry and marketing individualism.

Frequently situated in serene, wooded environments, Asian retreat centers offer a variety of choices designed to appeal to a wide swath of Americans. Some offer dormitory-style living or private rooms. Vegetarian meals are common, as are ample settings where adherents can escape the pressures of American life in nature trails with serene vistas. In the larger centers, emphasis is on healing and reintegration. Kripalu offers programs in detoxification, weight loss, post-cancer health, stress reduction, nutrition, and women's issues.[85] In Colorado, the Shambala Mountain Center provides mindfulness training, grief healing, and programs that incorporate Taoist teachings about health.[86] As some centers have expanded, borrowing extensively from a wide range of traditions, others have retained close ties with the gurus who initiated them. At the Arsha Vidya Gurukulam in Saylorsburg, Pennsylvania, the founding guru, Swami Dayananda, continues to maintain an active presence.[87]

While religious centers such as Kripalu, Arsha Vidya, Yogaville, and the Himalayan Institute are available to Americans from diverse ethnic and religious backgrounds, some centers define their presence primarily through specific communities. Vraj has developed its presence in Pennsylvania using this model, which principally relies on the Gujarati community for support. This is also the case with Siddhachalam (a Jain retreat center in northwestern New Jersey) and the Chaung Yen Monastery (a Chinese, Pure Land Buddhist facility in Carmel, New York). These centers exhibit a number of common characteristics. In each case their clientele is an ethnic, largely immigrant population including many first generation émigrés. Like Vraj, each site attracts a diverse body of devotees rather than a defined membership. Each institution is highly networked, reaching large populations of devotees over a wide geographical area. The three centers are all places of pilgrimage. Each institution is also residential and able to accommodate large numbers of devotees in facilities designed for retreats. Finally, each institution reaches a multi-generational community and develops a variety of programs on different levels to reach different generations.

SIDDHACHALAM

On a sprawling wooded compound near Blairstown, New Jersey, the Jain community has created a tirtha or pilgrimage site.[88] Identified as Siddhachalam ("an abode of liberated souls"), the site was founded in 1983 by Sushil Kumar, a Jain monk from the *Svetambara* Jain tradition. Kumar conceived the project as a place where devotees could practice Jain teachings and seek enlightenment. The campus contains a temple, dining hall, and cottages for pilgrims and is a thriving religious center.

Like Vraj, Siddhachalam is not built on a model of membership. There is no congregation of contributing members. Instead, the site offers much more. Devotees may worship in a fully equipped Jain temple where images of the *tirthankars* (beings who have escaped the suffering associated with rebirth) are worshipped in marble images. They may participate in an extensive nature walk, punctuated with rest stops where pilgrims can reflect and where they may encounter visiting monks. Many also attend conferences and participate in discussions of Jain principles. Devotees can join others in yoga and meditation camps, or use the facility for a more solitary experience. They may spend time in a library developed on the site, or traverse a microcosm of Shikharji—a miniaturized replica of a revered pilgrimage site in Jharkhand, India.[89]

In these aspects Siddhachalam is much like other retreat centers in the United States. The property includes a campus of buildings, with an ambiance that often accompanies retreats. Wooded areas and ponds are an important part of the facility. However, in envisioning Siddhachalam, American Jain developers have borrowed from the imagery of theme parks, which have become centers of secular pilgrimage. At the core of the comparison are nuances of transcendence and the attraction of places where the secular world can be abandoned and the ego jettisoned.

Alexander Moore argues that visitors to theme parks (secular centers of pilgrimage), like Walt Disney World, seek an overriding experience that he characterizes as play:

> The argument is *not* that the behavior within Walt Disney World is therefore religious or necessarily even explicitly ritual. Play and ritual together comprise a metaprocess ... in our post-modern world play seems to be gaining importance both at the expense of organized religion and obligatory rituals. That is, rites of passage and rites of intensification in the contemporary world are becoming voluntary rather than obligatory; religion definitely so.[90]

From this perspective, play is transformative and is deeply intertwined with ritual. For devotees at Shikharji, who seek to escape the rigors of mainstream American society, the two perspectives are also connected. In theme parks, visitors experience rituals connected with the American vacation, which is understood as a time of renewal and re-creation. In sites like Siddhachalam, pilgrims also enter a ritualized sacred space that also presents opportunities for renewal.

The comparison also applies to Vraj, where the metaphor of play is understood as lila. In daily darshans and during festivals Pushtimargiyas hope to catch glimpses of the lila of Krishna. The ambience of the environment is centered on this experience. Devotees may look for Krishna inside a circle of dancers performing a bhajan. Or, they may use binoculars to see the child deity play with his toys.

THE CHAUNG YEN MONASTERY

Situated in New York State not far from West Point, the Chaung Yen Monastery was established by the Buddhist Association of the United States.[91] Dedicated in May 1985, the facility was made possible by the donations from an industrialist in New York's China Town, C.T. Shen. Chaung Yen is a Pure Land monastery in the Chinese Mahayana form of Buddhism. The Chaung Yen Monastery is constructed in a secluded, wooded environment away from major population centers but easily reached through the interstate highway system. Constructed as a campus, it offers devotees a wide range of experiences.

Like Vraj and Siddhachalam, the Chaung Yen Monastery has become a place of pilgrimage. The center incorporates traditional symbols of the journey. On the long walkway to the Buddha Hall visitors pass a series of statues of Buddhist guardians (*lohans*). Once in the temple, they may circumambulate the central 37-foot-tall Buddha, passing reliefs of future Buddhas (*bodhisattvas*), paintings of saints (*arhants*), and sculpted figures of 10,000 Buddhas. Pilgrims can stay in Tai-Hsu Hall, near the Seven Jewels Lake, a serene wooded pond, fully stocked with Japanese Koi. Wildlife roam confidently through the grounds, aware that they will not be harmed, creating a serene environment conducive for meditation and reflection.

Pilgrims can visit the monastery unannounced, hike through the wooded environment on their own, or (with advanced registration) participate in a program. They may meditate in the Kuan Yin Hall, where they can sit beneath an ancient figure of the bodhisattva Kwan Yin. For a nominal price they can participate in a noon meal on weekends without advance reservations. They may also visit the Woo-Ju Memorial Library, a state-of-the-art facility overlooking the Seven Jewels Lake. In addition, families may also come to the monastery for pilgrimages to venerate deceased ancestors. Rituals are frequently performed on two large memorial terraces where cremains have been interred.

The monastery offers a vibrant programmatic life that is integrated with the work of the Buddhist Association of the United States, headquartered in the Bronx. Devotees can participate in meditation retreats, attend lectures and workshops (led by monks from Europe, the United States, and Asia), join dharma discussions, and even participate with Buddhist groups teaching in prisons in the area. Or they may participate in a Saturday afternoon film series held at the library. In these offerings, the monastery retains an ethnic focus but has also expanded, reaching a variety of other groups, including monastics from other traditions. Bhikkhu Bodi is an example. Born in New York City and ordained in the Theravada Buddhist Tradition in Sri Lanka, he offers cutting-edge programs in English including a library talk (2012), "A Buddhist Perspective on Occupy Wall Street."[92]

With the exception of the Bodhi Friends club (which requires completion of an online application to join), the programs, activities, retreats, and study groups developed by the Chaung Yen Monastery are available to the public. Little if any mention is made of membership or membership requirements. There is no injunction that participants be Buddhist—only interest is required. Although the monastery does not proselytize, free Buddhist literature (in English or Chinese) is provided to everyone, including texts written by Buddhist scholars. This program is made available through the BAUS book fund, which obtains texts from Taiwan for distribution in the United States in a fascinating reversal of American missionary practices.

Much like Siddhachalam and Vraj, the Chaung Yen Monastery depends on a diverse cadre of volunteers. The Buddhist Association looks for volunteers from a variety of professions who help prepare classes, work as computer consultants, and assist in maintaining the campus. Volunteers also work in the library and the monastery's kitchens. Others do flower arranging and provide transportation.

Some Conclusions

This chapter has demonstrated how Pushtimarg has adapted to the American religious landscape, sharing some of its characteristics. As one of the latest additions to the evolution of American Hinduism, it has extended the work of its predecessors in a parallel form of development. In the nineteenth century, Orientalist visions of Hinduism created a simplified, generic, but transportable faith that gathered increasing attention in the United States. This perception continued to be given voice through the mid-twentieth century, touting a vision of Hinduism that minimized the trappings of culture. In the early

Vedanta centers of the twentieth century and in the appeal of gurus to the "flower children" of the 1960s, it became a missionary tradition in a reversal of the American Protestant missionary efforts of the nineteenth century.

In a complementary pattern of development, immigrants began to practice their traditions, emphasizing ethnicity and cultural variation. Following modification of immigration restrictions in 1965, South Indian temples, ashrams, and broadly based ecumenical temples became part of the religious landscape as sectarian bhakti movements began to move into the diaspora. As American Hinduism matured, each form of Hindu tradition complemented the others by allowing them "space" in which to develop.

Throughout this period of evolution, Hindus began to adapt American denominational practices by defining memberships, organizing volunteers, and often developing congregational expressions of religion. Like their Christian predecessors, they sought to protect and preserve ethnicity. Havelis have become microcosms of Gujarati culture, replicating patterns of language and diet, and establishing educational programs that help preserve culture for the education of children. For Pushtimargiyas, this concentration on ethnicity has been part of its rapid growth, fulfilling Andrew Greeley's suggestion that "American religion ... is successful because American religious denominations are ethnic groups."[93]

The dedication of the Vraj temple in 2002 expanded American denominational tradition by creating a regional presence that functions as a retreat and pilgrimage center without a fixed membership base. Situated in rural Pennsylvania and insulated from the wider fabric of religion in America, Vraj attracts thousands of supporters, as do its counterparts in the Jain and Buddhist traditions.[94] Havelis constructed throughout the United States incorporate some of these same elements but on a smaller scale. As the next chapter will demonstrate, organizers have successfully used their backgrounds in international business and global commerce to develop and sustain the beginning of a thriving temple tradition.

7

The Challenges of the Diaspora

Happily Śyām spoke, "In my arbor home in the dense forest we shall meet again."[1]—Surdas

This text has argued that understanding the social history of Pushtimarg in India is necessary in order to comprehend its presence in North America. Part One demonstrated this by showing how Vallabha developed a unique tradition, differentiating seva from puja and elevating swarups above murtis. The first chapter showed how Vitthalnath sustained the faith, enshrining swarups and borrowing Mughal images of opulence. Havelis garnered the aura of palaces, and darshans acquired the image of royal audiences. Chapter 2 examined Vallabha's use of swarups through another lens, utilizing material culture and textual studies as padas transformed language into sensual experience through synaesthesia.

Part Two demonstrated the relevance of the historical processes that enabled the sampradaya to sustain the symbols of wealth and power through patronage. Royal favor facilitated the continued enthronement of Krishna in regional seats (gaddis), expanding the sect geographically. Chapter 3 showed how this process began when the sampradaya received support from Akbar and Shah Jahan. Receiving madad-i-ma'ash grants, the sect extended grazing rights for its cattle, increasing its ability to find adherents. Chapter 4 explored the way that the sect continued to cultivate royal favor in Mewar when Aurangzeb's iconoclastic policies made further expansion in Braj difficult. Relocating in a tiny village near Udaipur, the sect established Nathdwara as a center of pilgrimage and religious commerce. Under the tutelage of Raj Singh, Pushtimarg became the personal religion of the maharanas of Mewar. As Nathdwara grew in the seventeenth and eighteenth centuries, Pushtimarg influenced royal courts in Kishangarh, Kota, and Bundi, further expanding

7. The Challenges of the Diaspora

the sect. As the sampradaya developed, the seven sons of Vitthalnath created a sacred geography, installing nidhi swarups in independent and autonomous gaddis frequently supported by patronage.

Part Three continued the exploration of Pushtimargiya history, interpreting its expansion into the diaspora in the twentieth century. When patronage was eliminated in 1947, the sect found new avenues of support abroad. Pushtimargiya emigration expanded in East Africa and Great Britain, where it had already established roots, and also moved to the United Arab Emirates, Australia, and North America. Following the 1965 immigration reforms in the United States, Pushtimargiyas became part of Gujarati communities in metropolitan areas. American devotees began to direct further growth. Entrepreneurial laity created havelis, employing the same symbols of enthronement and opulence used in India.

Chapter 5 showed how the Vallabhkul became globalized, as goswamis followed their devotees into the diaspora. Chapter 6 explored the way that Pushtimarg became part of evolving Hindu traditions in America. Devotees used their influence to authorize new havelis, securing mukhiyas and kirtankars, locating swarups, and helping to plan construction. As havelis looked to the Vallabhkul for authorization, there was no uniform model of affiliation. Some sought traditional alliances with the goswamis that their leaders had known in India. Others looked to a range of visiting members of the Vallabhkul to meet their needs.

This chapter suggests that movement into North America has also posed a number of challenges, including the conflict between intrinsic and extrinsic religion, difficulties in the transposition of sacred space, challenges of assimilation, and the problems of maintaining the balance between religious experience and culture. Because the sampradaya is still in a formative period in its global evolution, Pushtimarg may not assimilate in America in the same way as earlier immigrant religions.

American sociologists first looked at the processes of immigration and assimilation when Will Herberg theorized a "triple melting pot" in which first generation immigrants retained the linguistic and cultural traditions of their homeland.[2] Members of the second generation often lost these traits. Herberg speculated that the third generation found renewed interest in the religion of their grandparents in a search for identity. Writing in the 1960s, Milton Gordon discussed a wider view of assimilation.[3] He defined cultural assimilation as a process through which groups adapt to patterns of dress, language, and customs of a dominant culture. Structural assimilation followed, in which ethnic groups intermarried with persons from the societal mainstream. Structural assimilation was also dependent on the elimination of previous patterns of discrimination and the establishment of overall acceptance of the group. In a final stage, patterns of conflict between the minority and the mainstream were eliminated.

As part of the flow of Gujarati immigrants to America, Pushtimargiyas have become part of American culture but have resisted structural assimilation. They show few signs of reducing their ethnic identity, which is defined globally. A number of factors allow resistance to structural assimilation to continue. Expansive international networks create frequent interactions with India, facilitated by the social media. Pushtimargiyas are increasingly connected not only on FaceBook and Twitter but also through Web sites set up by devotees. Some offer a virtual experience of darshan, available anywhere in the world.

The continuing flow of Gujaratis into the United States supports global patterns of ethnic and religious identification. There is little reason to suspect that this will cease. While leaders who established the first wave of havelis in the United States in the 1980s and 1990s are aging, there is scant evidence that their vacancy will be filled by the second generation, which struggles with questions of religious identity. Rather, as the flow of immigrant Gujaratis continues and burgeoning populations of first generation Pushtimargiyas fill ethnic communities through the country, new leaders emerge. For both generations there are many challenges in the diaspora.

The Challenge of Intrinsic and Extrinsic Religion

A recorded conversation (May 2011) with goswami Vrajarajkumarji, a 24-year-old member of the Vallabhkul, defines Pushtimarg: "Essentially Pushti marg [sic] is the way of complete surrender. It is the offering of oneself to the Lord without wanting anything in return."[4] This understanding of complete submission to deity is not just doctrine but is reflected in praxis in the sampradaya. Visitors to havelis notice the manner in which devotees may prostrate themselves in front of the deity in an expression of submission called dandavat. With arms outstretched on the carpeted floor, face down, the prostration is a mark of complete surrender. This physical act is voluntary, not done in unison, and quickly becomes one of the distinguishing symbols of the faith. Dandavat is not defined by gender, but due to cultural values of modesty it is usually only performed in a haveli by men.

Conversations with devotees often produce references to the same theme. A frequent comment is that seva performed at home becomes surrender of everything to Krishna. In this context there is no distinction between possessions that belong to him and those that do not.[5] The house, personal belongings, and even the family all belong to Krishna. Surrender is complete, with nothing remaining.

Pushtimarg is an intrinsic religion—self-surrender is the lens through which the relationship between devotee and deity is understood. The three traditional duties of all Pushtimargiya devotees—raag, bhog, and shringar (music, food offerings, and adornments to the deity)—are all rooted in this understanding of religion and have little meaning apart from it.

The concept of extrinsic and intrinsic forms of religion was first articulated by Gordon Allport.[6] Drawing heavily on the seminal work of William James on the individual role of religious experience, Schleiermacher's understanding of the encounter with the sacred as a "feeling of absolute dependence," and Rudolph Otto's understanding of the numinous, Allport posited that encounters with the sacred were intrinsic, based on complete submission.[7] He differentiated intrinsic religion from extrinsic forms, which were tied to social gratification or reward and often linked to personal development and gain. In advancing these ideas Allport assumed that intrinsic and extrinsic patterns of religion could be expressed on a continuum and that the intrinsic pattern was more mature.[8]

Since the introduction of these concepts, psychologists of religion have debated the relationship between intrinsic and extrinsic religion. Some have argued that the earliest forms of American Protestantism, with its emphasis on belief and complete submission to God, were intrinsic. Others, such as Daniel Batson, have contended that Allport's distinction between intrinsic and extrinsic religion is incomplete, advancing another pattern of religious expression called quest.[9] Religion as quest

> examined the degree to which a person finds doubt an important characteristic of his or her religion. It also sought to gauge a person's willingness to embrace the full complexity of the existential questions of life. Persons with Quest-oriented religion are unwilling to accept the "pat answers" provided by established religion. Finally, religion-as-Quest looked at a person's readiness to review his or her own beliefs.[10]

While discussion continues about such alternative theories as quest, Allport's approach remains useful, particularly in understanding expressions of Hinduism that emphasize direct experience rather than belief. As it is an intrinsic form of religion, the challenge for Pushtimarg is the societal pressure that it faces in twenty-first century America, where religion is associated with extrinsic patterns of development and reward.

The American religious marketplace is the domain of extrinsic religion. Frequently rooted in self-help and developmental traditions, the marketplace offers stress reduction and even claims to cure some of the more complex illnesses of our day. The language of the marketplace is centered on the individual and caters to self-fulfillment, spiritual achievement, and the ability of the individual to switch religious affiliations. According to a Pew Foundation study:

> More than one-quarter of American adults (28 percent) have left the faith in which they were raised in favor of another religion—or no religion at all. If change in affiliation from one type of Protestantism to another is included, 44 percent of adults have either switched religious affiliation, moved from being unaffiliated with any religion to being affiliated with a particular faith, or dropped any connection to a specific religious tradition altogether.[11]

This tendency of Americans to move through the religious landscape, changing religious loyalties at will, affects traditional forms of Christianity as well as transplanted traditions. American forms of yoga have been particularly susceptible to the lure of extrinsic patterns of religion. Yoga has become the purview of the health club, where it is devoid of religious context.

Classical yoga is a diverse tapestry of practices. Raja yoga, the traditional eightfold path, was codified by Patanjali in the second century BCE. Rooted in the *Sankhya* school of Hindu philosophy, which posited the separation of human souls from their true divine nature, practitioners sought to re-awaken the self. The process was cumulative and required knowledge of Sanskrit and immersion in the Vedas. Moral purity was also required, as seen in the first two steps of the path—*yama* (non-violence and ethical behavior) and *niyama* (purification). Following these stages, the initiate masters posture (*asana*) and breath control (*pranayama*) and focuses the mind so that all extraneous thoughts are removed in the stages of *pratyahara* and *dharana*. Only then does real meditation (*dhyana*) begin, opening the possibility for release (*samadhi*), eliminating the process of birth and rebirth. The process can last a lifetime.

In the second half of the twentieth century, the classical expression of yoga became immersed in a series of American approaches that emphasized extrinsic goals including self-determinism, autonomy, and success. Shifting the perception away from traditional precepts of yoga, new movements gave priority to the individual, focusing on personal development. Yoga became associated with well-being and a healthy lifestyle, and was frequently associated with integrative medicine. Even the Mayo Clinic acknowledges these connections, suggesting that practitioners of yoga can reduce stress, increase fitness, manage chronic health conditions, and achieve weight loss.[12]

For Pushtimargiyas, who also may practice yoga in conjunction with seva, the marketplace of developmental religion presents conflicting values. They see a bewildering variety of new forms of yoga all based on personal gain. *Ashtanga Yoga* promises "improved circulation, a light and strong body, and a calm mind."[13] Power yoga and "hot yoga" (Bikram Yoga) offer faster results and greater efficiency. Still others, including the Himalayan Institute, Sri Sri Ravi Shankar's Art of Living, and Swami Kriyananda's Ananda yoga, cater to a highly extrinsic, developmental lifestyle. In its breadth and totality the yoga marketplace is highly entrepreneurial, competitive, and ordered to fit within a fast-paced postindustrial society valuing individual achievement, success, and well-being. This complete absorption of yoga in the American marketplace has spawned a backlash among Hindus in the United States, affirming its religious roots.[14]

While extrinsic religion is well suited to the marketplace, religions with a dominant intrinsic orientation such as Pushtimarg have difficulty adapting to it. Because their focus is surrender rather than personal gain, they can invite but are unable to promise reward. They have little to say to Americans who seek self-development and who see religion as connected to the wider paradigm of success.

This problem is of particular concern for second generation Pushtimargiyas. While many first generation devotees have successfully adapted to life in the United States, and have retained the intrinsic form of their faith, their children grow up in a cultural environment in which India is the distant homeland of their parents. The intrinsic form of religion that their parents practice does not fit within their lifestyles. Even among the most traditional families, the second generation never completely experiences the Indian religious milieu.

These difficult issues are compounded by the emphasis on individualism in the second half of the twentieth century. In *Habits of the Heart*, Robert Bellah describes the nature of the changes that have propelled individualism:

> Perhaps the crucial change in American life has been that we have moved from the local life of the nineteenth century—in which economic and social relationships were visible and, however imperfectly, morally interpreted as parts of a larger common life—to a society vastly more interrelated and integrated economically, technically, and functionally. Yet this is a society in which the individual can only rarely and with difficulty understand himself and his activities as interrelated in morally meaningful ways with those of other, different Americans.[15]

This profound change has created even more social distance between the individual and the community in a process that Martin Marty, reflecting on Bellah's ideas, called "cancerous," concluding, "Having left home and church, people ground the self in whatever suits them, and concentrate more on 'feeling good' than on 'being good.'"[16]

Both Bellah and Marty wrote before the dominance of the Internet age. There is little doubt that the social media has accelerated the dominance of liberal individualism in which the common good is subsumed by the increasing centrality of self-expression. Some scholars have argued that the rise of social media is directly related to a phenomenon called network individualism, in which the needs of the individual are served with little reference to the common good. The new technology serves the need of the individual and moves beyond connections to place or to community:

> Changes in the nature of computer-mediated communication both reflect and foster the development of networked individualism in networked societies. Internet and mobile phone connectivity is to persons and not to jacked-in telephones that ring in a fixed place for anyone in the room or house to pick up. The developing personalization, wireless portability, and ubiquitous connectivity of the Internet all facilitate networked individualism as the basis of community. Because connections are to people and not to places, the technology affords shifting of work and community ties from linking people-in-places to linking people at any place. Computer-supported communication is every*where,* but it is situated no*where.* It is I-alone that is reachable wherever I am: at a home, hotel, office, highway, or shopping center. The person has become the portal.[17]

While the dramatic increase in the influence of American individualism has had significant effects on all forms of religion, transplanted religious traditions such as Pushtimarg are especially vulnerable to these changes. For Pushtimargiyas the overwhelming center of the tradition is the home, where daily seva take place and where the intimate relationship with a swarup of the child Krishna is formed. Yet, for most Gujaratis in the United States, the home also emphasizes self-determinism, the paradigm of success, and the viability of the American Dream. Children are motivated to excel academically and to find lucrative and meaningful career paths. At the same time, in the home and haveli, devotees are urged to practice surrender. The array of competing values is confusing and contradictory.

Conversations with college age adults (second generation) in Pushtimargiya families in different parts of the United States confirm the influence of an extrinsic worldview in which religion serves the need of personal development. A college student of Pushtimargiya heritage talks about how he has moved through a number of religions but retains those parts that make personal sense to him. His pattern of religious switching conforms to that of his peers and to what the Pew Foundation saw as a central characteristic of American religion. As an American, this student has learned to look at religion as part of his development, taking what he prefers from one tradition and abandoning those parts that may not suit his individual needs. Another student discusses darshan but is unable to understand the rite in terms of self-surrender. Still other youth are attentive in discussions that take place in the haveli, but once away from home quickly turn to the prevailing cultural model of individual achievement and the drive for economic and social success.

While these patterns of American individualism are increasingly common and are a deeply seated concern for many havelis, some more traditional Pushtimargiya youth have demonstrated that they are able to retain the intrinsic religion of their parents and still strive for individual success. Young adults interviewed in the Shreenathji Haveli in Toronto expressed their desire to continue in the tradition and fully understood the obligations that seva required.[18] Their perceptions were strengthened by the strong social network in the haveli, frequent intergenerational family and neighborhood gatherings and discussions (*satsang*), and by the pervasive sense of Pushtimargiya identity that had been fostered among the youth.

The Challenge of Recreating Pushtimarg Sacred Geography in the West

In the haveli, the replication of Braj is a transportable form of sacred space. Because havelis can be constructed virtually anywhere, recreating the aura of Braj is not difficult. However, Pushtimarg also depends on a fixed sacred geography in gaddis and baithaks in India. For first generation devotees, who have left this part of Pushtimargiya sacred geography behind, the secular landscape of the United States poses a difficult transition.

In the United States there is no sacred geography. The process of spatial transposition is difficult since the devotee cannot move through a continuous interconnecting web of sacred space but only from one secular location to another. Even when places carry names associated with Christianity such as Bethlehem, Nazareth, and Emmaus in Pennsylvania, there is no wider sacred geography that connects them. In America's secular landscape there are few places associated with theophanies, no public consensus about land that is sacred, and few historical associations between landscape and religion.

This creates anomalies when a secular space in the United States is substituted for a sacred place in India. An example of this difficult process of replacement has been the substitution by Hindus in the New York metropolitan area of Jamaica Bay for the Ganges River. In India, the Ganges is considered holy and is used for a variety of purposes from morning ablutions and pujas to the scattering of ashes following death and cremation:

"We call it the Ganges," one pilgrim, Madan Padarat, said as he finished his prayers. "She takes away your sickness, your pain, your suffering." Another devotee commented with " ... arms thrust toward foggy Jamaica Bay," "I love the water, I revere the water, it is my mother."[19]

Such instances of substitution are not understood by the public and can cause difficulties for the Hindus who practice them. When devotees began to place funerary ashes in the bay they were accused of polluting the natural environment.

Transplanted religions can also manufacture sacred space in a process of reversal, in which holy places are first recreated and then sanctified. This is quite different from the way in which sacred sites are discovered in India, where there are intrinsic associations between land and the divine:

> Pilgrims may ask, "How did this place come to be sacred?" The stories to be told are, in many instances, part of the implicit cultural knowledge they bring with them. Perhaps the place descended from heaven to earth like the rivers, or it was retrieved from the sea by the gods, like the coastlands. Perhaps the divine erupted from the earth here, like the many *jyotirlingas* of Shiva. Or perhaps this divine image was once put down here and then clung spontaneously to the earth and could not be moved by human hands. Perhaps this place is part of the body of the divine Goddess, distributed throughout the land. Perhaps this hill is a piece of the Himalayas transported to Gujarat; this river is the Ganga gushing up from underground in Orissa; this temple is Kāshī Vishvanāth, re-created in the south. All these ways of speaking of divine presence begin to constitute a linked landscape, patterned with sacred places.[20]

In the United States, where these connections do not exist, devotees may create a scaled-down replica of sacred space. This process is illustrated by Siddhachalam in northwestern New Jersey (described in chapter 6).[21] At Siddhachalam, Jain leaders have created an extraordinary project within their 120-acre compound. They have made a miniaturized replica of Shikharji, a group of Jain *tonks*, or holy places, in Jharkhand, India, where liberated souls (*siddha*) have achieved salvation.[22]

Securing a cartographer in India, American Jains have ascertained the latitude, longitude, and elevation of each of the tonks in Shikharji. They plan to recreate the path between the tonks with as much precision as possible. Although this project is Jain, not Hindu, it reaffirms the common ideas that both religions have about sacred geography in India and illustrates the difficulties in trying to recreate these levels of meaning in America. Attempts to replicate sacred geography in microcosm in the United States incorporate American rather than Indian perceptions of sacred space. This is the case at Siddhachalam, where devotees stress exact proportions, scale, and distance in creating a precise replica of Shikharji.

Such levels of precision are easily distinguished from Indian sites such as Varanasi or the forests of Braj, which do not depend on a linear, measurable understanding of sacred space. On the contrary, the Indian sites are often fluid. The Ban Yatra pilgrimage at Braj is an exercise in walking in circles with no single point of origin and no final destination:

7. The Challenges of the Diaspora   175

The forest ... is not a center. It is unmarked territory. There are no office buildings or permanent homes there; rather, one passes through the forest, sneaks into the forest, frolics within the forest. The darkness and density of the trackless forest shields one from the judgmental gaze of society. Life in the forest is characterized by aimless wandering and spontaneous play.[23]

In India, pilgrims are urged to lose themselves within the sacred space they traverse. This loss of self may be connected to a wider value of aimlessness, which is connected to the Hindu understanding of non-attachment. Aimlessness does not mean lack of intention or purpose but instead a wandering exploration of the holy that is not defined by a goal as much as it is by the process.

For Pushtimargiyas in America, the aimless experience of sacred space is not possible. Not only is a wider Hindu sacred geography absent, but the nuances of gaddi and baithak that are so much a part of the Pushtimargiya

Fig. 16. Recreation of Govardhan mountain inside the Shreenathji Temple, Phoenix, Arizona.

sacred geography are missing. These interconnecting aspects of sacred geography can only be experienced through costly patterns of international travel to return to India.

Havelis in the United States have attempted to fill this void with miniaturized replicas of Mount Govardhan in Braj (fig. 16). The largest of these is at Vraj in Pennsylvania, where a replica of Mount Govardhan has been constructed in a wooded area behind the haveli (fig. 17). Unlike its counterpart in the homeland, the American sacred mountain can be circumambulated quickly and with little difficulty. While a path has been constructed to allow devotees to walk barefoot around the perimeter of the mountain, the more arduous expressions of devotion defined by repeated prostrations over the course of months are not encountered.

This suggests that for devotees there is a qualitative difference between the Indian and American experiences and that the substitution is not complete. When queried if the American re-creation of Mount Govardhan had the same religious value as Mount Govardhan in India, devotees responded that if that was the case there would be little need to return to India.[24] Others spoke of

Fig. 17. Replica of Mount Govardhan at Vraj.

the stones that form the replica as being unlike the dirt that forms Govardhan, which is more of a hill than a mountain.

While most devotees would understand the qualitative differences between the originals and the American replicas of parts of Govardhan in India, others express strong positive emotions about the re-creations. One woman was in tears when she found the American Mount Govardhan under construction, making the circumambulation temporarily impossible.[25] Most devotees agree that for persons who are unable to travel to India to experience Govardhan firsthand, the American counterpart is a valuable addition to the faith in diaspora.

The partial substitution by American Pushtimargiyas of manufactured sacred space for the fuller examples in India is also evident in temporary attempts to recreate baithaks. When land was originally purchased near Pottsville for the Vraj campus, one of the first exhibits that devotees encountered was a miniature replica of Vallabha's 84 baithaks. Similarly, at the dedication of the temple in 2002, representations of baithaks were recreated for the occasion.

While manufactured sacred space fulfills a need, it does not replace Pushtimargiya sacred geography in India. The erection of havelis in the United States is governed by expediency. Havelis are constructed near large populations of Gujaratis and are not developed around places that have become sacred through association with founders of the faith. The process of manufacturing sacred space is complex and dependent on factors such as the availability of property, financing, zoning, and the ability of planning committees to secure the cooperation of an appropriate gaddi in India. While devotees may spend their summers visiting one haveli after another, the route between them bears little similarity to the stories of Krishna or to the Pushtimargiya religious landscape in India. While seva in homes and havelis can recreate the experience of Braj and are eminently transportable, the larger Pushtimarg sacred geography is not. Pilgrimage in America is not the same experience as in India. Most devotees still look to India for this part of the tradition.

The Challenge of the Shift from a Patronage-Based Tradition to American Denominationalism

In America, havelis are part of a religious landscape in which denominational identity is primary. As a form of institutional religion, denominations are quite different from traditional religious systems. Denominations originated as ethnic institutions and voluntary associations and have maintained an important public presence. They are independent of the secular government and exist as non-profit, tax-exempt institutions. Unlike traditional patterns of patronage that have historically supported Hindu temples in India, denominations in the United States derive from voluntary contributions privately sought through donations and pledges.

American Pushtimargiya entrepreneurs have successfully used these characteristics of denominational life to their advantage. They have sought charitable donations, raised voluntary support, elected officers, and structured non-profit, tax-exempt institutions. In so doing they have also lost elements of traditional support. Like their Indian counterparts, American havelis use the manorath system, in which donors support the expenses of the darshans. But they are unable to employ the larger *birat* system, which is a traditional form of supply from villages. As an extension of the Hindu *jajmani* system of service relationships in which hereditary, caste-defined occupations provide services for households, the birat system uses these connections to satisfy the haveli's needs. The temple is treated like a household and supplied with what it needs through traditional relationships. This pattern of support is evident in Nathdwara:

> The shrine of Nathdwara was also a household and a wide variety of services were required to be performed ranging from rituals, ceremonies to others pertaining to the supply of commodities and the performance of other services.... At Nathdwara this system is being operated on a much wider scale because of the supplies required to be made to the temple, for daily consumption as well as on special occasions.... The management had, therefore, to fall back upon the traditional *birat*-system for the fulfillment of its daily requirements. Efforts were made to invite certain families of potters, carpenters, ganchhas and baris from the adjoining area or from distant places. In course of time, the number of such families swelled.[26]

To address the absence of traditional service systems, the Vraj haveli has devised substitutes. Soon after the establishment of regular darshans, the haveli developed relationships with local milk producers, purchasing large quantities of dairy products for the operation of the temple on a regular basis. Farmers were recruited to take care of the fields in exchange for the produce they raised. In creative adaptations of the principles of the birat system, Vraj hired a traditional tailor from India to make the deity's clothing.[27] Living on site in a bedroom equipped with a sewing machine, he replicated a traditional pattern of service. While removed from the caste and familial patterns that characterize birat, he transplanted the pattern of a traditionally defined occupation to the temple. Vraj also used his skills to prepare the settings for the darshans, creating accoutrements and props that few persons outside of the Pushtimargiya tradition would have the knowledge to make.

While havelis have been successful in navigating the financial demands of American denominationalism, they have also experienced the cultural and religious isolation that are part of the denominational model. American religion has frequently isolated minority traditions, often relocating them to the frontier. The westward movement of the Mormon faith in 1846 became a symbol of the estrangement and the non-acceptance that non–Christian religions faced in the heartland. Similarly, decades earlier, Roman Catholics were targets of nativist riots in Boston and Philadelphia. Roman Catholic bishops even urged their congregations to move to the frontier to ensure their safety.[28]

While these movements are part of an older national history, the vestiges of the repression of religious and cultural differences remain. In the twentieth century this pattern of estrangement re-emerged with the proliferation of stereotypes about cults. The experiences of the Branch Davidians, the Unification Church, the Hare Krishna tradition, Guru Rajneesh, and a wide variety of other non–Christian faiths all are examples of the tendency in American religion to continue to engender a fear of differences. Following the attacks on September 11, 2001, Muslim communities in the United States were targeted as potential terrorists and experienced similar patterns of estrangement and rejection. Attempts to construct mosques encountered prolonged difficulties with local zoning commissions. Muslim Americans were under continuing scrutiny.[29] Immigration law reflected, and continues to reflect, a religious and cultural aversion to communities outside the Judeo-Christian tradition.

Following the 1965 immigration reforms, Hinduism, Buddhism, Sikhism, Jainism, and Islam gradually emerged as American religions. But for many new arrivals, well aware of the earlier history of oppression, the fear of not being accepted led to isolation from the mainstream. A Hindu temple founded in Allentown in 1978 first constructed a building in 1985 that did not appear to be a temple, omitting any signage that would publically identify it as Hindu. Protracted negotiations with zoning commissions were necessary when extensions to the building were planned.[30] Similarly, in 1992 when the organizers of a Hindu Navaratri festival in Edison, New Jersey, planned the event in a large exposition hall, resistance from the local community led to denial of permission for the festival.[31]

Throughout the United States, other transplanted Asian religions have experienced similar difficulties. Well before September 11, 2001, many Islamic societies had difficulty obtaining local permission to construct mosques. Following the attacks, these difficulties intensified. Hindus, Buddhists, Sikhs, and Jains have built temples in almost every state; the new religious climate also presented recurring difficulties.

Pushtimargiyas have felt many of the same tensions when they have attempted to construct havelis. Aware of the potential for difficulty, some havelis have been proactive, developed significant local relationships in successful attempts to avoid problems. The Vraj temple offered the community a corner of its land to help redesign the road in front of its campus.[32] In Chicago, trustees cultivated positive relationships with local officials during the construction of their temple.[33] In Sugar Land, Texas, developers of the Texas Nathdwara secured good rapport with the community, inviting the political leadership to their dedication ceremonies.[34] Havelis have held open houses for the community to help reduce the suspicion that accompanies the emergence of any non–Christian religion.

Many havelis have replicated longstanding American traditions of community support, maintaining youth camps for their children and developing programs for seniors. Vraj maintains an active youth camp program each July, teaching the fundamentals of Hinduism and assisting Pushtimargiya children to understand the faith. The Texas Nathdwara in Houston offers a "Seniors Tea Party" on the first and third Fridays of the month, hoping to initiate conversations between older members of the first generation.[35] *Satsang,* a traditional means for reinforcing Pushtimarg culture,[36] takes the form of neighborhood gatherings common in the United States.

The Challenge of Assimilation, Marriage and the Role of the Extended Family

In India, marriages are traditionally arranged by families. They take into account practical considerations far beyond the personal preferences of the couple. In the diaspora, the network of contacts that introduce "suitable" candidates for marriages is affected by dispersal of the community. In order to help alleviate this, Gujaratis participate in vast networks. Matrimonial conventions each year draw thousands of participants. Members of the extended family also help their children find suitable marriage partners. Yet, although most Pushtimargiya families resist the structural assimilation of their children, the complex patterns of traditional marital relationships are under considerable stress.

Members of the ethnic community may be able to preserve caste (jati) relationships and patterns of purity and pollution. Hypergamy, in which women are permitted to marry above their status, may also continue.[37] But even if these traditions are successfully met, the role of the extended family in America is considerably weaker than in India. Separated from the villages in which their parents and grandparents had ties, families have difficulty maintaining these structures. While many South Asians opt to bring their parents here, the American emphasis on the nuclear family draws many second and third generation families away from economic ties with the extended family. The hard reality is that most second generation Pushtimargiyas eventually conform to the dominant pattern of life in America. Most can speak their parents' language, but few are able to write it. Even among those who grew up in a Gujarati-speaking home, the majority will not continue the language with their sons and daughters. In patterns of diet, second generation youth are like other ethnic groups in America who eat traditional food at home but who revel in fast food once outside.

However, in a recent trend, some second generation South Asians are moving to India looking for economic opportunities. A case in point is Samir Kapadia, who

> seemed to be on the rise in Washington, moving from an internship on Capitol Hill to jobs at a major foundation and a consulting firm. Yet his days, he felt, had become routine.
>
> By contrast, friends and relatives in India, his native country, all in their early-to-mid–20s, were telling him about their lives in that newly surging nation. One was creating an e-commerce business, another a public relations company, still others a magazine, a business incubator and a gossip and events Web site.
>
> "I'd sit there on Facebook and on the phone and hear about them starting all these companies and doing all these dynamic things" recalled Mr. Kapadia, 25, who was born in India but grew up in the United States. "And I started feeling that my 9-to-5 wasn't good enough anymore."
>
> Last year, he quit his job and moved to Mumbai.[38]

When young second generation adults like Samir move to India, they often find they are stereotyped as Americans. The way that they walk, speak, and present themselves reveals their cultural orientation. Looking for economic opportunities, they encounter the urban, fast-paced world that Samir Kapadia found so attractive. Yet, in time, they will also encounter the internalized dynamics of Indian culture in which they will be seen as outsiders even though their familial heritage may be Indian. Raised in the United States with American values, devoid of ritual purity, their participation in a culture defined by caste and village is difficult at best. One child in a Pushtimargiya family discovered this when his parents sent him to India to complete a year in school. His new classmates immediately picked him out as different, asking who he was and why he was there.

These experiences leave second generation Gujaratis in a netherworld, in between the culture of their parents and life in the United States. They often are not completely accepted in either environment. For Pushtimargiyas the problem is compounded by the complex religious world of their parents. Many second generation youth are unaware of the complex history of the faith. They have come to know goswamis as visiting dignitaries but rarely have the kind of deep and lasting experiences of them that their parents have had. Some prefer to interpret seva through analogy as a more generalized service relationship rather than as daily ritual.

These challenges suggest that there is a dual Pushtimargiya culture in the American diaspora. Havelis continue to be managed and staffed by a steady stream of first generation immigrants. Mukhiyas, cooks, tailors, and temple attendants who serve the deity are members of the first generation. Most have lived in Pushtimargiya culture in India and are familiar with the corpus of traditions that inform the faith. However, their sons and daughters are rapidly assimilating and do not have the same background or experience. While they attend youth camps in the summer, many fail to return to the haveli as adults. Some retain the broader identification of Hindu but for others, the complex patterns of Pushtimargiya tradition are lost. Most also experience the uncomfortable scrutiny of their non–South Asian peers, who may consider them to be Hindus. Yet, many are not sure exactly what this means and find themselves in the precarious position of being expected to speak on behalf of their perceived religion.

Pushtimargiya leaders in the United States work hard to address these concerns, developing programs for both sides of the faith. Festivals recreate the homeland, offering members of the first generation the same experiences they knew in India. They connect the second generation to the first, teaching patterns of cultural identification. Educational programs such as Tavasm*i* offer curricula for children. Temples schedule retreats for young adults. At Vraj, gatherings in June and January offer discussions of the difficult issues related to family and religion. These efforts nurture both parts of the community, linking them together wherever possible, but recognizing dual levels of cultural identity.

The Challenge of Maintaining the Balance Between Religious Experience and Culture

In many religions, religious experience and culture are symbiotic and exist in a relationship that creates perceptions about the nature of reality. On one hand, culture creates the conditions for the perception of religious experience. On the other, religious experience is often threatened by culture, which has the possibility of consuming it and making it so ordinary that the experience of transcendence is lost or devalued. This tension is well known and was described by ethicist and theologian H. Richard Niebuhr, who posited a series of conditions in which religion was linked with culture, pitted against it, or elevated beyond it.[39]

For Pushtimargiyas, this dynamic is complicated by the reality that for many devotees in India the faith is predominantly cultural. In many homes seva has been practiced for generations. The morning rituals and the occasional visit to the haveli are normative and the mystical orientation of the faith is lost beneath accumulated cultural traditions. While older members of the family emphasize religion, India's rapid secular growth creates disinterest among younger generations.

The delicate balance between experiences of transcendence and the dynamics of culture is especially important among immigrant religions. For many transplanted Hindus, the greatest fear is the loss of culture through the inevitable processes of assimilation and the wane of traditional patterns of language, dress, diet, and social relationships. In order to survive in the new location, devotees must adapt to a very different way of life that is secular and demanding. At the same time they must transmit the essential qualities of their culture to their children. For many, this creates a paradox. By attempting to prevent erosion of culture, immigrant groups may so overemphasize it that the transformative, mystical experiences inside their religion risk becoming mundane.

As with most Hindu temples, the pressures on havelis to recreate the essential elements of their culture are significant. Temples work hard to maintain the delicate balance between spirituality and culture, attempting to replicate the same conditions for darshan and seva that first generation devotees experienced in India. Temples maintain educational programs that teach elements of belief and introduce pan–Hindu practices of art, dance, social values, and language. While these efforts may succeed in providing second and third generations with measures of Pushtimargiya identity, they risk minimizing the more intimate levels of mystical experience.

In most havelis, devotees attempt to retain the essential elements of seva through the priest. The mukhiya is the voice of the tradition. He represents a standard of purity and knowledge that devotees hope will safeguard the darshan and preserve its essential mystical nature. For this reason, if a mukhiya is older, a haveli may also hire a younger apprentice. Or, as has been the case in Phoenix, the haveli may employ two young mukhiyas, ensuring the continuity of tradition. Yet even in these carefully constructed recreations of religious tradition, the drive to establish both a Hindu and a Pushtimargiya identity in the West risks creating an imbalance in which the essential mysticism of the darshan is not widely understood.

Maintaining Boundaries

For many transplanted religions, finding a unique American identity has been an important part of movement to the United States. From the experiences of mainstream Protestantism to the uniquely American structures of Orthodox, Conservative, and Reformed Judaism, the process of adapting to life in the United States has changed traditional patterns of religious identity. While Pushtimarg is influenced by the same forces of acculturation, its evolution in the United States is so recent that any discussion of a unique American identity is premature. In only 24 years it has established regional networks of devotees and the beginnings of an American denominational presence. This rapid growth is supported by extensive social networks and the traditional role of the extended family; these have become boundaries, insulating the faith from the wider society.

Kenneth Pargament's work on boundaries in religion has shown how they both protect and conserve tradition.[40] In some cases, such as that of the Amish, boundaries have become extreme, secluding religions from the normal course of life. However, for Pushtimargiyas, seclusion is antithetical to their success. The first generation depends on high levels of interaction with American society in small businesses, franchises, and a number of professions. The second generation emphasizes American values and participation in the mainstream.

Yet at the same time, families and social networks insulate the tradition, establishing formidable boundaries. Transplanted families are linked in the United States and abroad. Retaining Gujarati as a medium of communication, they conduct business, arrange marriages, and bring their distant cousins to the United States in a continuing process that is invisible to the outside world.

Other immigrant networks also succeed through well-insulated linguistic networks. Felix Sanchez de la Vega Guzman is an example.[41] Emigrating from Mexico to the United States 40 years ago, Guzman became a highly successful entrepreneur with little reliance on English:

"The entire market is Hispanic," Mr. Sanchez said of his business. "You don't need English." "A deal," he said, "is only a cheap long-distance phone call or a few key strokes on the computer away." "All in Spanish," he added.[42]

Guzman represents a small but evolving part of the American economic landscape that has been able to prosper without English. Within his Spanish-speaking network, business interests are engendered across borders, and families move across them freely.

As Pushtimargiyas participate in the American mainstream, so family networks insulate the culture and provide assistance in living beyond borders.

Vast international networks reach all the way to the village. Because of this, unlike older expressions of religion in America that have resisted globalization, Pushtimargiyas have thrived within it. While their overall numbers are still small, they have succeeded in less than a quarter century in rooting their faith in the United States and Canada.

Born of patterns of patronage that supported it for over 300 years, the Vallabha Sampradaya now looks to a wider, affluent, and far more global future. Adapting to the paradigm of the American Dream, its future is wedded to the continued flow of immigrants to the United States. Protecting haveli and home as expressions of Pushtimargiya culture, American devotees look to the continued globalization of the Vallabhkul and to the presence of ritual specialists (mukhiyas and kirtankars) imported from India. These essential services are augmented through the social media, as devotees develop extensive Web sites, use blogs, and even offer virtual darshans.

All of this is consistent with heritage. Since the discovery of the stone swarup of Sri Nathji on Mount Govardhan, the faith has been nurtured by a metaphor of movement. Leaving Braj, Krishna moved into the heartland of the independent Raput states. Swarups were transported to the distant reaches of Rajasthan and the Gujarat. Baithaks were developed throughout the subcontinent. Now, 500 years after his emergence in a mountain, Krishna has moved again, this time to America.

Glossary

The terms below are first listed as they are used in the text. Diacritical marks are inserted in parentheses and may include alternative spellings.

acharya (acārya): a Hindu teacher who also functions as a guru. The term acharya is also used to describe the great teachers of the Hindu tradition such as Shankara, often identified as Shankaracharya.

adhikari (adhikārī): a temple manager in India. The word adhikar implies a right or a privilege.

Akshar Purushottam (Akṣar Purushottam/Puruṣottam): a philosophy developed by the Bochasanwasi Shri Akshar Purushottam tradition (BAPS) in the Swaminarayan faith. BAPS recognizes the highest form of ultimate reality as parabhahman or Purushottam, transcending Brahman.

alaukika (alaukika): the sacred realm of Krishna's play (lila) which is distinguished from the mundane or laukika world. In Vallabha's philosophy the alaukika realm can only be perceived by a person who has been initiated into the tradition and whose inner divine nature has been awakened.

ana (ānā): an older form of Indian currency equivalent to ¹⁄₁₆ of a rupee.

anand (ānand): bliss, which in Vallabha's philosophy is associated with the alaukika realm of Krishna.

anjali (añjali): A common Hindu greeting made with both hands pressed together and held at the chest with a slight bow. The anjali is also understood as a reference to the experience of divinity inside both participants. The term is also used to refer to water sipped from cupped palms before worship.

annakut (ānnakūṭ): "mountain of food," an important fall festival in the life of the Vallabha Sampradaya that is often celebrated with Diwali (the Hindu New Year) in America. During Annakut large quantities of sweets are presented to Krishna.

ashram (Asram): a Hindu retreat center, often having an integral relationship with a spiritual teacher.

Astachap (Aṣṭachāp/Aṣṭachhāp): a group of eight poets in the Vallabha Sampradaya including Surdas, Krishnadas, Parmanandadas, Kumbhandas, Nanddas, Chaturbhujdas, Chhitsvami, and Govindsvami. Astachap poets were brought into the sect by Vallabha and by Vitthalnath to enrich the music (raga) connected with seva. The Astachap poetry was understood to enhance the darshan by describing the play (lila) of Krishna and by setting a mood (bhava). In turn, this was meant to allow a glimpse of the divine realm. Padas are sung in a range of traditional melodies in the style of North Indian music called Dhrupad Sangeet.

baithak (baiṭhak): seat. Traditionally, a place where Vallabha or his descendants recited the *Bhagavata Purana* (or other significant scripture) is called a baithak. There are 142 bhaitaks in the Pushtimargiya tradition, located throughout India which are centers of pilgrimage. 84 baithaks are linked to Vallabha, an additional 28 to Vitthalnath, and 30 more are associated with Vitthalnath's seven sons.

balak (bālak): a descendent of Vallabhacharya also referred to as a goswami. Balaks have an important role in Pushtimarg as gurus whose hereditary link to Vallabhacharya generates spiritual authority.

Balkrishna (Bālakṛṣṇa): an iconographic form of Krishna as a child in which he is shown crawling with a butter ball in his right hand. There is innocent mischievousness of a baby in this form of Krishna. This is the most frequently worshiped swarup in Pushtimargiya homes.

Bania (Baniā): a mercantile caste (jati) with significant percentages of Vaishnava adherents in Rajasthan, Maharashtra, and the Gujarat. Historically, Banias have been both Jain and Hindu. Many Banias are Pushtimargiya and have formed an important segment of the Vallabha Sampradaya.

bhajan (bhajan): a devotional song.

bhakti (bhakti): devotion or spiritual attachment. Bhakti is often associated with an intense outpouring of emotion. Bhakti also refers to an historical movement beginning with the Tamil Alvars in South India (6th to 9th century CE) and continuing in North India, where in the sixteenth and seventeenth centuries, it produced a variety of sectarian forms.

Bhatia (Bhāṭia): a mercantile caste (jati) in Rajasthan, the Gujarat, and other parts of India whose members have supported Pushtimarg.

bhava (bhāva): emotion, feeling, mood. Socially constructed emotion associated with bhakti and in Pushtimarg with the ability to sense the alaukika realm of Krishna.

bhet (bhēṭ): gift. All offerings to the haveli or to the deity are made as a bhet, or loving gift. This is in keeping with the theme of grace and love espoused by the sect.

bhog (bhog): food offerings made to a swarup. There are different bhogs associated with each of the six darshans of the liturgical day in which Krishna is given a snack.

birat (birat): a traditional system of support for Pushtimargiya temples in India relying on economic relationships between the haveli and villages. The haveli is treated as a household and supplied with the foodstuffs and large quantities of dairy products that are necessary for the daily cycle of darshans.

brahman (*brahman*): in Hindu philosophy. "The One," all encompassing reality of the universe. Advaitan monist philosophy postulates oneness of the soul (atman) with brahman.

Brahmin (*Brahmin*): one of the four levels or varnas in the Hindu caste system as defined in the Vedas. In practice, caste is far more complex and involves hundreds of endogamous groups or jatis, whose level of purity and pollution is defined by birth. Jatis involve common occupations, social networks, ritual practices, and patterns of diet and marriage. Each jati is also given a rank within the fourfold varna system of priests (Brahmins), soldiers (Kshatriyas), merchants (Vaishyas) and laborers (Shudras).

Brahmsambandh (*Brahmsambandh*): the central rite of initiation in the Vallabha Sampradaya. Brahmsambandh is administered by a goswami who is a descendant of Shri Vallabha and authorizes the supplicant to practice seva.

Braj (Braj): Vaishnavas believe that Braj is the region where Krishna lived and herded his cows during his sojourn with his foster family. Currently, a number of religious sites in and around Mathura define the area popularly known as "Braj," which has traditionally been understood to exist in Uttar Pradesh and part of Rajasthan.

Braj Bhasha (*Braj Bhāṣā*): a dialect of Hindi used by the people of Braj (Bhasha = language). Astachap poets wrote their hymns in this local dialect. Braj Bhasha is an important aspect of the sect which has used it in allegorical literature and poetry to point to the hidden realm of Krishna. Goswamis, their families, priests and temple servants speak in Braj Bhasha.

Chaitanya (Chaitanya): (1486–1534)—a Bengali Vaishnava saint and contemporary of Vallabha whose bhakti tradition, called Gaudiya, emphasized the mystical union of Radha and Krishna.

chandan (*chandan*): sandalwood. A religious or sectarian mark applied to a deity and/or to the worshipper in the form of powder or paste.

Chandra Sarovar (*Chandra Sarovar*): ("moon lake")—a small lake in Braj associated with Krishna and an important baithak for Pushtimargiya pilgrims.

Chappan Bhog (*Chappan Bhog*): an important Pushtimargiya festival in which 56 kinds of foods are offered to Krishna, including many varieties of sweets and other foods including rice, puri, and daal.

chit (*chit*): in Vallabha's philosophy of Shuddhadvaita, the self is comprised of sat (being), chit (consciousness), and anand (bliss).

dandavat (*daṇḍavat*): the full prostration of a devotee in front of a deity or guru.

dargah (*dargāh*): a tomb of a Sufi saint.

darshan (*darshan*): seeing god. In Pushtimarg, darshan refers to a daily sequence of six to eight periods in a haveli when a swarup of Krishna is unveiled.

dharana (*dhāraṇā*): to hold. The sixth stage of Patanjali's Raja Yoga in which concentration is maintained, free from all external influences.

Dhrupad Sangeet (*Dhrupad Saṅgīt*): "fixed words." It is the oldest form of classical style of Indian music, having its roots in the chants of Vedic hymns. It has a rich vocal quality that seems to reverberate through the body of the singer, resonating with the bhava described in the hymn that he or she is singing. Haveli singing is the last bastion of this ancient style of music where padas written by the astachap poets are still sung in Dhrupad style during the darshans.

diksha (*dīkṣā*): Initiation in the Hindu tradition.

farman (*farmān*): an Imperial order issued at the discretion of the Mughal Emperor. Farmans were frequently followed by parwanas, which summarized the specific land assignments that were part of the order.

gaddi (*gaddī*): one of the seats of the Vallabha Sampradaya in Rajasthan, Gujarat and Uttar Pradesh where a patrilineal descendent of Vitthalnath's seven sons (balaks) serves one of the nidhi swarups associated with the sect.

Gaudiya (*Gauḍīya*): followers of the Vaishnava bhakti sect of Chatanya (1486–1534).

Gopal (*Gopāl*): cow-herd, he who looks after cows, a synonym for Krishna.

goswami (*goswāmī*): patrilineal descendants of Vallabha Bhatt (1479–1532) who have formed a dynasty (Vallabhkul) of spiritual leaders. Members of the dynasty are the only individuals who can administer Brahmsambandh, initiating devotees into the practice of seva. Other Vaishnava sects including the Gaudiya tradition also use the same term.

Govardhan (Govardhan): a hill and a town in Braj located 22 kilometers from Mathura. In Pushtimargiya mythology, Govardhan is associated with Krishna who magically lifted the mountain up so that his devotees could escape the wrath of Indra. The central deity of the tradition, Shri Nathji, is a shortened form of Shri Govardhannathji connecting the divinity of the god with the mountain.

Gujarat (Gujarat): an Indian state in the western part of the country defined by patterns of language, diet, dress, and culture.

Gval (*Gvāl*): the third darshan of the liturgical ritual in the day in which Krishna is taken into the field to tend his cattle. The term is also used to mean cowherd.

haveli (*haveli*): a large mansion. The term haveli became popular in the Mughal period and was used to define a mansion or large abode. The Vallabha Sampradaya frequently uses the term to refer to the house in which a swarup resides, as its layout and architecture resembles a mansion rather than a traditional temple. Vallabhacharya temples are also properly referred to as Nandalay—the house of Nanda, Krishna's father.

hindola (*hiṇḍolā*): swing used during the month-long monsoon festival. Made of tropical wood, it is painted or encased in gold or silver gilt. The infant Krishna swings in the *hindola* during the afternoon or evening darshan.

jagir (*jāgīr*): land grants given to soldiers and court favorites by the emperors and kings in lieu of salary. Jagir holders kept the profits from the land and were allowed to collect taxes. In exchange, they were expected to provide military service in proportion to the size of their jagir.

Jain (Jain): uniquely atheistic religion emphasizing karma and non-violence. Religious tradition now primarily concentrated in the state of Gujarat. The Jain religion was formed in the sixth century BCE through the teachings of Mahavira. However, Jains recognize a far older series of teachers including Mahavira called tirthankaras or liberated souls. Jainism teaches absolute non-violence (ahimsa), which influenced both Mohandas Gandhi and Dr. Martin Luther King, Jr., who followed Gandhian teachings.

jati (*jāti*): endogamous groups that are part of the Hindu caste system. Jatis share a common level of purity and pollution and hold common occupations. Jatis are ranked in the Hindu varna system, although the rankings are not precise and can vary slightly from village to village.

Jizya (*Jizya*): per capita tax levied on non–Muslims to allow them to practice their ancestral faith.

kirtan (*kīrtan*): lyrical devotional hymns, employing poetry and sung in the form of classical ragas. In Pushtimargiya worship, kirtans often use padas written by the astachap poets. Kirtans are set to music that corresponds to the season and time of day.

kirtankar (*kīrtankār*): musicians who perform kirtans during darshans in Pushtimarg and other bhakti traditions. Pushtimarg kirtankars are trained in the North Indian style of music called Dhrupad Sangeet.

Kripalu (*kripālu*): a term implying a kind or graceful person. Kripalu is a yoga center in western Massachusetts that was formerly housed on the site where the Vraj temple has been erected in Schuylkill Haven, Pennsylvania.

laukika (*laukika*): the mundane realm of everyday life that is distinct from the alaukika realm of Krishna.

Lila (*Līlā*): divine play or sport associated with Krishna.

Lohana (*Lohānā*): a mercantile caste (jati) with significant number in the Gujarat. Many Lohanas follow Pushtimarg.

madad-i-ma'ash (*madad-i-ma'ash*): Mughal charitable grants often given to religious figures and comprised of four component parts: (1) a statement of the conditions of the grant and the land assignment made, (2) a direction to the officers of the empire to carry out the conditions of the grant, (3) an exhortation for loyalty and continued prayers for the duration of the empire, and (4) an implicit assumption contained in the language of the document that the recipient of the grant would live and work on the assigned land.

maharana (*mahārāṇā*): a great king. In the Mughal Empire, vassal rulers were hereditary regents of their ancestral lands. Under the British, they were termed princes and native chiefs. The pilgrimage center of Nathdwara is located in the state of Mewar, whose *maharana* provided military protection and financial support for the sect.

mandir (*mandir*): a Hindu temple.

Mangala (*Maṅgala*): auspicious. The first darshan of the liturgical day in which Krishna is awakened and given some light food. In havelis, Mangala may also include arati (the ceremonial waving of lighted wicks in front of the deity). However, in sevas done at home, arati is not employed.

manorath (*manorath*): a donation often to cover the expenses of a darshan or festival, made by a manorathi. The function of manorathis is one of the oldest means of supporting expenses in Pushtimargiya havelis.

Mantra (*mantra*): a sacred Hindu incantation with very specific meaning and dedicated to specific deity. Some mantras are generally known, while others are passed secretly during initiation ceremonies and are not publicly revealed.

marjadi (*marjādī*): ultra orthodox worshipers, a term used by Pushtimargiyas to describe devotees who strictly adhere to stringent guidelines in practicing seva, often for long periods of time and with extensive patterns of ritual behavior that ensure absolute purity.

maryada (*maryādā*): a term used by Vallabha to denote non–Pushtimargiyas. It is especially applied to adherents of the Advaita followers of Shankara. Vallabha distinguished this from pravahi individuals who have no understanding of salvation, and pushti, souls who innately perceive Krishna's alaukika realm.

muafi (*muāfi*): charitable grants issued in the Mughal Empire that were frequently gifts of land.

Mughal: Muslim emperors who governed India from the time of Babur (1483–1530) through the last Mughal, Bahadur Shah Zafar II, who was unseated following the Sepoy Mutiny of 1857 when Britain assumed the direct governance of India.

mukhiya (*mukhiyā*): main/head priest. Mukhiyas frequently come from the region of Sanchore in Rajasthan, where their role has been defined through the use of hereditary traditions. While there is no formal training for mukhiyas, they are expected to be thoroughly versed in all rules of seva.
Mukhiyas are expected to be artistic providing evocative darshans for the laity, fluent in Braj Basha, knowledgeable of the nuances of haveli rituals and the astachap literature as well as the musical forms of Dhrupad Sangeet that accompany worship. Mukhiyas live a life of absolute purity in which they must refrain from touching any source of contamination prior to conducting seva. However, mukhiyas are viewed as temple servants and not the heads of the haveli.

murti (*mūrti*): a Hindu image usually constructed of bronze, a combination of five metals called panchaloha (comprised of gold, silver, copper, iron, and lead), or stone.

nandalay (*nandālay*): the house of Nanda, Krishna's father. Many Pushtimargiyas insist that nandalay is the correct term for a Pushtimarg temple rather than haveli.

Nathdwara (Nāthdwārā): the seat of the Tilkayat or the most senior goswami of Pushtimarg. The Tilkayat cares for the swarup of Shri Nathji, discovered by Vallabhacharya on his third pilgrimage. Nathdwara is near the city of Udaipur in Rajasthan and is associated with pilgrimage.

Nidhi swarup (*Nidhi swarūp*): swarups worshiped by Shri Vallabha, his sons or grandsons. The *swarups* that were specifically entrusted to the seven sons of Vitthalnath are referred to as nidhi swarups. Currently nidhi swarups are distributed across the states of Gujarat, Rajasthan and Uttar Pradesh.

niyama (niyama): the second stage of Patanjali's system of Raja Yoga in which the devotee maintains absolute moral purity through rules that govern spiritual practice.

pada (pada): a poem describing the play (lila) of Krishna and often used as a song or part of liturgy. Padas were written by the astachap poets associated with the early history of the Vallabha Sampradaya.

palana (pālanā): a swing for the infant form of Krishna used in the third darshan of the day in havelis and in home sevas in a miniaturized form.

Parabrahman (Parabrahman): the highest level of Brahman in bhakti philosophy. Brahman is the sum total of all forms of reality and is without gender, form, or ontology. Brahman is a universal reality that underlies everything.

parwana (parwānā): A specific direction of a Mughal emperor, often incorporating the names and descriptions of land that is granted. Parwanas often followed the imperial order or farman.

pichhavai (pichhavai): a temple hanging used as a backdrop for darshan in a haveli.

pranayama (prāṇāyāma): breath control, which forms the fourth stage of Patanjali's Raja Yoga.

prasad (prasad): blessed or consecrated food that has been offered to a deity.

pratyahara(pratyāhāra): the fifth state of Patanjali's Raja Yoga, involving the withdrawal of senses from external reality and permitting absolute concentration devoid of any outside influence.

puja (pūjā): worship offered to a Hindu god in iconographic form. Hindu murti worship focuses on bathing, feeding, anointing, and entertaining a deity.

pusht (pushṭ/puṣṭ): In Vallabha's philosophy of Shuddhadvaita, a type of mature soul (jiva) that innately recognizes Krishna as the supreme form of Brahman.

Pushtimarg (Puṣṭimārg): the way of grace. Name given to the spiritual tradition taught by Vallabha, who emphasized that salvation was freely offered by Krishna and could not be "earned."

raga (rāga): "color"—a sequence of notes in classical Indian music. Ragas are composed of at least five notes and denote an emotion, which is often translated into a time of day.

Raj Bhog (Rāj Bhog): Regal lunch / banquet. A large meal offered to a deity during the fourth darshan of the day at noon. In turn, this consecrated food is distributed to the devotees.

Raja Yoga (Rāja Yoga): a form of yoga based on eight steps, codified by Patanjali in the second century BCE.

Rajput (Rājpūt): descendants of princes (sons of kings). Historically, Rajputs have been nobility who have controlled small Hindu states in what is now the Indian state of Rajasthan. Rajput nobility played an important role in the spread of the Vallabha Sampradaya through the patronage that they provided to Vallabha's patrilineal descendants, or goswamis.

ras lila (*rās līlā*): a form of religious drama popular among Vaishnava bhakti sects, depicting episodes from Krishna's life.

rupee (*rupee*): a unit of Indian currency.

sadhu (*sadhu*): a Hindu holy man. Sadhus are renunciants who abandon their worldly lives, focusing entirely on meditation.

samadhi (*samādhi*): the final stage of yoga, in which the soul is released from further rebirth and suffering.

sampradaya (*sampradāya*): a Hindu sect.

sanad (*sanad*): orders issued with the authority of the Mughal Empire but not necessarily by the Emperor himself. These grants gave the Vallabha Sampradaya tax-free use of land it had previously acquired, a share in local commerce, grazing rights for its cattle, and perhaps most important, the favor and patronage of the Mughal aristocracy.

sat (*sat*): being or existence. Truth. In Vallabha's philosophy of Shuddhadvaita, part of the self that also includes consciousness (chit) and bliss (anand).

satsang (*satsang*): literally, "In the company of the true ones." Religious conversations and discourses. Satsang has become an important means of developing Pushtimarg in the West and often takes place in devotees' homes and in havelis.

seva (*sevā*): the daily routine of worshipping Krishna in Pushtimarg. Seva is conceived of as a completely selfless act and incorporates liturgical patterns that in havelis are seen as darshans. In home seva, darshans are condensed into a period of worship done in the morning.

shaiva (*shaiva*): Hindus who worship the god Shiva or other deities associated with him.

shayan (*shayan*): to sleep. The seventh darshan of the liturgical day, in which Krishna is fed before sleeping.

Shikharji (*Shikharjī*): a hill in Jharkhand, India, that is one of the most sacred sites for Jains.

Shri Balakrishnaji (*Śrī Bālakṛṣṇajī*): a small metal image of Krishna crawling and holding butter. Shri Balakrishnaji is similar in appearance to Shri Navanitpriyaji.

Shri Dwarakanathji (*Śrī Dvārakānāthjī*): a black stone image of Vishnu as Krishna with four arms.

Shri Gokulanathji (*Śrī Gokulanāthjī*): a metal image of Krishna with four arms.

Shri Gokulachandramaji (*Śrī Gokulachandramājī*): a wood image showing Krishna with a flute.

Shri Gusaiji (*Śrī Gusāījī*): a term used with affection to describe Vallabha's second son, Vitthalnathji.

Shri Madanamohanji (Śrī Madanamohanjī): an image of Krishna standing with a flute.

Shri Mahaprabhuji (Śrī Mahāprabhujī): "great lord"—a term of endearment and honorific title used by *Pushtimargiya* devotees to describe Vallabha. Some other Vaishnava sects also employ the term. For example, the Gaudiya Vaishnavas refer to the founder of the tradition, Chaitanya, as Mahaprabhu.

Shri Mathureshji (Śrī Mathureshjī): a stone, four-armed image of Krishna crawling while holding a butter ball.

Shri Mukundrayji (Śrī Mukundrāyājī): an icon of Krishna as an infant.

Shri Nathji (Śrī Nāthjī): a shortened version of Shri Govardhannathji, the central manifestation of Krishna in Pushtimargiya tradition. The swarup of Shri Nathji is housed in Nathdwara, Rajasthan, where it has become an important place of pilgrimage. The image is considered self-manifested and naturally formed.

Shri Navanitpriyaji (Śrī Navanītpriyajī): a small metal image of Krishna crawling, holding a butter ball.

Shri Vitthalnathji (Śrī Viṭṭhalnāthjī): a form of the god Vithoba, which is a manifestation of Vishnu. Vallabha named his second son after this deity (see Amit Ambalal, *Krishna as Shrinathji: Rajasthani Paints Form Nathdvara* [Ahmedabad, India: Mapin, 1987], 55).

Shri Yamunaji (Śrī Yamunājī): a female deity associated with the Yamuna River. In Pushtimargiya theology, Shri Yamunaji facilitated Vallabha's encounter with Shri Nathji on Govardhan hill outside Mathura. Shri Yamunaji is perceived as the daughter of the sun and sister to Yama—the god of death. Shri Yamunaji strongly represents the feminine side of devotion in Pushtimarg.

shringar (shriṅgār): the second darshan of the liturgical day, in which Krishna is washed, anointed, dressed, ornamented and fed a light meal.

Shuddhadvaita (Shuddhādvaita): Vallabha's philosophical system of pure monism. Shuddhadvaita challenged the tenets of Shankara's system of Advaita, which posited a level of illusion called maya. Vallabha argued that maya cannot exist as a separate entity since there was only one true reality.

Shyam (Shyam): "the dark one"—a name for Krishna.

swarup (swarūp) ("his own form"): an image of Krishna in Pushtimargiya is thought to be the deity's own, pure form. There are nine nidhi swarups, which are cared for by patrilineal descendants of Vallabha, who are termed goswamis.

Tavasmi (Tavasmi): "beloved." A movement within American expressions of Pushtimarg directed at the second and third generations, providing educational support and curricula.

thakorji (thākorjī): a term of endearment used to describe swarups that are worshipped at home and the personal responsibility of devotees.

Tilkayat (Tilkāyat): the eldest goswami of the first house (gaddi) of the Vallabha Sampradaya in Nathdwara, who cares for the swarup of Shri Nathji.

tirthankara (*tīrthankar*): in Jainism, beings who achieve spiritual liberation and release from the karmic cycle of birth and rebirth.

Utsava (*Utsava*): a Hindu festival.

Utthapan (*Utthāpan*): the fifth darshan of the liturgical day, in which Krishna is awakened from the afternoon siesta and given a snack.

Vaishnava (*Vaiṣṇava*): Hindus who venerate Vishnu or one of his incarnations (avatars), and their consorts. Pushtimargiyas frequently use the term Vaishnava to identify their faith and understand Vallabha to be an incarnation of Krishna. There are a variety of sectarian forms of Vaishnavism including the Gaudiya Sampradaya in Bengal and the Shri Vaishnava tradition in Southern India.

Vallabha (Vallabha): (1470–1532 CE). The founder of Pushtimarg. Vallabha was both a devotee of Krishna and a philosopher. He is often referred to as Vallabhacharya—using the title acharya or great teacher. He is also called Shri Mahaprabhuji or great Lord, recognizing him as an incarnation of Krishna.

Vallabhkul (*Vallabhkul*): the dynasty of Vallabhacharya.

Varna (*Varṇa*): five hierarchical levels that are defined in the Rig Veda for the organization of society. Varna is often popularly used to describe caste, which is culturally defined through jatis or endogamous groups sharing a common occupation and a common level of purity and pollution.

Vedanta (*Vedānta*): the monistic school of Hindu philosophy developed through the teachings of Shankara in the eighth century CE.

Vitthalnath (Viṭṭhālnāth) (Shri Gusaiji): the son of Vallabha Bhatt who became leader of his sect in 1543. Vitthalnath is credited with codification of the system of darshans, instituting the geographical spread of the sect, and organizing the hereditary tradition of goswami.

Vraj (Vraj): the North American counterpart of the Indian Braj and the abode of Krishna as Shri Nathji in the West.

VYO: Vallabh Youth Organization. A movement started by goswami Shri Vrajrajkumarji to help youth in the diaspora and in India understand Pushtimarg. In the United States, Vallabh Youth Organizations have been started in a variety of locations and have often been instrumental in organizing worshipping communities and havelis.

Yama (Yama): the Hindu god of death.

yantra (*yantra*): a geometrical design that is used as a focal point during the process of meditation.

Zakat—obligatory religious tax upon Muslim citizens by the Islamic state.

Appendix

Adapted from Vraj, *Global Vaishnav Convention on the Occasion of Vraj 20th Anniversary, July 3–4–5, 2009* (Schuylkill Haven, Pennsylvania, 2009).

Name and Title of Goswami	Gaddi/Residence
Pradhan Pithadhish Tilkayat HDH Goswami 108 Shri Rakeshji Maharajshri	Nathdwara/Mumbai
Trutiya Pithadhish HDH Goswami 108 Shri Vrajeshkumarji Maharajshri	Kankroli/Vadodara
Vakpati Pithadhish HDH Goswami 108 Shri Mathureshwarji Maharajshri	Surat/Vadodara
HDH Goswami 108 Shri Indirabetiji Mahodaya	Surat/Vadodara
HDH Goswami 108 Vrajeshkumarji Maharajshri	Kadi/Ahmedabad
Trutiyapith Yuraj HDH Goswami 108 Shri Vagishkumarji Mahodayshri	Kankroli/Vadodara
Shashthapithadhish HDH Gowami 108 Shri Dwarkeshlalji Maharajshri	Vadodara
HDH Goswami 108 Shri Drumilkumarji Mahoday	Amreli/Kandivali
Champaranyapith Yuraj HDH Goswami 108 Shri Dwarkeshlalji Mahoday	Amreli/Kandivali
HDH Goswami 108 Shri Dwarkeshlalji Mahoday	Kadi/Ahmedabad

Chapter Notes

Preface

1. The image of Krishna as the "dark god" is deeply seated in Hindu mythology. The deity is often identified as "*shyam*" or "black," connoting a dark color (Edwin F. Bryant, *Krishna: A Sourcebook* [New York: Oxford University Press, 2007], 4).
2. Cultural India, "Dwarkadhish Temple Mathura," http://www.culturalindia.net/indian-temples/dwarkadheesh.html (accessed April 8, 2011).

Introduction

1. The term *Vaishnava* refers to Hindus who worship Vishnu or one of his incarnations (*avatars*), including Rama and Krishna. Hindu tradition includes numerous Vaishnava sects, among them the Shri Vaishnava communities in South India as well as Pushtimargiya in the north. Pushtimargiya tradition frequently uses the term Vaishnava as a means of identification.
2. SALT, "Demographic Information," http://www.saalt.org/pages/About-the-South-Asian-Community.html (accessed January 1, 2012).
3. Gijsbert Oonk concludes, "The diaspora as a *type of consciousness* emphasizes the variety of experiences, a state of mind, and a sense of identity" (Gijsbert Oonk, ed., *Global Indian Diasporas: Exploring Trajectories of Migration and Theory* [Amsterdam: Amsterdam University Press, 2007], 18).
4. Pew Research Religion and Public Life Project, "Report 1: Religious Affiliation," http://pewresearch.org/pubs/743/united-states-religion (accessed January 1, 2012).

Chapter 1

1. Sūradāsa, Shyam Manohar Pandey, Norman H. Zide, and Anoop Chandola, *The Poems of Surdas: For Advanced Students of Hindi* (Chicago: University of Chicago, 1963), 56.
2. Karen Prentiss, *The Embodiment of Bhakti* (New York: Oxford University Press, 1999), 24.
3. Ibid.
4. Guy L. Beck, *Alternative Krishnas: Regional and Vernacular Variations on a Hindu Deity* (Albany: State University of New York Press, 2005), 70.
5. Ibid., 4.
6. Stephen Knapp, "Ancient Krsna Balaram Coins 200 BC," http://www.bibliotecapleyades.net/ciencia/esp_cienciaindia_3.htm (accessed January 1, 2012).
7. Wendy Doniger, *The Hindus: An Alternative History* (New York: Penguin, 2009), 24.
8. Prentiss, *Embodiment of Bhakti*, 26.
9. This text employs conventional references to time. In those instances when Pushtimargiya tradition uses the Hindu lunar calendar, the dates have been changed to correspond with Western usage.
10. Beatrice Pitney Lamb, *India: A World in Transition* (New York: Praeger, 1963), 30.
11. Ibid., 40.
12. John Keay, *India: A History* (New York: Atlantic Monthly, 2000), 275.
13. In Hindu philosophy, the non-dualistic tradition championed by the ninth century reformer Shankara is called Advaita.
14. James Tod, *Annals and Antiquities of Rajasthan, or The Central and Western Rajpoot States of India* (London: Smith, Elder and Co. [etc.], 1829), republished as *Annals*

Notes—Chapter 1

and Antiquities of Rajasthan or the Central and Western Rajpoot States of India, with a Preface by Douglas Sladen (New Delhi, India: KMN, 1971).

15. A helpful description of Vallabha's life can be found on the Web sites of the Kankroli and Nathdwara temples: Shuddhadvaita Trutiya Gruh of Pushtimarg (Kankroli), "Jagadguru Shree Mahaprabhu Shree Vallabhacharyaji," http://vallabhkankroli.org/achar yas_shree%20vallabhacharyaji.htm, and Shri Goverdhandharannavneetpriau Jayatah (Nathdwara), "Nikunj Nayak Shree Govardhannathji Shree Navneetpriyaji," http://www.na thdwara.in/.

16. Manilal Chhotalal Parekh, *Shri Vallabhacharya: Life, Teachings, and Movement; A Religion of Grace* (Rajkot, India: Shri Bhagavata Dharma Mission, 1969), 11.

17. The dates of Vallabha's first pilgrimage are taken from the Web site of the Kankroli temple: Shuddhadvaita Trutiya Gruh of Pshtimarg, "Jeevan Charitra (Life Sketch) of Shree Vallabhacharyaji," http://www.vallabh kankroli.org/shree%20vallabhacharyaji_ Managalacharan8.htm (accessed April 15, 2012).

18. Richard Barz suggests that there is some discrepancy about the role of Krishnadevaray, who did not realize the throne until 1509 CE. However, this discrepancy is not reported in the sectarian literature (R.K. Barz, Hariraya, and Gokulanātha, *The Bhakti Sect of Vallabhācārya* [Faridabad, India: Thomson, 1976], 44).

19. See R.G. Bhandarfkar, *Vaishnavism, Saivism and Minor Religious Systems* (Varanasi, India: Indological Book House, 1965), 77.

20. Barz, *Bhakti Sect*, 45.

21. The date of 1493 CE is taken from Shri Goverdhandharannavneetpriau Jayatah, "Vijayanagar," http://www.nathdwara.in/shree_ mahaprabhuji2.php. Sectarian sources differ on the sequence of events during Vallabha's pilgrimages. In order to provide consistency, references to the pilgrimage traditions of Vallabha have been taken from the narrative of the Nathdwara temple.

22. Ibid.

23. Ibid.

24. Parekh, *Shri Vallabhacharya*, 46. See also Jethalal Govardhandas Shah, *Shri Vallabhacharya: His Philosophy and Religion* (Nadiad, India: Pushtimargiya Pustakalaya, 1969), 47.

25. Shri Goverdhandharannavneetpriau Jayatah, "Vijayanagar," http://www.nathdwar a.in/shree_mahaprabhuji2.php (accessed April 15, 2012).

26. This final renunciation is described by the Kankroli temple authorities in "Jagadguru Shree Mahaprabhu Shree Vallabhacharyaji," Shuddhadvaita Trutiya Gruh of Pushtimarg, http://www.vallabhkankroli.org/acharyas_ shree%20vallabhacharyaji.htm: "Sri Vallabh had started his preparations for the passage to Goloka. He had decided to take the order of an ascetic to renounce the world he needed the permission of his wife. But his wife did not give the necessary permission to him. He is already known as a form of 'Agni' (fire). So by his supernatural power he had managed to ignite fire in the hut when he was inside. Seeing the hut burning his wife cried loudly: 'Run away! Run away!' Taking their granted [sic] as permission given for leaving the house, he emerged from it to accept 'Sanyasi.' In order to explain the form of renouncing the world under the system of devotion he had written an important book—titled 'Sanyasa Nirnaya.' He had been initiated into the order of a Sanyasi of Bhakti Marga on the 2nd day of dark half of the month of Hetha in the year 1530 A.D. or S.Y. 1578 at Hanuman Ghat in Kasi. He had assumed the name of 'Puranananda.' Then he gave up food, water and speech. He remained in a state of constant meditation on God for 15 days reciting the name of God day and night."

27. Beck, *Alternative Krishnas*, 70.

28. Parekh, *Shri Vallabhacharya*, 125.

29. Barz, *Bhakti Sect*, 71.

30. Bhagwat Shah, "Shodash Granth: Sixteen Treatises of Shri Vallabha," http:// pushti-marg.net/16-granth-intro.htm (accessed February 1, 2012); Shuddhadwait Shri Vallabhacharya Dwitiya Gruha Peeth, "Bethakji," http://www.pushtidwitiyapeeth. org/bethakji2.html (accessed February 1, 1012); Shuddhadvaita Trutiya Gruh of Pushtimarg, "Literary Works by Shree Mahaprabhuji," http://vallabhkankroli.org/granthas_ list%20of%20granthas.htm (accessed February 1, 2012).

31. Rupert Snell, *The Hindi Classical Tradition: A Braj Bhāṣā Reader* (London: University of London School of Oriental and African Studies, 1991), 37.

32. "Shri Gopinathji" in Shuddhadvaita Trutiya Gruh of Pushtimarg, http://www.val labhkankroli.org/acharyas_shree%20gop inathji.htm.

33. Peter Bennett, *The Path of Grace: So-*

cial Organisation and Temple Worship in a Vaishnava Sect (Delhi: Hindustan, 1993), 53.
34. Amit Ambalal, *Krishna as Shrinathji: Rajasthani Paintings from Nathdvara* (Ahmedabad, India: Mapin, 1987), 48. In keeping with Pushtimargiya convention the medial vowel in the names of the deities has been retained.
35. Bennett, *Path of Grace*, 94.
36. Bennett, *Path of Grace*, 93–94.
37. Ibid.
38. Paul M. Toomey, *Food from the Mouth of Krishna: Feasts and Festivities in a North Indian Pilgrimage Centre* (Delhi: Hindustan, 1994), 110.
39. Ibid., 57.
40. Barz, *Bhakti Sect*, 89–90.
41. Bennett, *Path of Grace*, 29.
42. See Kenneth E. Bryant, *Poems to the Child-God: Structures and Strategies in the Poetry of Surdas* (Berkeley: University of California Press, 1978), xi–xii.
43. John Stratton Hawley, *Three Bhakti Voices: Mirabai, Surdas, and Kabir in Their Time and Ours* (New Delhi, India: Oxford University Press, 2005), 28.
44. Bryant, *Poems to the Child-God*, 3.
45. Mircea Eliade and Willard R. Trask, *The Sacred and the Profane: The Nature of Religion* (New York: Harcourt, Brace, 1959).
46. Eliade and Trask suggest, "For religious man, space is not homogeneous; he experiences interruptions, breaks in it; some parts of space are qualitatively different from others. 'Draw not nigh hither,' says the Lord to Moses; 'put off thy shoes from off thy feet, for the place whereon thou standest is holy ground' (Exodus, 3, 5). There is, then, a sacred space, and hence a strong, significant space; there are other spaces that are not sacred and so are without structure or consistency, amorphous. Nor is this all. Religious man, this spatial nonhomogeneity finds expression in the experience of an opposition between space that is sacred—the only *real* and *real-ly* existing space—and all other space, the formless expanse surrounding it" (Eliade and Trask, *Sacred and Profane*, 20).
47. Diana L. Eck, *Banāras: City of Light* (New York: Knopf, 1982), 34.
48. Diana L. Eck, *India: A Sacred Geography* (New York: Harmony, 2012).
49. Ibid., 1.
50. Ibid., 283–284
51. David L. Haberman, *Journey Through the Twelve Forests: An Encounter with Krishna* (New York: Oxford University Press, 1994), 6.

52. Alan W. Entwistle, *Braj: Centre of Krishna Pilgrimage* (Groningen, Netherlands: E. Forsten, 1987), 9.
53. Edwin Bryant, "Krishna in the Tenth Book of the *Bhagavata Purana*," in Bryant, *Krishna: A Sourcebook* (New York: Oxford University Press, 2007), 189.
54. Bryant, *Poems to the Child-God*, 189–190.
55. Haberman, *Journey*.
56. Entwistle, *Braj*, 15.
57. Haberman, *Journey*, 71.
58. Eck, *Banāras*.
59. Haberman, *Journey*, 406.
60. Ibid., 409.
61. Entwistle, *Braj*, 354.
62. Ibid., 232.
63. Ibid., 245.
64. Ibid., 252.
65. Ibid., 261.
66. Ibid., 267.
67. Ibid., 268.
68. Pushtikul.com, "The Beithakji at HimGopal, near Mysore," http://www.pushtikul.com/topic.asp?TOPIC_ID=1484&FORUM_ID=2&CAT_ID=7&Forum_Title=%3Cb%3ENews+Column%3C%2Fb%3E&Topic_Title=The+Baithakji+at+HimGopal%2C+near+Mysore (accessed February 1, 2012).
69. Bennett, *Path of Grace*, 83.
70. Norbert Peabody, *Hindu Kingship and Polity in Precolonial India* (New York: Cambridge University Press), 74.
71. Bennett, *Path of Grace*, 52.
72. Barz, *Bhakti Sect*, 55.
73. Adapted from Prabhudayal Mital, *Brajsthān Vallbha Sampradāya kā Itihās* (Mathura, India: Sahitya Sanasthan, V.S. 2025), 64.
74. The Shikshapatra is attributed to the sixteenth century author Hariray. The Shikshapatra carries authority, drawing on Hariyay's status as a fourth generation descendant of Vallabhacharya and head of the second gaddi. Hariray is also associated with a large corpus of literature. See Paul Arney, "The *Bade Shikshapatra*: A Vallabhite Guide to the Worship of Krishna's Divine Images," in *Krishna: A Sourcebook*, ed. Edwin Bryant (New York: Oxford University Press, 2007), 511.
75. See Pravin Bhatia-Purecha, "How to Preform Nitya Seva of Thakorji," www.bhatiacommujnity.org (accessed February 1, 2013).
76. Although Pushtimarg recognizes a va-

riety of mantras, the Brahmsambandh is widely applied. Devotees repeat, "Shri Krishna Sharanam Mama" ("I surrender to Lord Krishna") as an expression of their complete submission.

77. Hasmukh Purushottam Shah, *Krishna Sewa Primer* (Greenwich, CT: Tavasmi, 2008).

78. Paul Arney, "The *Bade Shikshapatra*," in Bryant, *Krishna: A Sourcebook*, 526.

79. Toomey, *Food from the Mouth of Krishna*, 118; see also R.S. Khare, *Culture and Reality: Essays on the Hindu System of Managing Foods* (Simla: Indian Institute of Advanced Study, 1976).

80. Haberman, *Journey*, 169.

81. Barz, *Bhakti Sect*, 87–93.

82. In maan bhava, anger is portrayed when the lover's jealousy spills over and requires the guilty party to apologize profusely before being forgiven.

83. Toomey, *Food from the Mouth of Krishna*, 29.

84. Bennett, *Path of Grace*, 97.

85. Victor W. Turner, "Betwixt and Between: The Liminal Period in *Rites de Passage*," in *The Proceedings of the American Ethnological Society*, Symposium on New Approaches to the Study of Religion, ed. June Helm (Seattle: Proceedings of the American Ethnological Society, 1964), 4–20.

86. Ibid. See also Arnold van Gennep, *The Rites of Passage* (Chicago: University of Chicago Press, 1960).

87. Jonathan Z. Smith, "The Bare Facts of Ritual," in *Imagining Religion: From Babylon to Jonestown* (Chicago: University Chicago Press, 1982), 54.

88. Redheshyam Gor, interview with the author, Shrinathji Haveli, Toronto, Canada, May 2010.

89. Toomey, *Food from the Mouth of Krishna*, 53–54.

90. Ibid., 122.

91. Ibid., 122.

92. Personal observations, Vaishnav Samaj of Midwest, Addision, Illinois, July 2010.

93. This event was discussed by devotees during a visit to the Vaishanav Samaj of Midwest, July 2010.

94. Pushtimargiya is the plural form of the noun and is used throughout the text to refer to practitioners of the faith.

95. Kenneth I. Pargament, *The Psychology of Religion and Coping: Theory, Research, Practice* (New York: Guilford, 1997).

96. Ibid., 201.

97. The historical bhakti movement frequently eschewed caste and instead popularized a more open approach to the divine. However, this element of bhakti reform did not mean that devotional traditions were separated from mainstream Hindu culture. Rather, frequently drawing their followers from caste groups, they developed specific avenues of appeal. In the case of Pushtimarg, the tradition grew through direct appeal to several caste groups or jatis such as the banias and Bhatias.

Jatis are endogamous caste groups who observe a common level of ritualistic purity. Such patterns of caste-related behavior have often been misunderstood when Western observers equated caste solely with the fourfold scriptural division of priests, soldiers, traders and laborers that is found in the Vedas (Rig Veda 10:90). In reality, caste is far more complex and includes hundreds of endogamous groups whose identity is defined by a common livelihood and a shared pattern of purity and pollution. Jati members practice the same occupation and occupy the same strata in Indian society. In North India, they may also practice village exogamy—marrying within their jati but outside of their village.

David Mandelbaum ("Family, Jati, Village," in *Structure and Change in Indian Society*, ed. Milton B. Singer and Bernard S. Cohn [Chicago: Aldine, 1968], 35), suggests that the patterns of touch, purity, and pollution that are part of the *jati* system are learned in the family: "A child learns about pollution and purity in the round of household tasks, in the preparation of food, in the various degrees of purity of the separate precincts of the house, in the daily avoidances brought on by one's biological functions, and in the periodic avoidance brought on by his mother's menstrual cycle. The touch taboos observed between family members because of temporary pollution set the style for keeping permanent distance between members of different jatis. The household is the scene of stricter purity observance than is the village outside." This pattern of ritualistic purity is embedded in every facet of society. While to the casual observer the fast-paced Western lifestyle seems to have lost any connections with caste, the fact remains that India is a land of 70,000 villages where the majority of people, even outside the villages, retain the traditional culture.

98. Bennett, *Path of Grace*, 33; see also

James Tod, *History of the Sect of Maharajas or Vallabhacharyas in Western India* (London: Trubner, 1865), 44.
99. Ibid.
100. Bennett, *Path of Grace*, 53. Bennett concludes, "The dynasty is strictly exogamous, receiving wives and husbands from another lineage of the same Brahman caste (Tailanga) known as Bhatta-kul. Matrimonial relations between Vallabha-kul and Bhatta-kul originally commenced with Vitthalnathji's marriage to his second wife, Padmavati. The arrangement has a somewhat peculiar aspect in the context of Hindu marriage customs, for whereas Bhatta wives married to Vallabha Gosvamis live virilocally, Bhatta husbands married to daughters of the Vallabha Dynasty are expected to live uxorilocally."
101. Swami Agehananda Bharati, *The Ochre Robe* (London: George Allen and Unwin, 1961), 114.
102. Ibid., 124.
103. Ibid., 93
104. See Donald K. Swearer, *Becoming the Buddha: The Ritual of Image Consecration in Thailand* (Princeton, NJ: Princeton University Press, 2004).
105. Interviews were conducted with the family of Mahul Desai in Toronto.
106. Ibid.
107. Bennett, *Path of Grace*, 105.
108. Ibid., 106.
109. Ibid.
110. Kamlesh Shah., interview with the author, Vaishnav Samaj of Midwest, July 2010.
111. Gijsbert Oonk, ed., *Global Indian Diasporas: Exploring Trajectories of Migration and Theory* (Amsterdam: Amsterdam University Press, 2007), http://public.eblib.com/EBLPublic/PublicView.do?ptiID=419921.
112. Scott Levi, "Multanis and Shikapuris: Indian Diasporas in Historical Perspective," in Oonk, ed., *Global Indian Diasporas*, 31.
113. Ibid.
114. Ibid.
115. Ibid.
116. Scott Levi, "Multanis and Shikarpuris," in Oonk, ed., *Global Indian Diasporas*, 31.
117. Ibid., 33.
118. Hiral Dholakia Dave, "42% of U.S. Hotel Business Is Gujarati," *The Times of India* (U.S.), December 1, 2011, http://articles.timesofindia.indiatimes.com/2006-10-18/us/27810036_1_gujaratis-hotels-and-motels-hilton-and-starwood.
119. Redheshyam Gor, interview with the author, Shrinathji Haveli, Toronto, Canada, May and November 2010.

Chapter 2

1. Norman H. Zide, S.M. Pandey, and Anoop Chandola, *The Poems of Surdas: For Advanced Students of Hindi* (Chicago: University of Chicago, 1963), 71.
2. Diana L. Eck, *Darśan: Seeing the Divine Image in India* (New York: Columbia University Press, 1998).
3. Eck, *Darśan*, 9.
4. Richard H. Davis, *Lives of Indian Images* (Princeton, NJ: Princeton University Press, 1997), 35.
5. Ibid., 35–36.
6. Ibid., 36.
7. Some icons in the wider Hindu tradition are made for festival use. The god can be invited to reside in them temporarily, after which they may be stored away for the next time once the power of the deity has been dismissed. Still other festival icons are destroyed as part of the ritual and have a short life designed for a particular rite.
8. See Donald K. Swearer, *Becoming the Buddha: The Ritual of Image Consecration in Thailand* (Princeton, NJ: Princeton University Press, 2004).
9. June McDaniel, "Folk Vaishnavism and the Thakur Pancayat: Life and Status among Village Krishna Statues," in *Alternative Krishnas: Regional and Vernacular Variations on a Hindu Deity*, ed. Guy L. Beck (Albany: State University of New York Press, 2005), 33.
10. Ibid.
11. Davis, *Lives of Indian Images*, 248–252.
12. Diane Purkiss, *The English Civil War: Papists, Gentlewomen, Soldiers, and Witchfinders in the Birth of Modern Britain* (New York: Basic, 2006), 203.
13. See, for example, John Malcolm Russell, Judith McKenzie, and Stephanie Dalley, *From Nineveh to New York: The Strange Story of the Assyrian Reliefs in the Metropolitan Museum and the Hidden Masterpiece at Canford School* (New Haven, CT: Yale University Press in association with the Metropolitan Museum of Art, New York, 1997).
14. Davis, *Lives of Indian Images*, 178.
15. Susan M. Pearce, *Museums, Objects, and Collections: A Cultural Study* (Washing-

ton, DC: Smithsonian Institution Press, 1993).
16. Ibid., 27.
17. Ibid.
18. Michael Thompson, *Rubbish Theory: The Creation and Destruction of Value* (New York: Oxford University Press, 1979).
19. Ibid., 7.
20. Ibid.
21. Ibid.
22. Davis, *Lives of Indian Images*, 263.
23. Lynn Meskell, *Object Worlds in Ancient Egypt: Material Biographies Past and Present* (Oxford: Berg, 2004), 183.
24. Ibid., 184.
25. Davis, *Lives of Indian Images*, 177.
26. Ibid., 17.
27. Ibid., 222ff.
28. Ibid., 248.
29. Ibid., 249.
30. Ibid.
31. Ibid., 251.
32. Ibid., 256–259.
33. Ibid., 253.
34. Peter Bennett, *The Path of Grace: Social Organisation and Temple Worship in a Vaishnava Sect* (Delhi: Hindustan, 1993), 94.
35. Paul M. Toomey, *Food from the Mouth of Krishna: Feasts and Festivities in a North Indian Pilgrimage Centre* (Delhi: Hindustan, 1994), 77.
36. Ibid. In *The Path of Grace*, Bennett suggests that *murtis* can become elevated to the status of *swarups*. However, once that has been done, the *swarup* can never revert to the status of a *murti* (93).
37. John Marchese, *The Violin Maker: Finding a Centuries-Old Tradition in a Brooklyn Workshop* (New York: HarperCollins, 2007), 161–163.
38. Ibid., 131–132.
39. I am indebted to Bhagwat Shah for this observation.
40. R.K. Barz, Hariraya, and Gokulanātha, *The Bhakti Sect of Vallabhācārya* (Faridabad, India: Thomson, 1976), 70–71.
41. Ibid.
42. John Stratton Hawley, "Author and Authority in the Bhakti Poetry of North India," *Journal of Asian Studies* 74.2 (May 1988): 269.
43. Ibid.
44. Anoop Chandola, *Mystic and Medieval Love Poetry of Hindi* (New Delhi: Today and Tomorrow's, 1982), 4.
45. Ibid.
46. "The Rich Heritage of *Dhrupad Sangeet* in Pushtimarg," *Shree Vakpati Foundation*, Baroda, India, n.d., http://www.vallabhkankroli.org/Rich%20Heritage%20of%20 Dhrupad%20Sangeet%20in%20Pushtimarg.pdf (accessed January 1, 2012).
47. Author's translation of a pada composed in *Braj Bhasha* by Paramanandas (Goswami Shribrajbhushan Sharma, *Paramānand-Sāgar* [Mathura, India: Shridinadayalu Gupta, V.S. 2016, 1960 C.E.], 173).
48. Whitney A. Sanford, "Painting Words, Tasting Sound: Visions of Krishna in Paramānand's Sixteenth-Century Devotional Poetry," *Journal of the American Academy of Religion* 70.1 (March 2002): 56–57; see also Whitney A. Sanford, *Singing Krishna: Sound Becomes Sight in Paramānand's Poetry* (Albany: State University of New York Press, 2008).
49. Sanford, *Singing Krishna*, 28.
50. Owen Lynch, "Pilgrimage with Krishna, Sovereign of the Emotions," *Contributions to Indian Sociology* 22.2: 188–194, quoted in Sanford, "Painting Words," 57.
51. "The Rich Heritage of *Dhrupad Sangeet*."
52. Ibid.
53. Ibid.
54. Ritwik Sanyal and Richard Widdess, *Dhrupad: Tradition and Performance in Indian Music* (Aldershot, Hants, England: Ashgate, 2004).
55. Personal observations, Vaishnav Samaj of Midwest, Addison, Illinois, July 2010.
56. Sanford, *Singing Krishna*, 5.
57. Alan W. Entwistle, *Braj: Centre of Krishna Pilgrimage* (Groningen, Netherlands: E. Forsten, 1987).
58. Redheshyam Gor, interview with the author, Shrinathji Haveli, Toronto, Canada, May 2010.

Part Two

1. Karen Armstrong, *A Short History of Myth* (Edinburgh: Canongate, 2006), 7.
2. Joseph Campbell, *The Power of Myth* (New York: Anchor, 1991).
3. Armstrong, *Short History*, 10.
4. Peter Heehs, "Myth, History, and Theory," *History and Theory* 33.1 (Feb. 1994): 1.
5. Ibid., 1–19.
6. Richard Barz, "Khumbhandas: The Devotee as Salt of the Earth," in *Krishna: A Sourcebook*, ed. Edwin Bryant (New York: Oxford University Press, 2007), 490–491.

Chapter 3

7. Kanthmani Shastri, *Kānkrolī kā Itihās*, part two (Kankroli: Vidya Vibhag, V. 2116).
8. David L. Haberman, *Journey Through the Twelve Forests: An Encounter with Krishna* (New York: Oxford University Press, 1994), ix.

1. George Michell and Anila Verghese, *Vijayanagara: Splendour in Ruins* (New Delhi: Alkazi Collection of Photography, 2008), 30.
2. The tradition suggests this title was conferred on him by the Mughal emperor Akbar. However, there is little historical support for this assumption.
3. Darbars were open court receptions used by Mughal emperors for public audiences.
4. The establishment of the office of adhikara permitted the goswamis to spend the bulk of their time conducting darshans and performing functions associated with their increasingly elevated positions within the sect. They also continued to function as teachers and gurus, overseeing the swarups that were under their care.
5. David L. Haberman, *Journey Through the Twelve Forests: An Encounter with Krishna* (New York: Oxford University Press, 1994), 35.
6. The farmans, parwanas, and sanads discussed here appear in Hindi in Kanthmani Shastri, *Kānkrolī kā Itihās*, vol. 2 (Kankroli: Vidya Vibhag, V. 2116), 104–105. They are also discussed in James Tod's *Annals and Antiquities of Rajasthan* (all editions) and by a number of contemporary authors.
7. Like madad-i-ma'ash grants, these documents often have four component parts: (1) a statement of the conditions of the grant and the land assignment made; (2) a direction to the officers to carry out the conditions of the grant; (3) an exhortation for loyalty and continued prayers for the duration of the empire; and (4) an implicit assumption contained in the language of the document that the recipient of the grant would live and work on the assigned land. This relatively simple pattern differs from jagirs and other military grants that required service in the militia to compensate for the privileges and assignments of land granted.

However, Irfan Habib discusses the Vallabhacharya grants as a variant from the madad-i-ma'ash tradition. He observes, "There were certain grants, which were not in name madad-i-ma'ash but were in fact very similar.... We have a purely unconditional remission of revenue, which is illustrated by a series of sanads of the reigns of Akbar and Shah Jahan, issued to a family of Hindu divines in respect of two villages. The beneficiaries seem to have already held the land in their possession: they are in fact said to have purchased one of the villages from zamindars. The farmans exempted them from the revenue demand and all other cases, in language similar to that of the usual madad-i-ma'ash grants. A noteworthy difference, however, was the declaration that the grant was to be enjoyed not only by the first beneficiary but also by his descendents to come 'for generation to generation'" (Irfin Habib, *The Agrarian System of Mughal India [1556–1707]* [London: Asia Publishing, 1963], 397).

Habib's scholarship is thorough and well documented. Yet his conclusions in this instance are debatable. For example, six Vallabhacharya grants issued before 1633 were not declared to be transferrable and in all respects fit the madad-i-ma'ash category. Further, the author's criteria for defining madad-i-ma'ash as non-hereditary rest upon a 1690 edict ruling that the grants could be passed on from father to son. But there are very few madad-i-ma'ash grants extant that were issued before 1690. Hence, it is difficult to tell whether the edict simply legitimized previous practice or actively changed the structure of the madad-i-ma'ash system.

Hereafter, in consideration of this debate, the term madad-i-ma'ash (or in'am, which Habib equates with madad-i-ma'ash) is used to identify those Vallabhacharya documents that are similar to this general tradition, recognizing that they may or may not be an unidentified variant.

8. John F. Richards, *The Mughal Empire* (Cambridge: Cambridge University Press, 1993), 92.
9. Ibid., 93.
10. Author's translation. The grant is recorded in Hindi in Shastri, *Kānkrolī kā Itihāsa*, vol. 2, 104–105.
11. Ibid.
12. Ibid.
13. Ibid.
14. Sir Wolsley Haig, ed. and trans., *Muntakhabu-T-Tawarikh by 'Abdu-L-Qadir Ibn-I-Muluk Shah known as Al-Badaoni*, vol. III, revised Bramhadeva Prasad Ambeshthya (Patna, India: Patna Academic Asiatica, 1973), 128.

15. Ibid.
16. Ibid., 139.
17. Author's translation. Shastri, *Kānkrolī kā Itihāsa*, 104–105.
18. Ibid.
19. Ibid., 105–106.
20. National Archives of India, National Register of Private Records, *Descriptive Lists of Documents Available in Rajasthan (Based on Information Received in 1959–1960)*, Bikaner, 1972, no. 1, part 2, #792. The grant is also reprinted in all editions of James Tod's *Annals and Antiquities of Rajasthan, or The Central and Western Rajpoot States of India*. Many of the grants are also recorded in Hindi in Shastri, *Kānkrolī kā Itihās*.
21. National Archives of India, National Register of Private Records, no. 1, part 2, #794.
22. Alan W. Entwistle, *Braj: Centre of Krishna Pilgrimage* (Groningen, Netherlands: E. Forsten, 1987), 163–164.
23. See National Archives of India, National Register of Private Records, no. 1, part 2, #795, #796, and #797.
24. Ibid., #796.
25. Ibid., #797.
26. Entwistle, *Braj*, 164.
27. National Archives of India, National Register of Private Records, #801.
28. Ibid., #802.
29. D.L. Drake-Brockman, *Muttra [sic]: A Gazetteer Being Volume VII of the District Gazetteers of the United Provinces of Agra and Oudh* (Allahabad, India: Government Press, 1911), 192.
Much of Mahaban district still borders on the Jumna River; presumably in 1556 this was a large percentage of the total acreage as well. According to Drake-Brockman, in 1901 only 7.93 percent of the total district was uncultivable; the land is said to provide some of the best grazing in any of the areas adjacent to Mathura. By 1908, this highly desirable property encompassed 22 marketplaces. Of even greater significance is the fact that this pargana encompassed the village of Gokul, central to the mythology of Krishna and to the history of Pushtimarg in the region.
30. Entwistle, *Braj*, 177.
31. Norbert Peabody, *Hindu Kingship and Polity in Precolonial India* (New York: Cambridge University Press), 76; Entwistle, *Braj*, 183–184.
32. National Archives of India, National Register of Private Records, #799.
33. Peter Bennett, *The Path of Grace: Social Organisation and Temple Worship in a Vaishnava Sect* (Delhi: Hindustan, 1993), 180.
34. Emperor Shah Alam issued a farman in 1768—"From Emperor Shah Alam to Gosain Murlidhar. Regarding grant of Mauza Rasalpur (Gokul) by way of Inam-al-Timga to Murlidhar and his children; instructs all the officers to consider this as a strict order and a strong injunction and that they should not ask for a fresh deed every year" (National Archives of India, National Register of Private Records, #803).

Chapter 4

1. Kumbhandas, *Chaurasi Vaishnavan ki Varta*, quoted in Richard Barz, "Kumbhandas: The Devotee as Salt of the Earth," in *Krishna: A Sourcebook*, ed. Edwin Bryant (New York: Oxford University Press, 2007), 490–491.
2. Alan Entwistle summarizes the narrative as contained in the *Dwarkadhisji ki Prakatya*. See Alan W. Entwistle, *Braj: Centre of Krishna Pilgrimage* (Groningen, Netherlands: E. Forsten, 1987), 184. See also E. Allen Richardson, "Mughal and Rajput Patronage of the Bhakti Sect of the Maharajas, the Vallabha Sampradaya, 1640–1760" (Ph.D. Dissertation, University of Arizona, 1979), 59.
3. Entwistle, *Braj*, 59.
4. Ibid.
5. John Stratton Hawley, "Braj: Fishing in Sur's Ocean," in Bryant, *Krishna: A Sourcebook*, 232.
6. Diana L. Eck, *Banāras: City of Light* (New York: Knopf, 1982).
7. Cynthia Talbot, "The Mewar Court's Construction of History," in *Kingdom of the Sun: Indian Court and Village Art from the Princely State of Mewar*, ed. Joanna Gottfried Williams, Cynthia Talbot, and Kazuhiro Tsuruta (San Francisco: Asian Art Museum—Chong-Moon Lee Center for Asian Art and Culture, 2007), 20.
8. Ibid.
9. Ibid.
10. Ibid., 22.
11. John Stratton Hawley, *Three Bhakti Voices: Mirabai, Surdas, and Kabir in Their Time and Ours* (New Delhi, India: Oxford University Press, 2005), 89–98.
12. An interesting description of the uprising is contained in Laxman Burdak's "The Jat Uprising of 1669," http://www.jatland.com/home/The_Jat_Uprising_of_1669 (accessed March 1, 1012).

13. See also Robert C. Hallissey, *The Rajput Rebellion Against Aurangzeb: A Study of the Mughal Empire in Seventeenth-Century India* (Columbia: University of Missouri Press, 1977).
14. Richardson, "Mughal and Rajput Patronage," 61.
15. This reference is contained in a document of the period, the *Ranchhod* (Richardson, Mughal and Rajput Patronage," 63).
16. James Tod, *Annals and Antiquities of Rajasthan, or The Central and Western Rajpoot States of India* (London: Routledge and K. Paul), 1957), 296.
The balance of power that Mewar maintained with the Mughal Empire during this period make it unlikely, as Tryna Lyons suggests, that Raj Singh used this opportunity to "thumb his nose at the emperor"; see Tyrna Lyons, "Mewari Perspectives: Udaipur, Nathadwara, Basi," in Williams et al., *Kingdom of the Sun*, 36.
17. Talbot, "The Mewar Court's Construction," 24.
18. Richardson, "Mughal and Rajput Patronage," 78.
19. In eighteenth century Mewar, land tenure was of three principal types—jagir, bhum, and muafi. Jagir grants had a broad application and were usually given because of political favor. The holders of jagirs were most often Rajputs and were given land much in the same manner as the Mughal government assigned its jagirs. However, the jagir had become a way of ensuring the existence of a standing army and a class of fighting nobility who would defend their property in return for the favor of the emperor. Bhum grants in Mewar were also frequently given to Rajputs but carried a stipulation that the recipient pay a nominal rent and perform services as payment for the use of the property. The final category, muafi, was reserved for charitable organizations and was for the discretionary use of the recipient. It was this category of land that was repeatedly given to the Sampradya with the fewest restrictions on its use.
20. The unit of measurement called a gaj was equivalent to a yard. The size of the haveli given by the Maharana was an enormous structure—211 ft. by 17, 253 ft.
21. Kanthmani Shastri, *Kānkrolī kā Itihās*, 2 vols. (Kankroli: Vidya Vibhag, V. 2116).
22. Tod, *Annals and Antiquities of Rajasthan*, 577–578.
23. Ibid. Tod suggests that the order is undated. However, as it was issued by Maharana Bhim Singh, the grant clearly falls between 1778 and 1779. Bhim Singh was inaugurated in 1778 and died the following year.
24. Ibid.
25. Ibid.
26. See Rajendra Jindel, *Culture of a Sacred Town: A Sociological Study of Nathdwara* (Bombay: Popular Prakashan, 1976).
27. Richardson, "Mughal and Rajput Patronage," 78.
28. Tryna Lyons, *The Artists of Nathadwara: The Practice of Painting in Rajasthan* (Bloomington: Indiana University Press, 2004), 33.
29. The *hindola* (swing) is an important part of Pushtimargiya worship. The infant Krishna is placed on the swing during the darshan. In Pushtimargiya homes this practice continues with miniature hindolas.
30. Rajendra Jindel, *Culture of a Sacred Town*, 144.
31. Ibid.
32. Tod, *Annals and Antiquities of Rajasthan, or The Central and Western Rajput States of India* (London: Oxford University Press, 1920), 529.
33. Ibid., 555.
34. Raymond Brady Williams, *A New Face of Hinduism: The Swaminarayan Religion* (Cambridge: Cambridge University Press, 1984), 21.
35. Bhavanidas Narandas Motivala, *Karsondas Mulji: A Biographical Study* (Bombay: Karsondas Mulji Centenary Celebration Committee, 1935), 293.
36. Yadunathaji Vrajaratanaji, Karsondas Mulji, and N.R. Ranina, *Report of the Maharaj Libel Case and of the Bhattia Conspiracy Case, Connected with It* (Bombay, India: Union, 1882), http://galenet.galegroup.com/servlet/MMLT?af=RN&ae=Q4201586426&srchtp=a&ste=14&locID=ucblaw_boalt, 4 (accessed December 1, 2011).
37. Bhavanidas Narandas Motivala, *Karsondas Mulji: A Biographical Study*.
38. During this period Nathdwara was governed by a regency council; see Rajendra Jindel, *Culture of a Sacred Town*, 197–198.
39. Mysore Narasimhachar Srinivas, *Social Change in Modern India* (Berkeley: University of California Press, 1966).
40. Gov't of Rajasthan (India), *Report of the Nathdwara Inquiry Commission* (Jaipur: Government Central Press, 1959).
41. Ibid., 59.
42. *The Nathdwara Temple Rules 1973*

(Nathdwara: Govind Bhawan, Nathdwara Temple Board, 1973), 13, http://fx.sauder.ubc.ca/etc/USDpages.pdf (accessed March 1, 2012).
43. Ibid., 10ff.
44. For a discussion of the income of the temple also see Jindel, *Culture of A Sacred Town*, 147. See also Nathdwara Temple Board, "Nathdwara, Balance Sheet," http://www.nathdwaratemple.org/Management/Balance%20Sheet%202010-2011.pdf (accessed February 1, 2012).

Chapter 5

1. Sūradāsa, Shyam Manohar Pandey, Norman H. Zide, and Anoop Chandola, *The Poems of Surdas: For Advanced Students of Hindi* (Chicago: University of Chicago, 1963), 43.
2. The best source for a history of the role of goswamis in each of the gaddis is Kanthmani Shastri, *Kānkrolī kā Itihās*, 2 vols. (Kankroli: Vidha Vibhag, V. 2116).
3. Eric D. Beinhocker, Diana Farrell, and Adil S. Zainulbhai, "Tracking the Growth of India's Middle Class," *The McKinsey Quarterly* 3 (2007): 56.
4. Howard Spodek, *Ahmedabad: Shock City of Twentieth-Century India* (Bloomington: Indiana University Press, 2011), 94.
5. Ibid., 106.
6. Ibid., 118.
7. Ibid., 134–135.
8. Ibid.
9. K.J. Thankachan, "A Study on Demographic Trends in Gujarat" (Saurashtra University, Ph.D. Dissertation, 2007), 321, 325.
10. Ibid., 179.
11. Ibid.
12. Spodek, *Ahmedabad*, 184.
13. Ibid., 203.
14. Ibid., 229.
15. Ibid., 230.
16. Ibid., 231.
17. Ibid., 232.
18. Ibid., 169.
19. I am indebted to Amit Ambalal in Ahmedabad for his assistance in determining this information.
20. Ibid.
21. See "Shree Ji Holiday Resort," http://www.tripadvisor.in/Hotel_Review-g1162444-d1405427-Reviews-Shree_Ji_Holiday_Resort-Nathdwara_Rajasthan.html (accessed February 23, 2013).

22. See Alejandro Portes and Ruben G. Rumbaut, *Immigrant America: A Portrait*, 3rd ed. (Berkeley: University of California Press, 2006); see also Vivek Wadhwa, AnnaLee Saxenian, Ben Rissing, and Gary Gereffi, *America's New Immigrant Entrepreneurs* (Master of Engineering Management Program, Duke University; School of Information, UC Berkeley, 2007); Ivan Hubert Light and Parminder Bhachu, eds., *Immigration and Entrepreneurship: Culture, Capital, and Ethnic Networks* (Piscataway, NJ: Transaction, 2004); Hermann Achidi Ndofor, "Immigrant Entrepreneurs, the Ethnic Enclave Strategy, and Venture Performance," *Journal of Management* 37.3 (May 2011): 790–818. The role of immigrant entrepreneurs has also produced a popular literature: see Richard T. Herman and Robert L. Smith, *Immigrant, Inc.: Why Immigrant Entrepreneurs Are Driving the New Economy (and How They Will Save the American Worker)* (Hoboken, NJ: John Wiley and Sons, 2009).
23. See Robert D. Putnam, *Bowling Alone: The Collapse and Revival of American Community* (New York: Simon and Schuster, 2000).
24. See Arturs Kalnins and Wilbur Chung, "Social Capital, Geography, and Survival: Gujarati Immigrant Entrepreneurs in the U.S. Lodging Industry," *Management Science* 52.2 (Feb. 2006): 233–247.
25. Ibid.
26. Ibid.
27. See note #50 in chapter 1.
28. The fourfold Hindu varna system describes caste as the province of priests (Brahmins), soldiers (Kshatriyas), merchants (Vaishyas) and laborers (Shudras). This scriptural description of caste is often used to describe a social phenomenon that is far more complex and dependent on the role of jatis in a system of ritual purity and pollution.
29. Hotels Online, "Shamin Hotels Opens Its 4th and 5th Hotels at the Richmond International Airport—130 Room Hilton Garden Inn and a 143 Room Holiday Inn," http://www.hotel-online.com/News/PR2008_4th/Nov08_Shamin.html (accessed June 1, 2012).
30. Ancestry.com, "Schuylkill County Genealogy Ties—Village Names and Townships," http://www.rootsweb.ancestry.com/~paschuy2/villages.html (accessed January 6, 2011).
31. Personal observations, Vraj, Schuylkill Haven, Pennsylvania, May–June 2002.
32. F.S. Growse, *Mathura: A District*

Memoir (New Delhi: Asian Educational Services, 1979), 83.
33. The convention was described on the Vraj Web site: www.vraj.org.
34. Suresh Patel, interview with the author, Vallabh Priti Seva Samaj, Houston, Texas, 2005 and 2010.
35. Sureshbhai S. Patel, "The Inspiring Tale of Vallabh Priti Seva Samaj of Houston, Inc.," in *Pushti Ratna: A Jewel of Pushti Marg* (Houston, Texas: Vallab Priti Seva Samaj, 2010), 83.
36. Ibid.
37. Vallab Priti Seva Samaj, *Pushti Ratna*, 8.
38. Ibid.
39. Ibid., 87.
40. Ibid.
41. Ibid., 74.
42. VPSS, "Vallabh Priti Seva Samaj," http://www.vpsshaveli.org/ (accessed December 1, 2011).
43. Vallab Priti Seva Samaj, *Pushti Ratna*, 93.
44. Kamlesh Shah, interview with the author, Vaishnav Samaj of Midwest, Addison, Illinois, July 2010.
45. Ibid.
46. Ibid.
47. Dr. Hari Dave, interview with the author, Shreenathji Temple of Phoenix, Phoenix, Arizona, February 2012.
48. Hari Dave, "Vaishnav Samaj of Arizona—VSA," in *Panchamrut—Gloval Vaishnav Convention on the Occasion of Vraj 20th Anniversary*, July 3–5, 2009, ed. (Schuylkill Haven, PA: Vraj, 2009), 87–89.
49. Ibid., 87.
50. Ibid.
51. Peter Bennett, *The Path of Grace: Social Organisation and Temple Worship in a Vaishnava Sect* (Delhi: Hindustan, 1993), 32.
52. Gujarati migration patterns are centuries old but have been accelerated by natural disasters such as the famine in the early twentieth century; see Maritsa Poros, *Modern Migrations: Gujarati Indian Networks in New York and London* (Stanford: Stanford University Press, 2010), 1. In more recent periods, Gujarati Pushtimargiyas have migrated to parts of Africa (Kenya), the United Arab Eremites (Dubai), and Australia.
53. I am indebted to Bhagwat Shah for this observation.
54. Within the Vallabhkul, daughters of goswamis are identified as betiji until they marry.
55. These observations were made in havelis from 2008 to 2012, Shrinathji Haveli, Toronto, Canada, May 2010 and November 2010.
56. H.H. Pujya Goswami 108 Shri Vrajrajkumarji Mahodayshri, "O My Krishna," (Shri Goverdhannathji Haveli, Vadodara, India).
57. Ranjani Saigal, "In Conversation with Shri Vrajarajkumarji," Lokvani, May 10, 2011, http://www.lokvani.com/lokvani/article.php?article_id=7285 (accessed February 1, 2012).
58. Vallabh Youth Organization, http://www.vallabhyouth.org/index.php (accessed March 1, 2012).
59. Ibid.
60. Laura Legere, "Hindu Groups Plan New Spiritual and Cultural Center," *Times-Tribune* (Scranton, Pennsylvania), July 3, 2011.
61. Lokhvani, "In Conversation with Shri Vrajarajkumarji," http://paroolmodi67.blogspot.com/2011_07_01_archive.html (accessed February 1, 2012); Vallabh Youth Organization, http://www.vallabhyouth.org/index.php (accessed February 1, 2012).
62. Vrajrajkumarji Goswami, "Announcement of New Haveli in Boston, MA by VYO," http://www.facebook.com/note.php?note_id=171777549551715 (accessed March 1, 2012).
63. Shree Kalyan Pushti, "Biography—Jeevan Jharmar," http://www.shreekalyanpushti.org/hdhshashtpeet.html (accessed March 1, 2012).
64. James Clifford, "Diasporas," *Cultural Anthropology* 9.3: 311.
65. Mario Rutten and Pravin J. Patel, "Contested Family Relations and Government Policy: Linkages Between Patel Migrants in Britain and India," in *Global Indian Diasporas: Exploring Trajectories of Migration and Theory*, ed. Gijsbert Oonk (Amsterdam: Amsterdam University Press, 2007), 192. Other studies of South Asian diasporan traditions include Peter van der Veer, *Nation and Migration: The Politics of Space in the South Asian Diaspora* (Philadelphia: University of Philadelphia Press, 1995); Carla Petievich, *The Expanding Landscape: South Asians and the Diaspora* (New Delhi: Manohar, 1999); and Harold G. Coward, John R. Hinnells, and Raymond Brady Williams, *The South Asian Religious Diaspora in Britain, Canada, and the United States* (Albany, NY: State University of New York Press, 2000).
66. Personal observations made at the Shrinathji Haveli, Toronto, Canada, 2010.

67. I am grateful to Bhagwat Shah for this typology.
68. Suresh Patel, interview with the author, Texas Nathdwara, Houston, Texas, July 2010.
69. City of Toronto, "Toronto's Racial Diversity," Toronto, http://www.toronto.ca/toronto_facts/diversity.htm (accessed April 30, 2012).
70. Ibid.
71. This figure is commonly cited in discussions of Toronto's large South Asian population. See Balwant Jain, "Guajarati Diaspora Literature," *Generally About Books*, May 8, 2011, http://www.generallyaboutbooks.com/2011/05/gujarati-diaspora-literature.html (accessed April 27, 2012).
72. Shrinathji Haveli, "The Vaishnavs of Toronto," http://www.shrinathjihaveli.org/home.php?file=content&page=aboutus (accessed April 27, 2012).

Chapter 6

1. Quoted in John Stratton Hawley, "Braj: Fishing in Sur's Ocean," in *Krishna: A Sourcebook*, ed. Edwin Bryant (New York: Oxford University Press, 2007), 232.
2. Prema Kurien, *A Place at the Multicultural Table: The Development of an American Hinduism* (New Brunswick, NJ: Rutgers University Press, 2007), Part 1 of Kurien's text (pp. 119–186) discusses popular Hinduism while Part 2 (pp. 119–184) explores official Hinduism.
3. Vasudha Narayanan, "Creating the South Indian 'Hindu' Experience in the United States," in *A Sacred Thread: Modern Transmission of Hindu Traditions in India and Abroad*, ed. Raymond Brady Williams (Chambersburg, PA: Anima, 1992), 147–176.
4. Raymond Brady Williams, "Sacred Threads of Several Textures: Strategies of Adaptation in the United States," in *A Sacred Thread*, ed. Williams, 228–257.
5. See Thomas A. Forsthoefel and Cynthia Ann Humes, eds., *Gurus in America* (Albany: State University of New York Press, 2005).
6. Swami Vivekananda, "Hinduism," in *The World's Parliament of Religions: An Illustrated and Popular Story of the World's First Parliament of Religions, Held in Chicago in Connection with the Columbian Exposition of 1893*, ed. John Henry Barrows (Chicago: Parliament, 1893), vol. 2, 978.
7. Swami Vivekananda, "Final Address," in *The World's Parliament of Religions*, ed. Barrows, vol. 1, 170.
8. See David Gordon White, *Yoga in Practice* (Princeton: Princeton University Press, 2012), 20.
9. Swami Vivekananda, "Hinduism," in *The World's Parliament of Religions*, ed. Barrows, vol. 1, 975.
10. John A. Stevens, "Colonial Subjectivity: Keshab Chandra Sen in London and Calcutta," 1870–1884 (University College London: Ph.D. Dissertation, 2011), 112.
11. E. Allen Richardson, *East Comes West: Asian Religions and Cultures in North America* (New York: Pilgrim, 1984), 18–19.
12. Ibid.
13. Paramahansa Yogananda, *Autobiography of a Yogi* (New York: Philosophical Library, 1946).
14. Ibid.
15. Ibid.
16. Yogananda for the World, "Selected Early Works of Paramhansa Yogananda," http://yoganandafortheworld.com/wp-content/uploads/2012/03/yogananda-out-of-print-writings.pdf (accessed April 20, 2013).
17. Ibid., 243.
18. Ibid.
19. Ibid.
20. Ibid., 353.
21. Stevens, "Colonial Subjectivity."
22. Ibid.
23. Katheren Mayo, *Mother India* (San Diego: Harcourt, Brace, 1927).
24. *Gunga Din*, George Stevens, producer and director (Encino, CA: RKO Studios, 1939).
25. Aaron Terrazas and Cristina Batog, "Migration Information Source—Indian Immigrants in the United States," Migration Policy Institute, http://www.migrationinformation.org/usfocus/display.cfm?ID=785 (accessed June 2, 2013).
26. Ecumenical temples have been described by a number of authors including Raymond Brady Williams ("Sacred Threads of Several Textures," in *A Sacred Thread*, ed. Williams). The evolution of South Indian temples in the United States is explored by Vasudha Narayanan in the same volume.
27. Forsthoefel and Humes, eds., *Gurus in America*.
28. Richardson, *East Comes West*, 35–36.
29. Ibid.
30. Ibid.
31. "Temple Cook Withdraws from Lawsuit Against Flushing New York Hindu Tem-

ple," *Hinduism Today* (Hindu Press International), December 9, 2005.

32. Williams, "Sacred Threads of Several Textures," 239.

33. Lily Koppel, "Maharishi Mahesh Yogi, Spiritual Leader, Dies," *New York Times*, February 6, 2008, http://www.nytimes.com/2008/02/06/world/asia/06maharishi-1.html?pagewanted=all&_r=0 (accessed January 1, 2013).

34. Forsthoefel and Humes, eds., *Gurus in America*, 57.

35. "Bhagwan Shree Rajnesh, *The Oregonian*, July 1985, http://www.oregonlive.com/rajneesh/index.ssf/1985/07/rajneeshees_nurture_corporate.html (accessed January 1, 2013).

36. "Rush of Gurus," Pluralism Project (Harvard University), http://www.pluralism.org/ocg/CDROM_files/hinduism/rush_of_gurus.php (accessed January 5, 2013).

37. "Siddha Yoga Path," http://www.siddhayoga.org/teachings/essential (accessed January 5, 2013).

38. I am indebted to Dr. Alfreda E. Meyers for this observation.

39. Salagram.net, "Srila Prabhupad arrives in the USA 1965: 'Paschatya Desha Tarana Mahotsava,'" http://www.salagram.net/sp-arrival65.html (accessed January 5, 2013).

40. Thomas Hopkins, "Interview with Thomas J. Hopkins," in *Hare Krishna, Hare Krishna: Five Distinguished Scholars on the Krishna Movement in the West*, ed. Steven J. Gelberg (New York: Grove, 1983), 107.

41. Ibid.

42. Bhaktivedanta Memorial Library, "Srila Prabhupada Addresses The World Health Organization," http://www.bvml.org/ACBSP/19740606_who.html (accessed April 4, 2011).

43. In a study of this process, borrowing from H. Richard Niebuhr's dialectic of Christ and culture, Tamal Krishna Goswami and Ravi M. Gupta discovered three responses within Prabhupada's Vaishnavism—"Krishna *against* culture," "Krishna *of* culture," and a third alternative that "both distinguishes and affirms the two." See "Krishna and Culture: What Happens When the Lord of Vrindavana Moves to New York City," in *Gurus in America*, ed. Forsthoefel and Humes, 85. The researchers discovered that "Prabhupada and his followers oscillate between these alternatives—sometimes emphasizing opposition to culture, sometime agreement with it, sometimes both" (ibid.).

44. Ibid., 91.

45. Ibid., 88–89.

46. Travis Vande Berg and Fred Kniss, "ISKCON and Immigrants: The Rise, Decline, and Rise Again of a New Religious Movement," *The Sociological Quarterly* 49.1 (Winter 2008): 79–104, http://www.harekrsna.com/sun/editorials/10–11/editorials7861.htm (accessed February 1, 2013).

47. Henry Doktorski (Hrishikesh Dasa), "Kirtanananda Swami Bhaktipada: September 6, 1937–October 24, 2011," *Sampradaya Sun*, October 2011.

48. See Travis Vande Berg and Fred Kniss, "ISKCON and Immigrants," 79–104.

49. Ibid., 96ff.

50. Ibid., 94.

51. BAPS Swaminarayan Sanstha, "Yogji Maharaj," http://www.swaminarayan.org/yogijimaharaj/life/6.htm (accessed January 15, 2013).

52. BAPS Swaminarayan Sanstha, "Birth of Jinabhai," http://www.swaminarayan.org/yogijimaharaj/life/1.htm (accessed January 15, 2013).

53. I am indebted to Shree Patel for his assistance with these observations.

54. See A.D. Brear, "The Authority of Pramukh Swami Within the Swaminarayan Hindu Mission," *Diskus* 4.1 (1996): 23–33.

55. Raymond Brady Williams, *A New Face of Hinduism: The Swaminarayan Religion* (New York: Cambridge, 1984), 197.

56. Swaminarayan Info, "The Original Shree Swaminarayan Sampraday," http://www.swaminarayan.info/Temples/Display.asp?CatID=4&Chapter=23 (accessed January 20, 2013).

57. The Pluralism Project, "Center Profile, Shri Swaminarayan Mandir (BAPS) (2006)," http://www.pluralism.org/profiles/view/71207 (accessed February 1, 2013).

58. E. Allen Richardson, *Strangers in This Land: Religion, Pluralism, and the American Dream* (Jefferson, NC: McFarland, 2011), 185.

59. Pluralism Project, "Center Profile: Shri Akshar Purushottam Swaminarayan Temple (BAPS) (2006)," http://pluralism.org/profiles/view/68066 (accessed February 1, 2013).

60. BAPS Swaminarayan Sanstha, "Edison, USA 1991: Cultural Festival of India," http://www.swaminarayan.org/festivals/1991usa/index.htm (accessed February 1, 2013).

61. United Methodist Women, Western

North Carolina Conference, "Globalization Timeline: 1940–2005," http://www.wnccumw.org/PDF%20&%20Word%20Files/Globalization%20Timeline.pdf (accessed February 10, 2013).

62. Michael F. Martin and K. Alan Kronstadt, "CRS Report for Congress: India–U.S. Economic and Trade Relations" (Washington, DC: Congressional Research Service, 2007), 1.

63. BAPS Swaminarayan Sanstha: Shri Swaminarayan Mandir—Houston, "Mandir Construction," http://houston.baps.org/mandir_construction.html (accessed February 10, 2013).

64. BAPS Swaminarayan Sanstha, "Akshardham: Mahamandir Shilayanas Mahatsav," http://www.swaminarayan.org/news/usa/2011/10/njakshardham/index.htm (accessed February 10, 2013).

65. Kurien, *A Place at the Multicultural Table*, 103.

66. Pramod Amin, interview with the author, Vraj, Schuylkill Haven, Pennsylvania, 1990–2013.

67. Russell E. Richy, "Religious Organizations in the New Nation," in *Cambridge History of Religions in America*, ed. Stephen J. Stein (Cambridge University Press, 2012), vol. 2, 94.

68. Bill J. Leonard, "Dangerous and Promising Times: American Religion in the Postwar years" in *Cambridge History of Religions in America*, ed. Stein, vol. 3, 19.

69. See Timothy L. Smith, "Religious Denominations as Ethnic Communities: A Regional Case Study," *Church History* 35.2 (June 1966): 207–226.

70. Leonard, "Dangerous and Promising Times," 20.

71. Ibid., 16.

72. Martin Marty, "Visions of the Religious Future," in *The Cambridge History of Religions in America*, ed. Stein, vol. 3, 795.

73. Scott L. Thumma, "The Megachurch Phenomenon: Reshaping Church and Faith for the Twenty-First Century," in *The Cambridge History of Religions in America*, ed. Stein, vol. 3, 575–594.

74. Ibid., 797.

75. Ibid., 799–801.

76. The temple has established a regular membership of 300 members (Hindu Temple Society, letter to author, Sept. 5, 2012). However, along with 1,600 Indian families in the Lehigh Valley, it also attracts a variety of non-members from the Indian community. The temple repeatedly tries to close this gap as a means of increasing membership.

77. Internal Revenue Service, *Tax Guide for Churches and Religious Organizations: Benefits and Responsibilities under the Federal Tax Law*, IRS Publication 1828 (Washington, DC: Department of the Treasury, Internal Revenus Service, 2013).

78. Prema A. Kurien, "Multiculturalism and American Religion: The Case of Hindu Indian Americans," *Social Forces* 85.2 (December 2006): 723–741.

79. Personal observations, Shri Swaminarayan Mandir, Houston, Texas, 2010.

80. Kurien, *A Place at the Multicultural Table*, 145.

81. Ibid., 144.

82. Pramod Amin, interview with the author, Vraj, January 2013.

83. Hasmukh Shah, interview with the author, Vraj, January 2013.

84. Kripalu Healthy Living, "Featured Programs," http://healthyliving.kripalu.org/?sitelinks=HealthyLivingProgram&gclid=CNq2k5Hd47cCFZOk4AodgwsAWw (accessed June 1, 2013).

85. Kripalu Healthy Living, "Featured Programs," http://healthyliving.kripalu.org/?sitelinks=HealthyLivingProgram&gclid=CNq2k5Hd47cCFZOk4AodgwsAWw (accessed June 1, 2013).

86. Shambala Mountain Center, "Retreat and Renewal," https://www.shambhalamountain.org/program-category/retreat-and-renewal/ (accessed June 1, 2013).

87. Arsha Vidya Gurukalam, http://www.arshavidya.org/home.html (accessed June 1, 2013).

88. Siddhachalam, "The Layout of Siddhachalam Mirrors the Layout of Shikharji's Tonks," http://www.siddhachalam.org/shikharji/ (accessed February 28, 2013).

89. Ibid.

90. Alexander Moore, "Walt Disney World: Bounded Ritual Space and the Playful Pilgrimage Center," *Anthropological Quarterly* 53.4 (October 1980): 207.

91. Chaung Yen Monastery, http://www.baus.org/baus/about_us/intro_cym.html (accessed February 28, 2013).

92. Chaung Yen Monastery, http://www.baus.org/baus/programs/index.html (accessed February 28, 2013).

93. Andrew M. Greeley, *The Denominational Society: A Sociological Approach to Re-*

ligion in America (Glenview, IL: Scott Foresman, 1972), 108.

94. Scott L. Thumma, "The Megachurch Phenomenon: Reshaping Church and Faith for the Twenty-First Century," in *The Cambridge History of Religions in America*, ed. Stein, 575–594.

Chapter 7

1. Sūradāsa, Shyam Manohar Pandey, Norman H. Zide, and Anoop Chandola, *The Poems of Surdas: For Advanced Students of Hindi* (Chicago: University of Chicago, 1963), 67.
2. Will Herberg, *Protestant, Catholic, Jew: An Essay in American Religious Sociology* (Garden City, NY: Anchor, 1955), 32–34.
3. Milton Gordon, *Assimilation in American Life* (New York: Oxford University Press, 1964), 60–83.
4. Ranjani Saigal, "In Conversation with Shri Vrajarakumarji," Lokvani, May 2011 http://www.lokvani.com/lokvani/article.php?article_id=7285 (accessed January 1, 2012).
5. Similar sentiments have been expressed in each American haveli where research has been conducted.
6. The distinction between intrinsic and extrinsic religion evolved from a discussion about mature religion that Gordon Allport introduced in *The Individual and His Religion: A Psychological Interpretation* (New York: Macmillan, 1951), 52–74, and later refined in G.W. Allport and J.M. Ross, "Personal Religious Orientation and Prejudice," *Journal of Personality and Social Psychology* 5(1967): 432–443.
7. Ibid., 3.
8. See also G.W. Allport and J.M. Ross,"Religious Orientation and Prejudice," *Journal of Personality and Social Psychology* 5 (1967): 432–443.
9. Dabiel C. Batson and W. Larry Ventis, *The Religious Experience: A Social-Psychological Perspective* (New York: Oxford University Press, 1982), [PAGE].
10. Matthew D. Graham, "A Phenomenological Study of Quest-Oriented Religion," (Master of Arts Thesis, Trinity Western University, 2001), 8.
11. Pew Research Religion and Public Life Project: The Religious Landscape Survey, "Report 1: Religious Affiliation," http://religions.pewforum.org/reports (accessed January 15, 2012).
12. Mayo Clinic, "Yoga: Tap into the Many Health Benefits," http://www.mayoclinic.com/health/yoga/CM00004 (accessed December 15, 2011).
13. Ashtanga.com, http://www.ashtang.com (accessed December 1, 2011).
14. See Paul Vitello, "Hindu Group Stirs a Debate Over Yoga's Soul," *New York Times*, November 27, 2010, A1.
15. Robert Neelly Bellah, et al., *Habits of the Heart: Individualism and Commitment in American Life* (Berkeley: University of California Press, 1985), 50.
16. Martin E. Marty, "Habits of the Heart," http://www.religion-online.org/showarticle.asp?title=1921 (accessed November 1, 2011).
17. Barry Wellman, Anabel Quan-Haase, Jeffrey Boase, Wenhong Chen, Keith Hampton, Isabel Díaz, Kakuko Miyata,"The Social Affordances of the Internet for Networked Individualism," *Journal of Computer-Mediated Communication* 8 (April 2003): 16.
18. Conversations were held with members of the *haveli*'s youth in 2009 and 2010.
19. Sam Dolnick, "Hindus find a Ganges in Queens, to Park Rangers' Dismay," *New York Times*, April 21, 2011.
20. Diana L. Eck, *India: A Sacred Geography* (New York: Harmony, 2012), 18.
21. Siddhachalam, "The Making of a Tirth: A Brief Story of Siddhachalam," http://www.siddhachalam.org/tirth/making_of_siddhachalam.php (accessed November 1, 2011).
22. Siddhachalam, "Thirty Tonks Of Shri Shikharji," http://www.siddhachalam.org/shikharji/shikharji_tonks.php (accessed November 1, 2011).
23. David L. Haberman, *Journey Through the Twelve Forests: An Encounter with Krishna* (New York: Oxford University Press, 1994), 49.
24. Personal observations at Vraj, Schuylkill Haven, PA, June 2011.
25. Ibid.
26. Rajendra Jindel, *Culture of a Sacred Town: A Sociological Study of Nathdwara* (Bombay: Popular Prakashan 1976), 127–128.
27. Personal observations at Vraj, Schuylkill Haven, PA, 2005–2008.
28. E. Allen Richardson, *Strangers in This Land: Religion, Pluralism and the American Dream* (Jefferson, NC: McFarland, 2010), 68.

29. Ibid., 168ff.
30. Ibid., 203–05.
31. J.Z. Anand Vivodh et al., "Edison's Navratri: A Report on Religious Conflict in the Community," http://communityknowledge.net/navratri.html (accessed November 1, 2011).
32. Pramod Amin, interview with the author, Vraj, Schuylkill Haven, PA, June 2011.
33. Kamlesh Shah, interview with the author, Vaishnav Samaj of Midwest, Addison, IL, July 2010.
34. Suresh Patel, interview with the author, Vallabh Priti Seva Samaj, Sugar Land, TX, July 2010.
35. Vallabh Priti Seva Samaj, http://www.vpsshaveli.org/ (accessed January 20, 2012).
36. Satsang has become a common mechanism among teachers with strong international followings for cultivating a wider audience. For example, Asaram Bapu, a highly charismatic guru, has used the satsang as a means of reaching thousands of devotees around the world. His discourses can easily be found in the social media including on YouTube.

Other traditions, like Pushtimarg, that are not dependent on the teachings of a single guru utilize a broader understanding of satsang in which it can be used as a means of conversation with visiting goswamis, who frequently command large gatherings of followers. Most havelis host these gatherings, which provide times for devotees to receive regular teachings. However, in Pushtimarg, satsang can also be employed as a more informal kind of conversation among devotees. Frequently held in homes, satsangs are often intergenerational and provide a continuous way for members of the first generation, who have often grown up in Pushtimargiya culture, to share their insights with their grandchildren.

37. See Maritsa V. Poros, *Modern Migrations: Gujarati Indian Networks in New York and London* (Stanford, CA: Stanford University Press, 2011).
38. Kirk Semple, "Many U.S. Immigrants' Children Seek American Dream Abroad," *New York Times*, April 16, 2012.
39. H. Richard Niebuhr, *Christ and Culture* (New York: Harper, 1951).
40. Kenneth I. Pargament, *The Psychology of Religion and Coping: Theory, Research, Practice* (New York: Guilford, 1997).
41. Kirk Semple, "Moving to U.S. and Prospering, Without English," *New York Times*, November 9, 2011, 1.
42. Ibid.

Bibliography

Primary Sources

Includes sectarian publications and Web sites, imperial Mughal farmans and parwanas, texts containing Rajput grants, Pushtimargiya temple hangings, and related art connected to patronage of the sect in former Hindu states. Transliterated titles from Hindi texts published in devanagari script include diacritical marks. Texts and Web sites that use transliteration without diacritical marks appear in the same form in which they were published.

Akshardham. "What Is Akshardham." http://www.akshardham.com/whatisakdm/index.htm (accessed February 1, 2012).

Archer, W.G. *Indian Painting in Bundi and Kotah*. London: Her Majesty's Stationery Office, 1959.

Bhandarkar, R.G. "Bhaktamala." In *Vaisnavism, Saivism and Minor Religious Systems*. Varanasi: Indological, 1965.

Bhatta, Kaldhar. *Srīmad Vallabhācārya ke Dārshanika Acar kī Parampara (Eka Adhyayana)*. Ahmedabad: Shri Nagar Das ka Bambhaniya, V. 2021.

Bochasanwasi Shri Akshar Purushottam Swaminarayan Sanstha. http://www.14gaam.com/baps-swaminarayan-temple-usa.html (accessed February 1, 2012).

Cleveland Museum of Art. *Indian Art from the George P. Bickford Collection*. Cleveland: 1975.

Coomaraswamy, A.C. *Catalogue of the Indian Collections in the Museum of Fine Arts, Boston*. Cambridge, MA: Museum of Fine Arts, 1930.

Dave, Hari. "Vaishnav Samaj of Arizona—VSA." In *Panchamrut—Gloval Vaishnav Convention on the Occasion of Vraj 20th Anniversary, July 3–5, 2009*. Schuylkill Haven, PA: Vraj, 2009. 87–89.

Government of India. Central Publication Branch. *The Ruling Princes, Chiefs and Leading Personages in Rajputana and Ajmer*. 5th ed. Calcutta: 1924.

_____. Manager of Publications. *Rajputana and Ajmer, List of Ruling Princes, Chiefs and Leading Personages*. 7th ed. Delhi: 1939.

Government of Rajasthan (India). *Report of the Nathdwara Inquiry Commission*. Jaipur: Government Central Press, 1959.

Khandavala, Karl, ed. *Kishangarh Paintings*. New Delhi: Lalit Kala Akademie, 1971.

Lal, Rao Sahib Pandit Yamuna. *The Census of Mewar: The Village Directory*. Udaipur: Newal Kishore, 1942.

Low, D.A., M.D. Eltis, and M.D. Wainwright, eds. *Government Archives in South Asia: A Guide to National and State Archives in Ceylon, India and Pakistan*. Cambridge: Cambridge University Press, 1969.

Mahodayshri, H.H. Pujya Goswami 108 Shri Vrajrajkumarji. "O My Krishna." Vallabh Youth Organization, 2014.

Mital, Prabhudayal. *Brajasthān Vallabha Sampradāya kā Itihās*. Mathura: Sahitya Sanasthan, 1968.

Nathdwara Temple Board. "Nathdwara, Balance Sheet." http://www.nathdwaratemple.org/Management/Balance%20

Sheet%202010-2011.pdf (accessed February 1, 2012).

———. *The Nathdwara Temple Rules 1973*. Nathdwara, India: Govind Bhawan, 1973. http://fx.sauder.ubc.ca/etc/USDpages.pdf (accessed March 1, 2012).

Pandey, Shyam Manohar, Norman H. Zide, and Anoop Chandola. *The Poems of Surdas: For Advanced Students of Hindi*. Chicago: University of Chicago, 1963.

Paramānandadāsa. *Paramānanda Sāgara*. Ed. Govardhan Nath Shukla. Aligarh: Bharat Prakashan Mandir, 1948.

Parekh, Golok Vasi Dvarika Das. *Goswāmī Hari Rāyajī Pranīta Caurāsī Vaishnava kī Vārtā (Tīna Janma kī Līla Bhāvana Vālī)*. Mathura: Shri Govardhan Granthmala Karyalaya, V. 2027.

Parivar, Vaishnav. "Haveli List." http://www.vaishnavparivar.info/pushtimarg/haveli-list (accessed March 1, 2012).

Patel, Shreshbhai S. "The Inspiring Tale of Vallabh Priti Seva Samaj of Houston, Inc." In *Pushti Ratna: A Jewel of Pushti Marg*. Houston: Vallab Priti Seva Samaj, 2010. 83.

Portland Art Museum. *Rajput Miniatures from the Collection of Edwin Binney III*. Portland, OR: 1969.

Pushti Ratna: A Jewel of Pushti Marg. Houston: Vallabh Priti Seva Samaj, 2010.

Pushti, Shree Kalyan. http://www.shreekalyanpushti.org/hdhshashtpeet.html (accessed March 1, 2012).

Pushtikul.com. http://www.pushtikul.com/topic.asp?TOPIC_ID=1484&FORUM_ID=2&CAT_ID=7&Forum_Title=%3Cb%3ENews+Column%3C%2Fb%3E&Topic_Title=The+Baithakji+at+HimGopal%2C+near+Mysore (accessed February 1, 2012).

Republic of India. The National Archives of India. National Register of Private Records. *Descriptive Lists of Documents Available in Mysore, Orissa, Punjab, Rajasthan, Tamil Nadu and National Archives of India, New Delhi (Based on Information Received in 1959–1960)*. Document no. 1181, "Collection of Goswami of Govind Deoji Mandir, Jaipur," no. 1, part 3. Bikaner: Rajasthan, 1972.

———. *Descriptive Lists of Documents Available in Rajasthan (Based on Information Received in 1959–1960)*. Documents No. 792–805, "Collection of His Holiness Tilkayat Maharaj of Nathdwara," no. 1, part 2. Bikaner: Rajasthan, 1972.

Saran, P. *Descriptive Catalogue of Non-Persian Sources of Medieval Indian History*. New York: Asia Publishing, 1965.

Shah, Jethalal G. *Shri Vallabhacharya: His Philosophy and Religion*. Nadiad: Pustimargiya Pustakalaya, 1969.

Sharma, Braj Bhusan, ed. *Paramānand Sāgar*. Kankroli: Vidya Vibhag, V. 2019.

Sharma, G.N. *A Bibliography of Medieval Rajasthan*. Agra: Laksmi Narain Agarwal, 1965.

———. "Ekling Mahatmya." In *Mewar and the Mughal Emperors (1526–1707)*. Agra: Shiva Lal Agarwal, 1962. 162.

———. "Jagat Singh Kavy." In *Mewar and the Mughal Emperors (1526–1707)*. Agra: Shiva Lal Agarwal, 1962. 133.

———. *Mewar and the Mughal Emperors (1526–1707)*. Agra: Shiva Lal Agarwal, 1962.

Sharma, Ram. "Ranchhod." In *Maharana Raj Singh and His Times*. Delhi: Motilal Banarsidass, 1971. 16.

Shastri, Kanthmani. *Astachāp* Kankroli: Vidya Vibhag, V. 2009.

———. *Kānkrolī kā Itihās*. 2 vols. Kankroli: Vidha Vibhag, V. 2116.

Shreeji Arpan. Phoenix: Shreenathji Temple Phoenix, 2009.

Shree Vakpati Foundation. "The Rich Heritage of *Dhrupad Sangeet* in Pushtimarg." Baroda, India: n.d. http://www.vallabhkankroli.org/Rich%20Heritage%20of%20Dhrupad%20Sangeet%20in%20Pushtimarg.pdf (accessed January 1, 2012).

Shrimad Bhagvat Saptah. Phoenix: Shreenathji Temple Phoenix, 2010.

Shuddhadwait Shri Vallabhacharya Dwitiya Gruha Peeth. "Bethakji." http://www.pushtidwitiyapeeth.org/bethakji2.html (accessed February 1, 2012).

Shuddhadvaita Trutiya Gruh of Pushtimarg, "Literary Works by Shree Mahaprabhuji." http://vallabhkankroli.org/granthas_list%20of%20granthas.htm (accessed February 1, 2012).

Shyam Das, Asim Krishna Das, and Tulsi Krishna Das. *The Amazing Story of Shri Nathji: A Translation of Srinathji Ki Prakatya Varta.* [India]: Pratham Peeth, 2007.

Siddhachalam. http://www.siddhachalam.org/tirth/making_of_siddhachalam.php (accessed November 1, 2011).

Snell, Rupert. *The Hindi Classical Tradition: A Braj Bhāṣā Reader.* London: School of Oriental and African Studies, University of London, 1991.

Spink, Walter. *Krishnamandala: A Devotional Theme in Indian Art.* Special publications no. 2. Ann Arbor: University of Michigan, Center for South and Southeast Asian Studies, 1971.

———. *The Quest for Krishna: Paintings and Poetry of the Krishna Legend.* Ann Arbor: privately published, 1972.

State Government of Rajasthan. Directorate of Archives. *A Descriptive List of Farmans, Manshuras and Nishans.* Bikaner, India: 1962.

———. Government Central Press. *Report of the Nathdwara Inquiry Commission.* Jaipur, India: 1959.

Tod, James. *Annals and Antiquities of Rajasthan or the Central and Western Rajpoot States of India.* Vol. 1. Calcutta: Indian Publication Society, 1899.

Vallabh Priti Seva Samaj. http://www.vpsshaveli.org/ (accessed December 1, 2011).

Vallabh Youth Organization. "Index." http://www.vallabhyouth.org/index.php (accessed February 1, 2012).

Vallabhacarya. *Śrīsubodhinī.* Ed. Nand Kishor Sharma. Nathdwara: Vidya Vibhag, 1928.

———. *Shrīmadbrahmasūtrāṇubhāṣyam.* Ed. Hari Shankar Shastri. Bombay: Trustees of Seth Narayan Das Asanmala Trust, 1942.

———. *The Tattvartha-Dipa-Nibandha with Prakasha.* 2 vols. Ed. Hari Shankar Onkar Shastri. Bombay: Trustees of Seth Narayan Das, 1943.

———. *The Tattvadipanibandha with Prakasha.* 2 vols. Ed. Sita Ram Shastri. Bombay: Shridhara Shivalalaji, 1905–1908.

Vanchamrt: Global Vaishnav Convention on the Occasion of Vraj 20th Anniversary July 3–4–5, 2009. Schuylkill Haven, PA: Pushti Margiya Vaishnav Samaj of North America, 2009.

Varma, Dhirendra, ed. *Sūrasāgara-Sāra.* Allahabad, India: Sahitya Bhavan, 1970.

Vraj Tavasmi: Krishna Seva Sada karya. Schuylkill Haven, PA: Pushti Margiya Vaishnav Samaj, 2002.

Vrajaratanaji, Yadunathaji, Karsondas Mulji, and N.R. Ranina. *Report of the Maharaj Libel Case and of the Bhattia Conspiracy Case, Connected with It.* Bombay, India: Union, 1882. http://galenet.galegroup.com/servlet/MMLT?af=RN&ae=Q4201586426&srchtp=a&ste=14&locID=ucblaw_boalt (accessed December 1, 2011).

Secondary Sources

Abdur-Rashid, Sheikh. "Madad-i-ma'ash Grants Under the Mughals." *Journal of the Pakistan Historical Society* 9 (1961): 98–108.

Agraval, Bovind Das Ram Narayan. *Braja aura Braja-Yātnā.* Delhi: Bhartiya Vishva Prakashan, 1959.

Allport, G.W., and J.M. Ross. "Religious Orientation and Prejudice." *Journal of Personality and Social Psychology* 5 (1967): 432–443.

Allport, Gordon W. *The Individual and His Religion: A Psychological Interpretation.* New York: Macmillan, 1950.

Ambalal, Amit. *Krishna as Shrinathji: Rajasthani Paintings from Nathdvara.* Ahmedabad: Mapin, 1987.

Anand Vivodh, J.Z., et al. "Edison's Navratri: A Report on Religious Conflict in the Community," http://communityknowledge.net/navratri.html (accessed November 1, 2011).

Ancestry.com. "Schuylkill county Genealogy Ties—Village Names and Townships." http://www.rootsweb.ancestry.

com/~paschuy2/villages.html (accessed January 6, 2011).

Archer, William George. *Indian Painting in Bundi and Kotah*. London: Her Majesty's Stationery Office, 1959.

———. *The Loves of Krishna in Indian Painting and Poetry*. New York: Grove, [1957].

Aziz, Ahmad. *Studies in Islamic Culture in the Indian Environment*. Oxford: Clarendon, 1969.

Babb, Lawrence A. *The Divine Hierarchy: Popular Hinduism in Central India*. New York: Columbia University Press, 1975.

Bacon, Jean. *Life Lines: Community, Family, and Assimilation Among Asian Indian Immigrants*. New York: Oxford University Press, 1996.

Banerjee, Anil Chandra. *Lectures on Rajput History: Raghunath Prasad Nopany Lectures, 1960*. Calcutta: Firma K.L. Mukhopadhyay, 1962.

———. *The Rajput States and the East India Company*. Calcutta: A. Mukherjee, 1954.

Banerjee, Jitendranath. *The Development of Hindu Iconography*. Calcutta: University of Calcutta Press, 1956.

Banerji, Adris. "Kishangarh Paintings." *Roopa Lekna* 25 (1925): 13–18.

Barz, R.K., Harirāya, and Gokulanātha. *The Bhakti Sect of Vallabhācārya*. Faridabad, India: Thomson, 1976.

Barz, Richard. "Early Developments Within the Bhakti Sect of Vallabhācārya According to Sectarian Tradition." Ph.D. dissertation, University of Chicago, 1971.

———. "Kumbhandas: The Devotee as Salt of the Earth." In *Krishna: A Sourcebook*, ed. Edwin Bryant, 490–491. New York: Oxford University Press, 2007.

Batson, Daniel C., and W. Larry Ventis. *The Religious Experience: A Social-Psychological Perspective*. New York: Oxford University Press, 1982.

Beck, Guy L. *Alternative Krishnas: Regional and Vernacular Variations on a Hindu Deity*. Albany: State University of New York Press, 2005.

Bellah, Robert Neelly, et al. *Habits of the Heart: Individualism and Commitment in American Life*. Berkeley: University of California Press, 1985.

Bennett, Peter. *The Path of Grace: Social Organisation and Temple Worship in a Vaishnava Sect*. Delhi: Hindustan, 1993.

Bhandarkar, R.G. *Vaisnavism, Saivism and Minor Religious Systems*. Varanasi: Indological, 1965.

Bhatt, G.H. "A Further Note on Vishnusvami and Vallabhacarya." In *Proceedings and Transactions of the Eighth All-India Oriental Conference*, Mysore, December 1935, 322–328. [Mysore: M.H. Krishna, Local Secretary, Eighth All-India Oriental Conference].

———. "Pusti-marga of Vallabha." *Indian Historical Quarterly* 9 (1933): 300–306.

———. "The School of Vallabha." In *The Cultural Heritage of India*, vol. 3, ed. H. Bhattacarya, 347–359. Calcutta: Calcutta Institute of Culture, Ramakrishna Mission, 1973.

Bryant, Edwin F. *Krishna: A Sourcebook*. Oxford: Oxford University Press, 2007.

Bryant, Kenneth E., and Sūradāsa. *Poems to the Child-God: Structures and Strategies in the Poetry of Sūrdās*. Berkeley: University of California Press, 1978.

Burdak, Laxman. "The Jat Uprising of 1669." http://www.jatland.com/home/The_Jat_Uprising_of_1669 (accessed March 1, 1012).

Chandola, Anoop. *Mystic and Love Poetry of Medieval Hindi: With Introduction, Texts, Grammar, Notes, Translations and Glossary*. New Delhi: Today and Tomorrow's Printers and Publishers, 1982.

Chaturvedi, Jawaharlal, ed. *Pusti Mārgāya Grantha Ratna Kosa*. Calcutta: Ramchand Dau Dayal, n.d.

Clifford, James. "Diasporas." *Cultural Anthropology* 9.3: 311.

Coward, Harold G., John R. Hinnells, and Raymond Brady Williams. *The South Asian Religious Diaspora in Britain, Canada, and the United States*. Albany: State University of New York Press, 2000.

Dashora, Yamuna Lal, ed. *Census of Mewar 1941, Vol. 1: The Village Directory*. Ajmer: Newal Kishore, 1942.

Dave, Hiral Dholakia. "42% of U.S. Hotel Business Is Gujarati." *The Times of India (US)*. December 1, 2011. http://articles.

timesofindia.indiatimes.com/2006-10-18/us/27810036_1_gujaratis-hotels-and-motels-hilton-and-starwood.
Davis, Richard H. *Lives of Indian Images*. Princeton, NJ: Princeton University Press, 1997.
Dehejia, Harsha V. *A Festival of Krishna, Featuring Under the Kadamba Tree, Paintings of a Divine Love and Ateliers of Love, a Film on DVD: A Journey of Poets, Painters and Patrons*. New Delhi: Roli, 2008.
Derrett, J. Duncan M. "The Reform of Hindu Religious Endowments." In *South Asian Politics and Religion*, ed. Donald E. Smith, 311–336. Princeton: Princeton University Press, 1966.
Desai, Lallu Bhai Chaganlal. *Svarūpa Darśana*. Ahmedabad, India: Bombay Printers, 1923.
Dhamija, J. "Pecchawais of Nathdwara." *Times of India Annual* (Bombay), 1965, 173–188.
Dieter-Evers, Hans. *Monks, Priests and Peasants: A Study of Buddhism and Social Structure in Central Ceylon*. Leiden: E.J. Brill, 1972.
Dolnick, Sam. "Hindus Find a Ganges in Queens, to Park Rangers' Dismay." *New York Times*, April 21, 2011.
Doniger, Wendy. *The Hindus: An Alternative History*. New York: Penguin, 2009.
Drake-Brockman, D.O. *Muttra [sic]: A Gazetteer, Being Volume VII of the District Gazetteers of the United Provinces of Agra and Oudh*. Allahabad, India: Government Press, 1911.
Eck, Diana L. *Banāras, City of Light*. New York: Knopf, 1982.
———. *Darśan: Seeing the Divine Image in India*. New York: Columbia University Press, 1998.
———. *India: A New Sacred Geography*. Bourbon, Indiana: Harmony, 2012.
Eliade, Mircea, and Willard R. Trask. *The Sacred and the Profane: The Nature of Religion*. New York: Harcourt, Brace, 1959.
Entwistle, Alan W. *Braj: Centre of Krishna Pilgrimage*. Groningen, The Netherlands: Egbert Forsten, 1987.
Erskine, K.D., ed. *Rajputana Gazetteer Vol. II-A: The Mewar Residency*. Ajmer: Scottish Mission Industries, 1908.

Frykenberg, Robert Eric, ed. *Land Control and Social Structure in Indian History*. Madison: University of Wisconsin Press, 1969.
Gahlot, Jagdish Singh, and K.N. Dikshit. *The History of Rajputana*. Jodhpur: Hindi Sahitya Manoir, 1937.
Gangoly, O.C. "A Group of Vallabhacarya or Nathdwara Paintings." *Bulletin of the Baroda State Museum and Picture Gallery* 1 (1944): 31–40.
Goetz, H. "The First Golden Age of Udaipur, Rajput Art in Mewar During the Period of Mughal Supremacy," *Ars Orientalis: The Arts of Islam and the East* 2 (1957): 427–437.
———. "Notes of the Vallabhacarya Paintings from Udaipur and Jodhpur in the Baroda State Museum." *Bulletin of the Baroda State Museum and Picture Gallery* 1 (1944): 41–46.
Gokulanātha, Harirāya, Shyam Das, and Vallabhdas. *Krishna's Inner Circle: The Ashta Chaap Poets*. [Kota]: Pratham Peeth, 2009.
Gold, Ann Grodzins, and Ann Grodzins Gold. *Fruitful Journeys: The Ways of Rajasthani Pilgrims*. Prospect Heights, IL: Waveland, 2000.
Gopal, Lallanji. *The Economic Life of Northern India c. AD 700–1200*. Delhi: Motilal Banarsidass, 1989.
Gordon, Milton. *Assimilation in American Life*. New York: Oxford University Press, 1964.
Goswamy, B.N., and J.S. Grewal. *The Mughal and the Jogis of Jakhbar*. Simla: 1967.
———. *The Mughal and Sikh Rulers and the Vaisnavas of Pindori*. Simla: Indian Institute of Advanced Study, 1969.
Government of India, Surveyor General of India. *Survey of India Map Catalogue*. Calcutta: 1945.
Graham, Matthew D. "A Phenomenological Study of Quest-Oriented Religion." Master of Arts thesis, Trinity Western University, 2001.
Gray, B. *Treasures of Indian Miniatures from the Bikaner Palace Collection*. Oxford: B. Cassirer, 1951.
Growse, F.S. *Mathura: A District Memoir*. Oudh: Oudh Government Press, 1883.

Gupta, Beni. "The Vallabha Sect in Rajasthan." *Journal of the Rajasthan Institute of Historical Research* 9 (April–June 1972): 12–20.

Gupta, Din Dayal. *Astachap aur Vallabha-Sampradāya*. 2 vols. Allahabad: Hindi Sahitya Sammelan, 1948.

Haberman, David L. *Journey Through the Twelve Forests: An Encounter with Krishna*. New York: Oxford University Press, 1994.

Habib, Irfan. *The Agrarian System of Mughal India (1556–1707)*. London: Asia Publishing House, 1963.

———. "The Social Distinction of Landed Property in Medieval India." *Institut fur Orientforschung, Mitteilungendes* 13 (1967): 107–135. Berlin: Akademie der Wissenschaften.

Hallissey, Robert C. *The Rajput Rebellion Against Aurangzeb: A Study of the Mughal Empire in Seventeenth-Century India*. Columbia: University of Missouri Press, 1977.

Hanslal, Jadunath Sarkar. *Maāsir-i-'Alāmgiri: A History of the Emperor Aurangzeb-'Alamgir (Reign 1658–1707 AD) of Sagi Mushad Khan*. Calcutta: Bibliotheca Indica, Royal Asiatic Society of Bengal, 1947.

Hawley, John Stratton. *At Play with Krishna*. Princeton: Princeton University Press, 1981.

———. "Author and Authority in the Bhakti Poetry of North India." *Journal of Asian Studies* 74.2 (May 1988): 269.

Hawley, John Stratton, and Mark Juergensmeyer. *Songs of the Saints of India*. New York: Oxford University Press, 1988.

Hein, Norvin. *The Miracle Plays of Mathura*. New Haven: Yale University Press, 1972.

Helweg, Arthur W. *Strangers in a Not-So-Strange Land: Indian American Immigrants in the Global Age*. Belmont, CA: Wadsworth/Thomson Learning, 2004.

Helweg, Arthur W., and Usha M. Helweg. *An Immigrant Success Story: East Indians in America*. London: Hurst, 1990.

Herberg, Will. *Protestant, Catholic, Jew: An Essay in American Religious Sociology*. Garden City, NY: Anchor, 1955.

Hinnells, John R. *Religious Reconstruction in the South Asian Diasporas: From One Generation to Another*. Basingstoke, Hampshire: Palgrave Macmillan, 2007.

His Majesty's Secretary of State for India in Council. (Great Britain.) *The Imperial Gazetteer of India XXIV: Travancore to Zira*. Oxford: Clarendon, 1908.

Hopkins, Thomas J. "The Social Teachings of the Bhagavata Purana." In *Krishna: Myths, Rites and Attitudes*, ed. Milton Singer, 3–22. Chicago: University of Chicago Press, Phoenix Books, 1966.

Ikrarn, S.M. *Muslim Civilization in India*. Ed. Ainslie T. Embree. New York: Columbia University Press, 1964.

Jindal, Rajendra. *Culture of a Sacred Town: A Sociological Study of Nathdwara*. Bombay: Popular Prakashan, 1976.

Kagal, Carmen. "The Painters of Nathdwara." *Span* (New Delhi) 11 (July 1970): 2–7.

Keay, John. *India: A History*. New York: Atlantic Monthly Press, 2000.

Khandavala, Karl, ed. *Kishangarh Paintings*. New Delhi: Lalit Kala Akademie, 1971.

Knapp, Stephen. "Ancient Krsna Balaram Coins 200 BC." http://www.bibliotecapleyades.net/ciencia/esp_cienciaindia_3.htm (accessed January 1, 2012).

Kumar, Ravinder. "The Rise of the Rich Peasants in Western India." In *Soundings in Modern South Asian History*, ed. D.A. Low, 25–59. Berkeley: University of California Press, 1968.

Lamb, Beatrice Pitney. *India: A World in Transition*. New York: Praeger, 1963.

Legere, Laura. "Hindu Groups Plan New Spiritual and Cultural Center." *Times-Tribune* (Scranton, Pennsylvania), July 3, 2011.

Lokhvani. "In Conversation with Shri Vrajarajkumarji." http://paroolmodi67.blogspot.com/2011_07_01_archive.html (accessed February 1, 2012).

Lynch, Owen. "Pilgrimage with Krishna, Sovereign of the Emotions." *Contributions to Indian Sociology* 22.2: 188–194.

Lyons, Tryna. *The Artists of Nathadwara: The Practice of Painting in Rajasthan*. Bloomington: Indiana University Press, 2004.

Majumdar, R.C. *An Advanced History of India*. New York: Macmillan, 1967.

Mandelbaum, David G. *Society in India: Change and Continuity*. Vol. 2. Berkeley: University of California Press, 1970.

Marchese, John. *The Violin Maker: Finding a Centuries-Old Tradition in a Brooklyn Workshop*. New York: HarperCollins, 2007.

Marfatia, Mridula I. *The Philosophy of Vallabhācārya*. Delhi: Munshiram Manoharlal, 1967.

Marty, Martin E. "Habits of the Heart." http://www.religion-online.org/showarticle.asp?title=1921 (accessed November 1, 2011).

McDaniel, June. "Folk Vaishnavism and the Thakur Pancayat: Life and Status Among Village Krishna Statues." In *Alternative Krishnas: Regional and Vernacular Variations on a Hindu Deity*, ed. Guy Beck, 33. New York: State University of New York Press, 2005.

Mehta, R.N. "An Annakuta Pichhavai." *Bulletin of the Baroda State Museum and Picture Gallery* 20 (1968): 33–35.

———. "A New Pichhavai in the Baroda Museum." *Bulletin of the Baroda State Museum and Picture Gallery* 14 (1962): 19–22.

———. "Picchavais [sic]: Temple Hangings of the Vallabhacarya Sect." *Journal of Indian Textile History* 3 (1957): 4–14.

Meskell, Lynn. *Object Worlds in Ancient Egypt: Material Biographies Past and Present*. Oxford: Berg, 2004.

Michell, George, and Anila Verghese. *Vijayanagara: Splendour in Ruins*. New Delhi: Alkazi Collection of Photography, 2008.

Motiwala, B.N. *Karsondas Mulji, A Biographical Study*. Bombay: Karsondas Mulji Centenary Celebration Committee, 1935.

Mulji, Karsondas. *History of the Sect of Maharajas or Vallabhacharyas in Western India*. London: Trubner, 1865.

———. *Report on the Maharaj Libel Case*. 2nd ed. Bombay: n.p., 1882.

Neralla, Mayank S., Mandar S. Neralla, and Dewang S. Neralla. *Jagad Guru Shrimad Vallabhacharya*. Mumbai: Shri Gusainji Charitable Trust, 2002.

Niebuhr, H. Richard. *Christ and Culture*. New York: Harper, 1951.

Oonk, Giijsbert. *Global Indian Diasporas: Exploring Trajectories of Migration and Theory*. Amsterdam: Amsterdam University Press, 2007. http://public.eblib.com/EBLPublic/PublicView.do?ptiID=419921.

Paliwal, Devi Lal, ed. *Mewar Through the Ages*. Udaipur: Sahitya Sansthan, 1970.

Pandey, S.M., and N. Zide. "Surdas and His Kirshnabhakti." In *Krishna: Myths, Rites and Attitudes*, ed. Milton Singer, 173–199. Chicago: University of Chicago Press, Phoenix Books, 1966.

Parekh, Bhai Manilal C. *Shri Vallabhacharya: Life, Teachings and Movement: A Religion of Grace*. Rajkot: Shri Bhagavata Dharma Mission, 1969.

Pargament, Kenneth I. *The Psychology of Religion and Coping: Theory, Research, Practice*. New York: Guilford, 1997.

Peabody, Norbert. *Hindu Kingship and Polity in Precolonial India*. New York: Cambridge University Press, 2003.

Pearce, Susan M. *Museums, Objects, and Collections: A Cultural Study*. Washington, DC: Smithsonian Institution Press, 1993.

Pechilis, Karen. *The Embodiment of Bhakti*. New York: Oxford University Press, 1999.

Petievich, Carla. *The Expanding Landscape: South Asians and the Diaspora*. New Delhi, India: Manohar, 1999.

The Pew Forum on Religion and Public Life. *The Religious Landscape Survey, January 2012*. Part 1, Religious Affiliation. http://religions.pewforum.org/reports (accessed January 15, 2012).

Pinhey, A.F. *History of Mewar*. Government of India, Superintendent of Government Printing, 1906.

Poros, Maritsa V. *Modern Migrations: Gujarati Indian Networks in New York and London*. Stanford, CA: Stanford University Press, 2011.

Prentiss, Karen. *The Embodiment of Bhakti*. New York: Oxford University Press, 1999.

Purkiss, Diane. *The English Civil War: Papists, Gentlewomen, Soldiers, and Witch-

finders in the Birth of Modern Britain. New York: Basic, 2006.

Raghavan, Victor. *The Great Integrators: The Saint-Singers of India.* Patel Memorial Lecture. Delhi: Government of India, Publications Division, Ministry of Information and Broadcasting, 1966.

Richards, John F. *The Mughal Empire.* Cambridge: Cambridge University Press, 1993.

Rudolph, Susanne Hoeber, and Lloyd I. Rudolph. *The Modernity of Tradition: Political Development in India.* Chicago: University of Chicago Press, 1967.

Rukmani, T.S. *Hindu Diaspora Global Perspectives.* New Delhi: Munshiram Manoharlal, 2001.

Sanford, Whitney A. "Painting Words, Tasting Sound: Visions of Krishna in Paramānand's Sixteenth Century Devotional Poetry." *Journal of the American Academy of Religion* 70.1 (March 2002): 55–81.

———. *Singing Krishna: Sound Becomes Sight in Paramānand's Poetry.* Albany: State University of New York Press, 2008.

Sanyal, Ritwik, and Richard Widdess. *Dhrupad: Tradition and Performance in Indian Music.* Aldershot, Hants, England: Ashgate, 2004.

Saran, P. *Studies in Medieval Indian History.* Delhi: Ranjit, 1952.

Sax, William S. *The Gods at Play: Līlā in South Asia.* New York: Oxford University Press, 1995.

Semple, Kirk. "Moving to U.S. and Prospering, Without English." *New York Times*, November 9, 2011, 1.

Shah, Bhagwat. "Shodash Granth Sixteen Treatises of Shri Vallabha," http://pushti-marg.net/16-granth-intro.htm (accessed February 1, 2012).

Shah, Jethalal Govardhandas. *Shrimad Vallabhacharya: His Philosophy and Life.* Mumbai: Shri Subodhini Prakashan Sanstha, 2003.

———. *Shri Vallabhacharya: His Philosophy and Religion.* Mumbai: Vaishnav Mitra Mandal, 2003.

Shah, Rajiv. "Ahmadabad Population Hits Half Crore." *The Times of India* (Ahmadabad), March 11, 2012. http://articles.timesofindia.indiatimes.com/2010-09-23/ahmedabad/28226772_1_population-sq-km-surat.

Shain, Barry Alan. *The Myth of American Individualism: The Protestant Origins of American Political Thought.* Princeton, NJ: Princeton University Press, 1994.

Sharma, Dasharath. *Lectures on Rajput History and Culture: Raghunath Prasad Nopany Lectures, 1966.* Delhi: Motilal Banarsidass, 1966.

Sharma, G.N. *A Bibliography of Medieval Rajasthan (Social and Cultural).* Agra: Lakshmi Narain Agarwal, 1965.

———. *Mewar and the Mughal Emperors (1526–1707).* Agra: Shiva Lal Agarwal, 1962.

———. *Social Life in Medieval Rajasthan 1500–1800 with Special Reference to the Impact of Mughal Influence.* Agra: Lakshmi Narain Agarwal, 1968.

Sharma, Gopi Nath. *Rajasthan Studies.* Agra: Lakshmi Narain Agarwal, [1970].

Sharma, Goswami Shribrajbhushan. *Paramanand-Sagar.* Mathura, India: Shridinadayalu Gupta, V.S. 2016, 1960 CE.

Sharma, Satya Kumari. *Pustimārgīya Vārtā Sāhitya kā Saidhāntika tathā Bhakti Paraka Adhyayana.* Aligarh: Prabhat Prakashan, V. 2028.

Sharma, S.R. *The Religious Policy of the Mughal Emperors.* London: [PLACE], 1940.

Sharma, Sri Ram. *Maharana Raj Singh and His Times.* Delhi: Motilal Banarsidass, 1971.

Shastri, Brajnath R. *Shrimad Vallabhacharya and His Doctrines.* Baroda, India: Shri Vallabha, 1984.

Shukla, Sandhya. *India Abroad: Diasporic Cultures of Postwar America and England.* Princeton: Princeton University Press, 2003.

Siddiqi, I.H. "Wajh-i-Ma'ash Grants Under the Afghan Kings." In *Medieval India: A Miscellany*, vol. 2, 19–44. Aligarh: Aligarh Muslim University Press, 1972.

Singer, Milton, and Bernard S. Cohn, eds. *Structure and Change in Indian Society.* Chicago: Aldine, 1968.

Skelton, Robert. *Rajasthani Temple Hangings of the Krishna Cult from the Collec-*

tion of Karl Mann, New York. New York: American Federation of Arts, 1973.

Skop, Emily. "Asian Indians and the Construction of Community and Identity." In *Contemporary Ethnic Geographies in America,* ed. Ines M. Miyares, Christopher A. Airriess, 271–290. Lanham, Maryland: Rowman and Littlefield, 2007.

Smith, Donald E., ed. *South Asian Politics and Religion.* Princeton: Princeton University Press, 1966.

Snell, Rupert. *The Hindi Classical Tradition: A Braj Bhāṣā Reader.* London: School of Oriental and African Studies, University of London, 1991.

Somani, Ram Vallabhi. *History of Mewar from Earliest Times to 1751 AD.* Jaipur: C.L. Rank, 1976.

Spink, Walter. *Krishnamandala: A Devotional Theme in Indian Art.* Special publications no. 2. Ann Arbor: University of Michigan, Center for South and Southeast Asian Studies, 1971.

———. *The Quest for Krishna: Paintings and Poetry of the Krishna Legend.* Ann Arbor: privately published, 1972.

Srinivas, M.N. "Mobility in the Caste System." In *Structure and Change in Indian Society,* ed. Milton Singer and Bernard S. Cohn, 189–201. Chicago: Aldine, 1968.

Srinivas, Mysore Narasimhachar. *Social Change in Modern India.* Berkeley: University of California Press, 1966.

Swearer, Donald K. *Becoming the Buddha: The Ritual of Image Consecration in Thailand.* Princeton, NJ: Princeton University Press, 2004.

Tandon, Guru Prasad. *Materials for the History of Pustimarg.* Prayag: University of Allahabad Press, n.d.

Tandon, Harahari Nath. *Vārtā Sāhitya.* Aligarh: Bharat Prakashan Mandir, V. 2017.

Thompson, Michael. *Rubbish Theory: The Creation and Destruction of Value.* New York: Oxford University Press, 1979.

Tod, James. *Annals and Antiquities of Rajasthan, Or the Central and Western Rajpoot States of India.* Vol. 1. London: Smith, Elder, 1829.

———. *Annals and Antiquities of Rajasthan or the Central and Western Rajpoot States of India.* Vol. 1. Calcutta: Indian Publication Society, 1899.

———. *History of the Sect of Maharajas or Vallabhacharyas in Western India.* London, Trubner, 1865.

———. "On the Religious Establishments of Mewar." *Journal of Oriental Research,* December 1828, 270–320.

Toomey, Paul Michael. *Food from the Mouth of Krishna: Feasts and Festivals in a North Indian Pilgrimage Centre.* Delhi: Hindustan, 1994.

Toothi, N.A. *The Vaisnavas of Gujerat.* Calcutta: Longmans, 1935.

Vaidya, Chimanlal M. *Shri Vallabhacharya and His Teachings.* Baroda, India: Shri Vallabha, 1984.

Van Buitenan, J.A. "On the Archaism of the Bhagavata Purana." In *Krishna: Myths, Rites and Attitudes,* ed. Milton Singer, 23–41. Chicago: University of Chicago Press, Phoenix Books, 1966.

Veer, Peter van der. *Gods on Earth: The Management of Religious Experience and Identity in a North Indian Pilgrimage Centre.* London: Athlone, 1988.

Visharad, Brajnath R. *Shrimad Vallabhacharya and His Doctrines.* Baroda: Shri Vallabha Publ, 1984.

Vrahrajkumarhi Goswami. "Announcement of New Haveli in Boston, MA By VYO." http://www.facebook.com/note.php?note_id=171777549551715 (accessed March 1, 2012).

Vrajratna, Yadunath. *A History of the Sect of Maharajas or Vallabhacharyas in Western India.* London: Trubner, 1865.

———. *Report on the Maharaj Libel Case.* Bombay: n.p., 1862.

Wellman, Barry, Anabel Quan-Haase, Jeffrey Boase, Wenhong Chen, Keith Hampton, Isabel Díaz, and Kakuko Miyata. "The Social Affordances of the Internet for Networked Individualism." *Journal of Computer-Mediated Communication* 8 (April 2003): 0.

Williams, Joanna Gottfried, Cynthia Talbot, and Kazuhiro Tsuruta. *Kingdom of the Sun: Indian Court and Village Art from the Princely State of Mewar.* San Francisco: Asian Art Museum, Chong-Moon Lee Center for Asian Art and Culture, 2007.

Williams, Raymond Brady. *A New Face of Hinduism: The Swaminarayan Religion.* Cambridge: Cambridge University Press, 1984.

Wilson, H.H., ed. *Essays on the Religion of the Hindus.* London: Trubner, 1861.

Index

abhyang 35
acharya 19–20, 74–75, 187, 196
Addison (Illinois) 116–117, 160, 204, 209, 214
adhikara 75
Advaita 20–21, 199
Agiaras 118
Agra 1, 70, 78, 80, 87, 90, 206
Ahmedabad 64, 102–106, 195, 197, 201, 208
Ahmedabad Management Association 105
Ajmer 95
Akbar 18, 27, 70, 73–81, 88, 166, 205
akshar 6, 149, 187, 211
Akshardham 7, 151–152
alaukika 27, 63–65, 187–188, 191–192
Al-Badaoni 78–79, 205
Allentown (Pennsylvania) 142, 156, 179
Ambedkar 103
American Dream 172, 185, 214
Amin, Pramod C. 109, 212, 214
Amma 145
Amreli 119, 197
anand 187
Anglo Indian law 60
Annakut 25, 110, 118, 187
Aravalli Mountains 87
arhants 163
Arizona 8, 112, 119, 123, 132, 175, 206, 209
Armstrong, Karen 204
Arsha Vidya Gurukulam 161
Arya Samaj 136
asana 170
ashram 109, 142, 144, 160
Ashtanga yoga 170
Asotiya 90–92
assimilation 9, 115, 130, 159, 167–168, 183
Astachap 26–27, 64–65, 71, 188–189
atman 22, 189
Aurangzeb 18, 82, 85–86, 89–90, 166, 207
auratic 59–61
auratic objects 61
Australia 49, 112, 123, 167, 209

Avadhi 64
Ayodhya 21, 105, 158

Babur 17–18, 192
Bachha 84
Bade Shikshapatra 34, 201
Bahadur Khan 80
Bai, Mira 88
baithak 31, 111, 175, 188–189
Bal Vihar 130, 157
balak 82, 153, 188, 190
Balakrishnaji see *goswami*
Ban Yatra 174
Bangalore 103
Banu, Hamida 80
Baroda 49, 95, 104, 109, 113, 117, 204; see also Vadodara
Bellah, Robert Neelly 171, 213
Bengal 13, 16, 55, 97, 196
Bhagavad Gita 5, 11, 14, 135
Bhagavata Purana 5, 11, 23, 28, 71, 188, 201
bhajan 12–13, 163
Bhaktamala 20
bhakti 5–7, 9, 11–16, 18, 21, 23–25, 34, 39, 40, 42–44, 64, 66, 69, 74–75, 78, 80, 83, 89–91, 93, 96, 134, 145–146, 165, 188–191, 193–194, 202
Bharatpur 28, 95
Bhatta 24, 203, 215
bhog 40, 41, 67, 169
birat 178
bodhisattva 163
Bombay Presidency 104
boundaries 7, 14, 42, 51, 124, 184
brahmacharya 21
Brahman 22–23, 53, 57, 61, 71, 86, 187, 189, 193, 203
Brahmin 45, 47, 78–79, 117, 147, 189
Brahmsambandh Mantra 38, 43, 45, 127, 190
Braj 3, 8, 12–14, 20, 26–31, 34, 39, 52, 64–66, 71–78, 81–83, 86, 89, 96, 99, 111, 130, 166,

173–177, 185, 189–192, 196, 200–201, 204–206, 210
Braj Bhasha 31, 64, 130, 189, 204
Brajbhusanji see *goswami*
Brajbhusanji (II) see *goswami*
Brajray 83
British India 49, 104; colonialism 97; imperialism 88, 103, 135, 137
Buddhism 45, 163, 179
Bundi 85–86, 95–96, 166

caste 14–15, 24, 42–43, 47, 71, 74, 89, 97, 103–104, 107–108, 117, 135–136, 147, 178, 180–181, 188–189, 191, 196, 202–203, 208
Chaitanya 6, 26, 75, 146, 189, 195
Champaranya 119
Chandra Samovar 112
Chandrikabetiji see *goswami*
Chappan Bhog 25, 98, 115, 124, 129, 189
Charlotte (North Carolina) 125
Chaturbhooj Das 26
Chaung Yen Monastery 161, 163–164, 212
Chaurasi Vaishnavan ki Varta 23, 86, 206
Chennai 103, 125
Chicago (Illinois) 7, 41, 49, 116–118, 135, 138, 148, 151, 160, 180, 199, 202–203, 208, 210, 213
chit 189
Chitaswami 26
Christian missions 56
communitas 40
Council of Hindu Temples of North America 158
cultural assimilation 167
Cultural Festival of India 150–151, 211

Dahod 125
Damodar Lal 87
dandavat 35, 168
darbars 70
darshan 1, 23–28, 40, 45–48, 52–54, 63–67, 70–71, 86, 91, 95, 122, 153, 159, 168, 172, 183, 188–196
Das, Nagari 96
Das, Nand 26
Das, Paramanand 26, 64
Dave, Dr. Hari 118, 209
Dayananda 136, 161
Daytona Beach (Florida) 125
denomination 154–155, 157
denominationalism 157, 179
Desai, Amrit 109
Detroit (Michigan) 125
dharana 170
dharma 55, 164
Dharma Association of North America 158
dharmshala 106
Dhrupad Sangeet 66, 129, 188, 190–192
dhyana 170
diaspora 7, 44, 49–50, 66, 99, 106, 112–114, 125–130, 139–140, 145–146, 152–154, 158, 165–168, 177, 180–182, 196, 210
diksha 43–44, 160
Dilwara 92
Diwali 118, 187
Do Sau Bavan Vaishnavan ki Varta 24
Drumilkumarji see *goswami*
Dubai 49, 123, 209
Dwarka 106
Dwarkadhish (Dvarkadhish): diety 24, 33, 91–92, 94, 106; temple 1, 199
Dwarkeshji see *goswami*
Dwarkeshlalji see *goswami*

East Africa 49, 167
East India Company 18, 97
Eck, Diana 27
Edison (New Jersey) 49, 150, 179, 214
Ekling 88, 90–92
Eklingji 88, 91
Eliade, Mircea 27, 201
Emerson, Ralph Waldo 135
entrepreneurs 8, 102, 105, 107, 109, 122, 127, 131, 153, 178
extended family 38, 48, 71, 108, 126, 153, 180–181, 184
extrinsic 167, 169–172, 213

farman 77, 79–84, 193, 206; October 9, 1633 82; March 13, 1658 82; April 30, 1658 82
farman 1 77
farman 2 79
farman 3a 80
Fatephur Sikri 70
Federation of Hindu Associations 158

gaddi 25, 33–34, 49, 67, 74–75, 83–85, 104, 113–124, 153, 175–177, 201
Gandhi 103, 139, 142, 191
Ganges River 21, 173, 213
Gaudia Sampradaya 134
Gaudiya Vaishnavism 75, 145, 195
Ghanashyamji see *goswami*
ghats 30
Girdhari Lal see *goswami*
Girdharilal see *goswami*
Girdharji 24, 34
Giridharji see *goswami*
globalization 99, 101, 114, 120, 123, 149, 185
globalized 8–9, 122, 131, 151, 156, 167
Gokul 5, 19–20, 34, 64, 77–79, 81–82, 84, 87, 89, 206
Gokulanathji see *goswami*
Gokulchandramaji 24
Gopinath 21, 24
gopis 28, 53, 118
Gordon, Milton 213
goswami 3, 9, 23–24, 32–35, 41–45, 49, 63, 66, 70, 74–77, 81–86, 90–94, 98–99, 102, 111–116, 119–127, 130–133, 153, 167, 182,

Index

188–189, 192–196, 205, 208–209, 214; Balakrishnaji 24, 34; Brajbhusanji 92; Brajbhusanji (II) 23; Chandrikabetiji 119; Drumilkumarji 114, 119, 131, 133; Dwarkeshji 23; Dwarkeshlalji 119, 121–122, 125, 197; Ghanashyamji 24, 34; Girdhari Lal 98; Girdharilal 82–84; Giridharji 34; Gokulanathji 24, 34; Govindarayji 24, 34; Indirabetiji 113, 117, 119, 123–125; Jadunathji Maharaj 98; Mathureshwarji 49, 113–114, 123, 197; Pranvallabhaji 90; Pritirajabetiji 119; Raghunathji 24, 34; Rajkumarji 119; Vrajrajkumarji 119, 125, 133, 168; Yadunathji 24, 34; Yogeshkumarji 119
Govardhan hill 20, 26, 29, 121, 195
Govardhana-lila 29
Govardhannathji 190, 195
Govind Dev 30
Govind Swami 26
Govindarayji see *goswami*
grants 73–77, 81, 84–85, 90, 92–94, 166, 190–192, 194, 205–207, 209
Great Britain 49, 112, 167
grihastha 21
Gujarat 8, 16–21, 26, 34, 47, 51, 64, 72–75, 84, 88, 94–97, 102–106, 109, 118, 124–126, 149, 151–152, 174, 185, 188–193, 208
Gujarati diaspora 49, 127
Gujarati Immigrant Entrepreneurs 107, 208
Gujarati Sultanate 103
Gunatitanand 149
Gunjamani mala 64–65
Gunning 98
Gupta and Pallava dynasties 73
Guru Rajneesh 179
Gval 46–47, 190

Hamida, Banu 80
Hare Krishna 6, 14, 147–148, 179, 211; see also International Society for Krishna Consciousness
havelis 2–3, 8–9, 25, 33–34, 40–41, 46–48, 51–52, 66–67, 70, 74–75, 84–85, 99, 101–102, 106–108, 111–114, 117–118, 121–132, 145, 152–154, 159–160, 167–168, 173, 177–180, 183, 191–196, 209, 214; see also temples
Herberg, Will 167, 213
Himalayan Institute 160–161, 171
Hindola Raga 95
Hindu diaspora 7–8, 73
Hindu lunar calendar 127
Hindu Renaissance 97, 135, 139–140, 143
Hindu Students Council 158
Hinduism 7, 9, 14–16, 25, 45, 50–54, 73–75, 91, 97, 101, 105, 119, 132–140, 143–146, 151, 154, 157–159, 164–165, 169, 179–180, 207, 210–212
Hindus 7, 13, 16, 27, 49–50, 55, 61, 75–76, 89–90, 103, 105, 136–140, 143, 158, 161, 165, 171, 173, 179, 182–183, 194, 196, 199, 213

hindutva 105, 158
Holi 118
hot yoga 170
Houston (Texas) 49, 111, 113, 115, 124, 129, 151, 180, 209–210, 212
Humayun 18
Hyderabad 103

idols see *murti*
immigrant entrepreneurs 9, 51, 107, 208
immigrant networks 184
Indirabetiji see *goswami*
individualism 22, 138, 144, 161, 171–172
International Society for Krishna Consciousness (ISKCON) 6, 119, 144, 146–148, 152–153, 211; see also Hare Krishna
International Swaminarayan Satsang Organization (ISSO) 150
Internet 66, 145, 151, 171–172, 213
intrinsic 57, 167, 169, 171, 173–174, 213
Islam 18, 179
Islamic 27, 157, 179, 196

Jadunathji Maharaj see *goswami*
Jagat Singh 89–91
jagirs 76, 205, 207
Jahangir 18, 88
Jain 103, 118–119, 131, 143, 160–162, 165, 174, 179, 188, 191, 194, 210
Jainism 179, 191, 196
Jaipur 34, 71, 75, 95–96, 111, 207
jajmani 178
Jamaica Bay 173
James, William 169
Janmastimi 118
japiji 35–36, 45–46
jati 108, 189, 191, 196, 202, 208
Jhala Rajput 94
Jodhpur 87, 96
Judaism 120, 154, 184

kahlsa 80
Kandiwali 119
Kankroli 33–34, 64, 91–92, 197, 200, 205, 207–208
Kāṅkrolī kā Itihās 71, 205–208
Karauli 95
Kenya 112, 123, 209
Khan, Bahadur 80
Khan, Mukramat 84
Kirtananda 148
kirtankar 40
kirtans 40–41, 63–64, 66, 191
Kishangarh 75, 85–87, 95–96, 166
Kolkata 103
Kota 33, 86–87, 96, 166
Kripalu 191
Kripalu Yoga Ashram Retreat 109, 160–161, 191, 212
Krishna Das 26
Krishna Sewa Primer 37

228 INDEX

Kriyananda 171
Kumar, Sushil 162
Kumbhan Das 26
Kurien, Prema A. 134, 156–158, 210, 212

laukika 38, 187
liminality 39–40
Lohana 94, 191
lohans 163
lunar festivals 118
lila 5, 12, 22, 30, 39, 44, 62–63, 163, 187–188, 193

madad-i-ma'ash 76, 77, 92, 166, 205
Madanamohanji 24, 34
Madhuyra bhava 39
Madvha 20, 22
Mahabharata 5
maharajas 32, 73, 86
maharanas of Mewar 86, 88–89, 93, 166; Bhim Singh 93, 207; Chattar Sal 95; Jagat Singh 89–91; Pratap Singh 88; Raj Singh 89–91, 95–96, 166, 207; Sangram Singh 88
Mahavan 80
mala 122
Man Singh 71, 86
mangala 191
manorathis 84, 160, 178, 192
mantra 35, 43, 45, 54, 66, 192
Maratha 96–97
Marathi 104
marjadi 42
marriage 24, 43, 95, 180, 189, 203
Marty, Martin E. 155, 171, 212–213
Marwar 90
maryada 23
Mathura 1, 2, 5, 64, 70, 78–79, 82–83, 89, 190, 195, 199, 201, 204, 206, 208
Mathuramahatmya 31
Mathureshji 24
Mathureshwarji see *goswami*
maya 22, 63, 195
Melbourne (Australia) 131
Mewar Regency Council 98
Mewar 20, 25, 33, 70, 75, 85–98, 166, 191, 206–207
Mira Bai 88
Mount Govardhan 21, 28–30, 34, 70, 87, 110, 112, 121, 175–177, 185
mrdangam 66
muafi 92–93, 207
Mughal 9, 16–17, 24–27, 70–71, 73–79, 81–85, 88–92, 96, 103, 166, 190–194, 205–207
mukhiyas 42, 47–48, 112, 117, 123, 153, 158, 167, 183, 185, 192
Mulji, Karsondas 98, 207
Mumbai 28, 74, 99, 103–105, 125, 152, 181, 197
murti 54–55, 57–61, 193, 204
Muslim Americans 179

Muslims 16, 77–78, 89–90, 103, 105, 157, 191
mystical experiences 138, 183

Nadiad 125, 200
Nagari Das 96
Nagpur 125
Nand Das 26
nandalay 25, 114, 192
Narayanan, Vasudha 134, 210
Nathdwara 8, 18, 23, 33–34, 46, 64, 85–90, 92–99, 102, 106, 111–113, 115, 129, 166, 178, 191–192, 195, 197, 200, 207–208, 213
Nathdwara Temple Act of 1959 99
Navaratri 179
network individualism 172
New Delhi 1–2, 7, 28, 103, 151, 200–201, 205–206, 209
New England 120, 125, 155, 160
New Vrindaban 148
New Zealand 112
Newington 120, 122
NGOs see nongovernmental organizations
nidhi swarup 24–25, 33–34, 61, 74, 82, 104, 167, 190, 193, 195
Niebuhr, H. Richard 183, 211, 214
Nimbarka 13, 22, 28
nirguna Brahman 22
Nirma 105
niyama 170
nongovernmental organizations 125

order issued in 1696 92
Orientalist 97, 136, 164
Otto, Rudolph 169

padas 26–27, 41, 63–67, 122, 166, 190–191
Parabrahman 23, 193
Paramanand Das 26, 64
Pargament, Kenneth I. 42, 184, 202, 214
Parikh, Atul 111
parikrama 114
Partabgarh 95
parwana 77, 80, 84
Patanjali 170, 189, 193
Patel, Suresh 112, 115, 124, 129, 209–210, 214
Pathur Nataraja 60
patronage 7, 9, 15–16, 18, 24–26, 70–74, 81, 83–86, 91, 94–99, 101–103, 110, 123, 156, 166–167, 178, 185, 194
Patutsava 129
Pew Foundation 170, 172
Phoenix (Arizona) 118–119, 121, 124, 132, 175, 183, 209
pichhavai 95
power yoga 170
Prabhupada 6, 144, 146–148, 211
Pramukh Swami 149–152, 211
pranayama 170
Pranpratistha 45
Pranvallabhaji see *goswami*
Prasad 40, 144, 193, 205

Index

pratyahara 170
pravaha 23
Pritirajabetiji see *goswami*
puja 37–38, 40, 57, 81, 143, 166
pujaris 156
Pune 103
purity and pollution 15, 132, 180, 189, 191, 196, 208
Purushottam 149, 187, 202, 211
pusht 23, 45, 193
Pushti 34, 50, 101, 113, 118, 123, 125–126, 130, 132, 153, 159, 168, 171–172, 201, 209
Pushtimarg 1–11, 23–33, 40–44, 48–54, 63, 66, 70–83, 87, 91–97, 101–106, 109, 112, 117, 120, 125–134, 145, 149, 152–154, 158, 164–173, 177, 180, 184, 188–206, 214
Pushtimarg Vaishnava Samaj 131

quest 169

raag 40–41, 169
Radha 5–6, 12–13, 39, 66, 87, 189
raga 66, 191, 193
Raghunathji see *goswami*
raj (emotion) 67
Raj Bhog (Darshan) 40, 159, 193
Raj Samand Lake 91
Raj Singh 89–91, 95–96, 166, 207
Raja Yoga 189, 193
Rajasthan 8, 13, 16–21, 26, 28, 34, 51, 64, 72–75, 84, 87–89, 95, 102, 112, 126, 185, 188–195, 199–200, 205–208
Rajkumarji see *goswami*
Rajnagar 83, 92
Rajput 9, 18, 70–71, 74–75, 83, 85, 87–89, 91, 96, 193–194, 206–207
Rama 13, 31, 88, 90, 199
Ramanuja 22
Ramayana 88
Ras Lila 12–13, 194
rituals 2, 30, 33, 35, 40, 44, 47, 52, 55, 60–61, 66–67, 117, 143, 152, 162, 178, 183, 192
Roy, Ram Mohan 97, 136
Rubbish Theory 58, 204

sacred geography 27, 31–33, 88, 158, 167, 173–177
sadhu 22, 149
Sadri 94
saguna Brahman 22
Samadhi 194
sanad 76, 205
Sandhya-Arati 47
Sankhya 170
sannyasi 21
sat 61
satsang 119, 132, 134, 150, 173, 214
Satya Prakash 98
Savant Singh 96
Schleiermacher, Friedrich 169
Scranton (Pennsylvania) 125, 209

second generation 114–115, 118, 130, 132, 157, 167–168, 171–172, 181–182, 184
self-determinism 146, 170, 172
seva 11, 21–26, 34–48, 62, 66–67, 70–71, 84, 113, 117, 127, 130–133, 160, 166–173, 177, 182–183, 188–194
Shah, Govindbhai 109
Shah Alam 85, 206
Shah Jahan 18, 81–82, 84, 90, 166, 205
Shankar, Sri Sri Ravi 171
Shankara 20–22, 63, 187, 192, 195–196, 199
Shantiniketan 142–143, 156
Sharia 90
Shikharji 162, 174, 194, 212–213
Shilpashastras 54
shilpis 54, 57, 141
Shiva 13, 55, 60, 88, 174, 194
Shodash Granth 23, 200
Shree Kalyan *haveli* 125
Shreenathji Temple (Phoenix, Arizona) 118–119, 132
Shri Krishna Stuti 37
Shri Yamunaji 5, 37, 112, 195
Shrinathji Haveli (Toronto, Canada) 102, 131–133, 202–204, 209
shringar 40–41, 169
Shuddhadvaita 21, 23, 189, 193–195, 200
Shyam Dhak 31
Shyan 47
Siarh 87, 92–93
siddha 144, 174, 211
Siddhachalam 161–164, 174, 212–213
Sikhism 179
Singh, Jagat 89–91
Singh, Man 71, 86
Singh, Savant 96
Sisodia 88–91
smriti 15, 23
South Asians 7, 49, 108, 181, 209
South Indian temples 141–142, 165
spatial transposition 28, 30, 88, 173
Sri Vallbhacharitra 19
srinagar 67
Stone Mountain 109
Stony Mountain Manor 109
structural assimilation 168, 180
Subbodhini 23
success 170–173
Sugar Land (Texas) 114, 180, 214
sultanate 16
Surat 34, 64, 83, 104–106, 113, 118–119, 123, 197
Surdas 12, 21, 26–27, 52, 87, 102, 134, 166, 188, 199, 201, 203, 206, 208, 213
Surendranagar 125
surrender 13–14, 21, 38, 39, 44–45, 53, 67, 168–169, 171–172, 202
Sursagar 26
Sushil Kumar 162
Svetambara 162
Swami Dayananda 136, 161

Swami Kriyananda's Ananda yoga 171
Swami Vivekananda 135–136, 138–140, 210
Swaminarayan 6, 50, 97, 113, 119, 131, 134, 145, 149–150, 152–153, 156, 187, 207, 211–212
Swaminarayan Sanstha 6, 97, 149, 211–212
swarup 24, 32–34, 37–38, 42, 61–63, 83, 88, 123, 126, 154, 166–167, 192–195, 204–205; Shri Balakrishnaji 5, 34, 83, 104, 194; Shri Dwarkadhishji 6, 34; Shri Gokulanathji 5, 34, 194; Shri Gopinathji 34, 200; Shri Madanamohanji 5, 195; Shri Mathureshji 5, 33–34, 195; Shri Mukundarayji 6, 34, 195; Shri Nathji 5, 20, 25, 33–34, 37, 67, 70–71, 85–87, 91–97, 102, 109–111, 120–123, 153–154, 190–196; Shri Natvarlalji 34; Shri Navanitpriyaji 5, 34, 194–195; Shri Vitthalnathji 5, 33–34, 195
synaesthesia 65, 166

Tailanga 24, 203
Tailangana Brahmin 19, 43, 95
Tavasmi 37, 118, 130, 182, 195, 202
temple landlords 75
temples 1, 6–8, 15–16, 25, 33, 37–38, 47, 59, 70–78, 83, 86, 89–91, 97, 106–108, 119, 122–123, 126, 130–134, 140–143, 148–152, 156–160, 165, 178–179, 183, 188–190, 199–200, 210; see also *havelis*
Texas Nathdwara 112–116, 124, 129, 180, 210
textile industry 103, 105
Thakorji 41, 46, 195, 201
third generation 167, 181, 183, 195
Thoreau, Henry David 135
Tilkayat 92, 98–99, 111–112, 153, 192
tirtha 27, 162
Todd, James 97
tonks 174, 213
Toronto (Canada) 7, 50, 112, 123–124, 131–133, 173, 203, 210
transplanted religions 158, 184
triple melting pot 167
Tulsidasa 34

Udaipur 87, 90, 95, 97–98, 166, 192, 207
Ujjain 89, 122–123
United Arab Emirates 167
utsava 127, 196
Utthapan 47, 196

Vadodara 64, 99, 104, 106, 121–122, 125–126, 197, 209; see also Baroda
Vaishnav Samaj of Midwest 116–118, 160, 202–203, 209, 214

Vaishnava 16, 19–23, 28, 49, 57, 74, 78–80, 90, 95–96, 106, 111–113, 116, 119–122, 126–127, 141–142, 146, 158, 188–190, 194–196, 199–201, 204–206, 209
Vaishnava Samaj of Phoenix 119
Vaishnavism 20–21, 71, 91, 102, 145–147, 196, 200, 203
Vaishya 106, 108
Vallabh Priti Seva Samaj 112, 209, 214
Vallabh Vidya Mandir 115
Vallabha (Vallabhacharya) 5, 9, 16–17, 19–26, 61, 63, 75, 82, 86–87, 121, 166, 188–189, 192, 195–196, 200, 203; birth 16, 19–20, 118
Vallabha Sampradaya 2, 9, 11–12, 15, 25, 42, 50, 69–104, 109–112, 185–194
Vallabha Youth Organization (VYO) 125, 196, 209
Vallabhdham (Newington, Connecticut) 120, 122, 160
Vallabhkul 24–25, 31–35, 41–43, 71, 85, 114, 123, 153, 167–168, 185, 190, 196, 209
Vatsalya bhava 39
Vedanta 136, 165
Vietnamese Buddhist 114
Vijayanagar 16, 19, 73, 200
Vishnuswami 20, 22
Vitthalnath 6, 20–26, 31–35, 64, 73–88, 166–167, 188–196; birthday 118
Vitthalray 73, 77, 79–82
Vivekananda 135–136, 138–140, 210
voluntary association 154, 158, 177
Vraj 2, 8, 39–41, 47, 50, 107–114, 133, 153, 158–165, 176–182, 191, 196–197, 208–209, 212–214
Vrajabhaktivilasa 31
Vrajrajkumarji *see goswami*
Vrindaban 30, 67, 78, 89, 148
wat 55

Williams, Raymond Brady 97, 134, 143, 207, 209–211
World Parliament of Religions 135

Yadunathji *see goswami*
Yallamagaru 19
yama 170
Yavatmal 125
yoga 136, 139, 143–144, 161–162, 170–171, 191, 193–194, 213
Yogeshkumarji *see goswami*
Yogiji Maharaj 149

zarukas 111

www.ingramcontent.com/pod-product-compliance
Ingram Content Group UK Ltd.
Pitfield, Milton Keynes, MK11 3LW, UK
UKHW041944140426
5217IPUK00014B/645